Transformation, Development, and
Regionalization in Greater Asia | 4

The Series

Transformation, Development, and
Regionalization in Greater Asia

is edited by

PD Dr. Christoph Schuck,
Department of Political Science,
Friedrich-Schiller-University Jena

Prof. Dr. Reimund Seidelmann,
Department of Political Science,
Justus-Liebig-University Gießen

Prof. Dai Bingran | Dr. Jian Junbo (eds.)

The Enlarged European Union

Prospects and Implications

 **Nomos**

Die Deutsche Nationalbibliothek verzeichnet diese Publikation in
der Deutschen Nationalbibliografie; detaillierte bibliografische Daten
sind im Internet über http://www.d-nb.de abrufbar.

Die Deutsche Nationalbibliothek lists this publication in the Deutsche
Nationalbibliografie; detailed bibliographic data is available
in the Internet at http://www.d-nb.de.

ISBN 978-3-8329-4005-8

1. Auflage 2008
© Nomos Verlagsgesellschaft, Baden-Baden 2008. Printed in Germany. Alle Rechte,
auch die des Nachdrucks von Auszügen, der fotomechanischen Wiedergabe und der
Übersetzung, vorbehalten. Gedruckt auf alterungsbeständigem Papier.

The EU-Network of European Studies Centres in Asia (NESCA) Research Dialogue

This is the fifth volume in the EU-NESCA Research Dialogue Book Series, which contains the revised versions of papers presented at 4th EU-NESCA Workshop *"The Enlarged EU as an International Actor: Prospects and Implications"*, which was held together with the 4th EUSA-Asia Pacific[1] Conference on 11-13 October 2007 in Shanghai. Included are also some contributions that were written specially for this book.

Volume 1 of the book series ("EU's Foreign Governance: CSFP and ESDP and its Impact on Asia") and Volume 2 ("EU-Asian Relations: State of Affairs, Problems and Perspectives"), which contain selected papers from conferences in Macao/China hosted by EU-NESCA Consortium Member Institute of European Studies Macao, have been published by the Institute of European Studies Macao. Volume 3 of the book series ("European Union Identity: Perceptions from Asia and Europe") with revised papers from the EU-NESCA workshop in July 2006 in Christchurch/New Zealand hosted by EU-NESCA Consortium Member National Centre for Research on Europe at University of Canterbury/New Zealand has been published by Jessica Bain and Martin Holland at Nomos Publishing House. Volume 4 ("European Union and Asia: A Dialogue on Regionalism and Interregional Cooperation") with revised versions of selected papers presented at EU-NESCA workshops and conferences, as well as new contributions has been published by Reimund Seidelmann and Andreas Vasilache at Nomos. Further volumes are in preparation.

The project *EU–Network of European Studies Centres in Asia (NESCA): A Research Dialogue* was launched in April 2006 as a project funded by the 6th Framework Programme of the European Commission and consists of a series of conferences and workshops plus related research and cooperation activities on EU-Asian relations. In particular, this project aims at widening and deepening the research cooperation between the European research area, the Network of European Studies Centres in Asia (NESCA), and the European Studies associations in Asia.

---

1 The regional European studies association is composed of 10 national or regional European studies associations in the Asia Pacific region.

The project's main objectives are to

(1) transfer and disseminate latest research on issues relevant for Asia to the Asian European Studies community, to Asian politics, and in particular to the Asian public;
(2) transfer Asian research in European Studies in general and on EU-Asian cooperation in particular to the European Research area and to widen and deepen European interest and engagement in Asia;
(3) promote sustainable cooperation between universities and research institutions in the European Research area as well as in Asia; and
(4) involve the European and the Asian academic successor generation with special attention to gender equality in such activities.

The project's consortium consists of four European and five Asian universities/ institutes with special academic excellence, expertise in cooperation, and related infrastructure in European Studies as well as in European-Asian cooperation:

Consortium member organisation	Representative of consortium member organisation
Justus-Liebig-University Giessen/Germany	Prof.Dr. Reimund Seidelmann, Project Coordinator Prof.Dr. Andreas Vasilache, Junior-Coordinator and Executive Director
Institut d'Etudes Européennes, Université Libre de Bruxelles/Belgium	Prof.Dr. Mario Telò
Fondation Nationale des Science Politiques Paris/France	Prof.Dr. David Camroux
University of Warwick/United Kingdom	Prof.Dr. Shaun Breslin
Institute of European Studies Macao/China	Prof.Dr. José Luis Sales Marques
Centre for European Studies at Fudan University Shanghai/China	Prof.Dr. Dai Bingran
Korea University Seoul/Korea	Prof.Dr. Sung-Hoon Park
Interdisciplinary Department of European Studies at Chulalongkorn University Bangkok/Thailand	Prof.Dr. Apirat Petchsiri
National Centre for Research on Europe at University of Canterbury/New Zealand	Prof.Dr. Martin Holland

Further information can be obtained through the project website:
http:/www.ieem.org.mo/nesca/

6

Acknowledgement

As editors of this volume, we would like to take this opportunity to give our heartfelt thanks to the participants of the 4th EU-NESCA Workshop and the 4th EUSA-Asia Pacific Conference and many others. It is due to their contributions that the Workshop and Conference was a great success and this volume is possible.

Our thanks go also to the EU-NESCA consortium members, whose guidance and support are invaluable for the carrying-out of the whole programme, of which this Workshop and Conference is part.

We must also thank the Institute of European Studies of Macau for its publication support, and Nomos, the prestigious German publishing house, for rendering us their expertise services.

Dr. Jian Junbo
Prof. Dai Bingran
Centre for European Studies, Fudan University
25 June 2008, Shanghai

Contents

Part III: External Implications

Part I:

General Aspects

The Impact of the Recent EU Enlargements on the EU as an International Actor[1]

Ali M El-Agraa

I. Introduction

The theme announced for the conference, the presentations at which have been developed into the constituent chapters of this book, is 'the enlarged EU as an international actor: prospects and implications'. This is a very wide ranging theme. The term 'international actor' would encompass areas where the EU speaks with one voice to the outside world, such as the Common Commercial Policy where the EU Trade Commissioner, now Peter Mandelson, is in charge; the Common Foreign and Security Policy (CFSP) currently with Javier Solana entrusted with its Security leg; and External Relations and European Neighbourhood Policy which are entrusted to single Commissioner, presently Benita Ferrero-Waldner. The term would also include the role of the EU in international politics, but political science considerations lie outside my remit since they are not my area of expertise[2]. Moreover, it would also include areas where EU decisions undertaken for purely 'domestic' or 'internal' purposes nevertheless have international repercussions. Examples of these would be new developments in the Internal Market (and Services), now under Charlie McCreevy, which may infuriate some non-member countries so much as to revive the 'Fortress Europe' accusations[3], and actions under Competition, also entrusted to a Commissioner, currently Neelie Kroes, aggravating affected foreign multinational enterprises[4].

---

1   I wish to express my thanks to Dr David G Mayes, Adviser to the Board of the Bank of Finland and Adjunct Professor in the National Centre for Research on Europe at the University of Canterbury, New Zealand, for helpful comments and suggestions on earlier drafts of this paper. However, only I remain responsible for any errors or false arguments.—by Ali M El-Agraa

2   On this, see Elgström and Smith (2006), who acknowledge in their conclusion that there are many unanswered questions concerning the impact of the EU's role on international activities and indeed uncertainties about the relationship between the internal generation of role conception and their pursuit in institutional and political arenas.

3   When the Single European Act was being finalised in 1985 and before it became operative on 1 July 1987 the whole world broke loose, accusing the European Communities of erecting barriers against imports from non-member nations; hence the term Fortress Europe. These accusations became vehement and lasted for a long time before the accusers, especially the United States and Japan, realised that they were being far off the mark on the nature and extent of the Single European Market.

4   For a comprehensive survey of EU case-rulings under Competition and a full discussion of their significance and implications, see Sauter and Langer (2007). One case that has been attracting attention for a number of years and will continue to do so for several more, is the ruling against Microsoft Corporation, which was fined €497 million (about $613 million) by the EU Commission in 2004, under its anti-trust law, for not giving EU consumers real freedom of choice over the media software they are being offered. Microsoft has been continuously and persistently

Moreover, and arguably, it could include a discussion of whether the enlargements have coloured or solidified the type and/or nature of the decisions reached by the EU in the areas where the EU has an international take. An example of these would be decisions undertaken under the CFSP, even though the EU has no 'policy' in this area: this pillar of the EU is conducted on an ad hoc inter-governmental basis. In this context, Lee argues that because the recent enlargements have added mainly small nations, this will ensure that the EU will persist with its 'soft security' stance with regard to countries like North Korea[5].

Under the sub-heading, the 'prospects' would cover future EU enlargements, requiring a discussion of whether the latest enlargements have dampened or enhanced the chances for further enlargements. If so, then the case of Turkey[6] and its ilk would be upper most in one's mind. The prospects would also invite a discussion of whether these recent enlargements, whatever their consequences on the EU, have increased the chances of an enhanced future global role for the EU acting as one bloc or pursuing internal policies with international repercussions along the lines just mentioned.

Finally, the 'implications' in the sub-heading would call for similar considerations to those in the case of the 'prospects'. But they would also extend to a discussion of whether the costs incurred by the EU in readying the countries involved in the recent enlargements for joining could be repeated in the case of future candidates, vitally especially Turkey, in which case an evaluation of the nature and feasibility of *Agenda 2000*-type[7] budgetary arrangements[8] for the future would be warranted.

---

challenging this ruling but the European Court of Justice upheld; Microsoft has appealed against the ruling.

5   According to Lee (2007), the nature and constraints of the CFSP, whose decisions are reached through inter-governmental cooperation at the levels of the European Council and Council of Ministers, have led to a 'soft security' EU policy towards North Korea. He attributes this to the existence of small states because their very nature inclines them that way since they are lacking in military prowess. Due to this, he concludes that because the recent enlargements have added to the EU mainly small nations, the continuation of the EU's soft policy towards North Korea and countries like it is ensured. I should add that in so arguing, Lee believes that he is building on the established positions of Archer (2004) and Berkofsky (2003) rather than on contradicting them.

6   One may wonder why Turkey is singled out and the answer would be that not all EU citizens or member nations regard Turkey as 'European'. Many are also worried about a combination of factors concerning the country. One of these is its predominantly Muslim population, even though it claims to be secular nation. Another is its large population size which would make it the largest EU member nation if it were to join in 2015. Yet another is its low level of real per capita GNI. Last, but by no means least is its human rights record and denial of its squaring up to accusations of genocide of minorities in the past. It is indeed these factors together with fears regarding an excessive influx of Turkish workers that has prompted France to decide to hold a referendum on Turkey's EU membership if the negotiations between it and the EU end up successfully in 2015. Also, Germany is more or less inclined towards negotiating a 'special partnership', rather than full EU membership for Turkey.

7   See EU Commission (1997; 2000).

8   I am not referring to the policy costs such as the initial calculations regarding the impact of all the ten countries joining the EU in 2004 being equal to 11 billion ECUs per year by 2005 on the

Here I shall confine my paper to a consideration of the 'impact' of the 2004 and 2007 enlargements on the EU[9] 'as it acts as one bloc in the global arena'. I think this book will be set to offer an embracive discussion of the various manifestations of this vital topic.

II. The enlargements reality

In order to discuss the impact of the 2004 and 2007 EU enlargements on the EU as an international actor, I must begin by enumerating what these enlargements have entailed in terms of my declared limited focus. As Table 1 clearly reveals, consequent on the enlargements:

1. EU total membership has increased from 15 to 27 countries;
2. EU population has increased by just over one quarter;
3. EU GNI as measured by PPP rates has increased by just over 12%, or by about 6% using straight market exchange rates;
4. EU member nations' global ranking in per capita GNI terms has changed from a range of 1-50 to 1-86 using PPP rates or from 1-47 to 1-98 using market exchange rates; and
5. EU eurozone has acquired 12 'committed' members.

How do these changes impact on the EU as an international actor? Let me consider them in turn.

Guarantee section of EAGGF alone (EU Commission, 2000, vol. 2, p. 42). What I have in mind is the 'pre-accession aid' item in the general budget, random samples of which are the 1,203.4 million ECUs for 2000, €2,239.8 million for 2003, €3,052.9, etc. See Ardy and El-Agraa (2007), Armstrong (2007) and Mayes (2007a) for full details and discussion, and the European Court of Auditors annual reports on the EU budget.

9 For a general and detailed coverage of these enlargements, see, inter alia, O'Brennan (2006).

Table 1 The Enlargement Reality: Sheer Nubmer, Populaion and GNI, 2005								
	Population	Gross national income (GNI)				per capita GNI		
Country	(million)	($b)	Rank	PPP ($b)	Rank[1]	($)	Rank	PPP ($)	Rank
Austria	8.20	306.2	21	272.90	34	37,190	16	33,140	12
Belgium	10.50	378.7	18	342.00	26	36,140	17	32,640	14
Denmark	5.40	261.8	26	181.80	45	48,330	6	33,570	11
Finland	5.20	196.9	29	163.50	49	37,530	14	31,170	20
France	61.00	2,169.2	6	1,859.10	7	34,600	19	30,540	22
Germany	82.50	2,875.6	3	2,408.90	4	34,870	18	29,210	27
Greece	11.10	220.3	28	262.30	34	19,840	38	23,620	41
Ireland	4.10	171.1	35	144.40	51	41,140	9	34,720	8
Italy	59.00	1,772.9	7	1,690.20	8	30,250	26	28,840	28
Luxembourg	0.46	26.3	71	29.80	89	58,050	1	65,340	1
Netherlands	16.30	642.0	15	530.10	22	39,340	11	32,480	15
Portugal	11.00	181.3	31	208.10	40	17,190	47	19,730	50
Spain	43.00	1,095.9	8	1,120.50	11	25,250	34	25,820	33
Sweden	9.00	369.1	19	283.50	32	40,910	10	31,420	17
United Kingdom	60.60	2,272.7	4	1,968.80	6	37,740	13	32,690	13
EU (15)	**387.36**	**12,940.0**		**11,465.90**				
Bulgaria	7.80	26.7	70	66.80	65	3,450	98	8,630	86
Cyprus	0.80	13.6	86	16.50	110	18,430	54	22,230	43
Czech Republic	10.20	114.8	41	206.10	41	11,220	56	20,140	49
Estonia	1.40	12.2	98	20.80	101	9,060	63	15,420	60
Hungary	10.10	101.6	46	170.90	48	10,070	59	16,940	56
Latvia	2.30	15.6	88	31.00	87	6,770	74	13,480	67
Lithuania	3.40	24.6	76	48.60	73	7,210	72	14,220	62
Malta	0.40	5.5	128	7.70	132	13,610	53	18,960	52
Poland	38.20	273.1	25	514.90	23	7,160	73	13,490	66
Romania	22.00	84.6	50	193.40	42	3,910	93	8,940	85
Slovakia	5.40	42.8	60	84.90	59	7,950	68	15,760	58
Slovenia	2.00	34.9	62	44.30	74	17,440	45	22,160	44
EU enlargement (12)	**104.00**	**750.0**		**1,405.90**				
EU (27)	**964.02**	**26,695.1**		**25,128.70**				
% increase on EU (15)	**26.85**	**5.8**		**12.30**				
EU candidates								
Croatia	4.40	36.9	61	56.70	68	8,290	65	12,750	69
Turkey	72.00	342.0	20	606.80	17	4,750	86	8,420	88
EFTA countries								
Iceland	0.30	14.4	97	10.30	125	48,570	5	34,760	7
Liechtenstein	0.04							
Norway	5.00	281.5	24	186.90	43	60,890	2	40,420	4
Switzerland	7.00	411.4	17	275.80	33	55,320	3	37,080	5
NAFTA countries								
Canada	32.00	1,052.6	9	1,040.70	13	32,590	21	32,220	16
Mexico	103.00	753.4	12	1,034.00	14	7,310	71	10,030	3
United States	296.00	12,912.9	1	12,434.40	1	43,560	7	41,950	3
NAFTA total	**431.00**	**14,718.9**		**14,509.10**				3
Comparators								
Australia	20.00	673.2	13	622.30	15	33,120	20	30,610	21
China	1305.00	2,269.7	5	8,609.70	2	1,740	128	6,600	107
India	1095.00	804.1	10	3,787.30	5	730	158	3,460	143
Japan	128.00	4,976.5	2	4,013.40	3	38,950	12	31,410	18
New Zealand	4.00	106.3	44	94.40	51	25,920	32	23,030	42
Russian Federation	143.00	638.1	16	1,522.70	10	4,460	90	10,640	79
South Korea	48.00	765.0	11	1,055.20	12	15,840	49	21,850	45

Note: 1 the ranking for the countries with very low figures is not exact since the World Bank does not provide it and their list is not exhaustive, but the relative positions are fairly close to what they may be.
Source: the data is collected from various tables in the World Bank's *World Development Indicators*, 2007.

III. Increased EU Membership

The enlargements have added twelve new member nations to the EU of fifteen. If sheer numbers were the only or main preoccupation, then total EU membership has not only been boosted by an impressive 80%, but has also become so extensive as to edge towards encompassing practically the whole of Europe. These enlargements have therefore brought the EU much closer to the founding fathers' dream of an ever closer union of the peoples of Europe, much to the elation of all of us who view EU integration within such a perspective[10].

It may then seem natural to conjecture that this boosting of EU membership has enhanced the position of the EU as a global actor. This is because the more members the EU comprises, the more it would be listened to by the outside world. The EU would therefore be able to influence future world developments, steering them in directions favourable to it or along lines it deems commensurate with its priorities, if not its vision. Unfortunately, we live in a world where the sheer number of member nations in a bloc does not impact greatly in this respect. What really does matter are economic clout, military prowess, political influence in international organisations and forums and, some would add, population size.

Population size and economic clout are in the list so I shall turn to them in a moment. As to military prowess, the EU as such does not have it; it remains the domain of the individual member nations: the EU neither has an army nor does it have a true common defence policy. Hence, given this reality, the enlargements have in this respect obviously not impacted on the EU as an international actor.

One may be quick to counter by stating that that is a very narrow representation, if not an utter misrepresentation, of the situation since it misses the point that the EU has a formidable presence within NATO[11]. Of course, as Table 2 shows, 22 of the 26 NATO member states come from the EU; a staggering 84.6 per cent. The 22 however do not comprise a solid bloc in terms of having one policy stance within NATO. Not only that, but NATO is for all intents and purposes heavily dependent on the US followed by a very long distance by the UK, Germany, France and Italy[12]. Furthermore,

---

10 One should of course point out that presently, and in the not so distant past, there are politicians as well as individual persons and nations who do not share this dream, wanting to reduce the EU to a purely economic organization. Indeed, the devout 'Eurosceptics' exploit every possible opportunity to claim that this change in sentiment applies to practically the entire EU population, which is a far cry from reality. For example, witness their assertion that the rejection in referendums by the French (on 29 May 2005) and Dutch (on 1 June 2005) of the Constitutional treaty had nothing to do with disenchantment of these countries citizens with 'domestic' political woes for which they held their national politicians responsible (see, inter alia, Chapters 2 and 28 of El-Agraa, 2007b).

11 On the relationship between the EU and NATO, see, inter alia, Reichard (2006).

12 By this I do not mean the share contributed by the US towards the costs of running NATO, which is given and explained in the Appendix to this paper. Rather, the overall 'stock' of 'military capability' which lies at the very heart of NATO defence; see the Appendix for documentation, and NATO (2007) and US Congressional Budget Office (2007) for explanation.

and importantly, NATO remains largely a defence organisation, although in today's world the dividing line between 'defensive' and 'offensive' prowess is a very thin one indeed[13]. Moreover, and more pertinently: (a) Austria, Finland and Ireland, the neutral states, whatever neutrality may mean in this day and age, remain outside NATO; (b) the Czech Republic, Hungary and Poland, the most significant of the 12 EU enlargement nations in this regard, joined NATO on 12 March 1999, i.e. well before accession to the EU on 1 January 2004; and (c) Cyprus and Malta are not members. Thus, with the enlargements having added to NATO seven very 'small' nations, as measured by whatever criteria one wishes to employ, it is difficult to perceive any impact either on the EU's influence as one bloc within NATO or on 'club' NATO itself.

Table 2 NATO Membership			
Member Country	Date	Member Country	Date
Belgium	04 April 1949	Turkey	18 February 1952
Canada	04 April 1949	Germany	09 May 1955
Denmark	04 April 1949	Spain	30 May 1982
France	04 April 1949	Czech Republic	12 March 1999
Iceland	04 April 1949	Hungary	12 March 1999
Italy	04 April 1949	Poland	12 March 1999
Luxembourg	04 April 1949	Bulgaria	29 March 2004
Netherlands	04 April 1949	Estonia	29 March 2004
Norway	04 April 1949	Latvia	29 March 2004
Portugal	04 April 1949	Lithuania	29 March 2004
United Kingdom	04 April 1949	Romania	29 March 2004
United States	04 April 1949	Slovakia	29 March 2004
Greece	18 February 1952	Slovenia	29 March 2004

With regard to EU political clout in international organisations, one must be thinking mainly of influence in the United Nations. As Table 3 makes evident, all 27 EU nations have been members of the UN for a very long time, with the last two joining the organisation as long ago as 1993. Therefore, the enlargements are of no consequence whatsoever, again unless the 27 act as one solid bloc, but without a common EU foreign policy this is not in the offing, not even if the original draft of the Constitutional Treaty had been adopted[14]. Moreover, the enlargements are not going to boost

---

13 Witness the on-going discussion in Japan concerning the 'nature' of their Self Defence Force, now elevated to a Ministry of Defence Force, in the light of missiles coming from North Korea, the extending of assistance to units of United States fleet on their way to Iraq by supplying them with energy and the never-ending call for a revision of Article 9 of the Japanese Constitution.

14 The first draft (EU Commission, 2003), attributed almost entirely to Valéry Giscard d'Estaing, Chairman of the *Convention for the Future of Europe*, proposed the streamlining of the EU foreign policy apparatus by the creation of a single post of ,EU Foreign Minister' to replace the two roles then held by Javier Solana, EU foreign policy chief, which he still holds, and Christopher Patten, then EU Commissioner in charge of External Relations. Since neither of the mentioned

Germany's chances of becoming a permanent member of the UN Security Council (UNSC), raising the UNSC total membership to six and enhancing EU representation in it to 50 per cent (three out of six nations). That chance is heavily dependent not only on Germany's own persuasive endeavours, but on compromises at the UN which afford similar chances to Japan, India and Brazil and some would add South Africa. That is to say that instead of the EU nations comprising 40 per cent (two out of five) of the permanent UNSC, they would represent only 30 per cent (three out of ten) if all of these nations were to be so accommodated. Therefore, again I fail to detect any impact of these enlargements on the EU's clout as an international actor in this regard.

Table 3 Dates when the EU nations joined the United Nations			
EU Country	Date joining the UN	EU Country	Date joining the UN
Denmark	24 October 1945	Italy	14 December 1955
France	24 October 1945	Portugal	14 December 1955
Greece	25 October 1945	Romania	14 December 1955
Luxembourg	24 October 1945	Spain	14 December 1955
Poland	24 October 1945	Cyprus	20 September 1960
United Kingdom	24 October 1945	Malta	01 December 1964
Netherlands	10 December 1945	Germany	18 September 1973
Austria	14 December 1945	Estonia	17 September 1991
Belgium	27 December 1945	Latvia	17 September 1991
Sweden	19 November 1946	Lithuania	17 September 1991
Bulgaria	14 December 1955	Slovenia	22 May 1992
Finland	14 December 1955	Czech Republic	19 January 1993
Hungary	14 December 1955	Slovakia	19 January 1993
Ireland	14 December 1955		

Here, again, some would counter by asking: what about the partnership between the UN and the EU? To respond to this, some background information is of the essence. The EU member nations, Council and Commission do meet regularly to *coordinate* their positions on a variety of issues. Indeed, they are asked by the Treaty on European Union to uphold common positions so that their collective weight can have more

---

two positions entailed freedom for the person in charge to make own decisions, the recommended amalgamation was in a sense purely cosmetic. In the final draft (EU Commission, 2004), which the French and Dutch rejected, this was slimmed down to the creation of a post of 'EU Foreign Minister', who will head a newly established EU diplomatic service; hence largely subject to the same reservation. In the version agreed in Brussels in June 2007 (Council of the European Union, 2007a) and finalised as the 'Reform Treaty' in October 2007 (Council of the European Union, 2007b) during the informal meetings of the Council in Lisbon, the title has been altered to a 'High Representative of the Union for Foreign Affairs and Security Policy', which is surprisingly not very different from that in the Amsterdam Treaty, and the holder would speak on behalf of the EU, but only if the EU has agreed on a 'position', i.e. he/she will not have any 'own powers'. Note that despite this, Openeurope (2007) believes that there is not an iota of difference between what was in the rejected agreed constitutional draft treaty, let alone the initial Giscard d'Estaing version, and the latest; the Reform Treaty.

impact in the world. This coordination now encompasses the six main committees of the UN General Assembly (UNGA), including the Economic and Social Committee (ECOSOC) and its subsidiary functional commissions. Over a thousand internal EU coordination meetings are conducted every year in both New York and Geneva[15].

EU member nations work together with the EU Council and Commission to prepare and finalise EU statements and the member state holding the EU presidency presents the EU stance at the UNGA, whether in negotiations or debates, in the form of a presidency statement. Also, the Commission can take the floor as a permanent observer at the UNGA and speaks on behalf of the EU in matters concerning trade policy (see below). Nevertheless, all this is about coordination which is of course highly desirable but the fact remains that the EU has no UN policy as such, a fact made patently clear when the United Kingdom backed the US invasion of Iraq and both France and Germany distanced themselves from it. More pertinently still is that the recent enlargements definitely have no impact on the EU as an international actor in this respect because the largest acceding member nations were already involved in this activity prior to that.

IV. Increased EU population Size

As Table 1 clearly shows, EU population has increased by 26.8 per cent to exceed that of the United States by about 200 million and of NAFTA (Canada, Mexico and the US) by 60 million. Needless to add, none of these population sizes are a close match to those of our host nation China or India, with 1.3 and 1.1 billion respectively. Note that China's increasing international ascendance has nothing to do with population size; rather with a combination of GNI, military capabilities and 'historically determined' position, i.e. its holding of a permanent seat in the UNSC[16]. India is on its way to emulating China, but is not yet there in terms of these counts. All of this suggests that the act of adding another 100 million to the EU's population, though impressive on other grounds, is of no great or particular significance with regard to its impacting on the EU's role as an international actor.

V. Increased EU GNI

Increased EU GNI would have significance for the EU as an international actor in terms of clout within the Wold Trade Organisation (WTO) and the Group of Eight (G8). As Table 1 shows, EU GNI as measured in PPP rates has increased by 12.3 per

---

15 See United Nations (2007) for details, especially on the relationship between the EU Commission and UN.

16 Those countries that are hoping to join this 'elite' group (see Section III) stand no chance of ever succeeding without securing China's sympathy.

cent, or by 5.8 per cent using straight exchange rates, but any international comparison based on mere exchange rates should not be taken seriously; it is provided here for only those who would like to see it. Although the recent enlargements have taken the EU GNI to beyond that of the United States (on both measures), EU 15 is only 7.79 per cent behind the US in PPP terms (just ahead of the US using market exchange rates). Hence, in terms of sheer magnitude, the enlargements have not led to any appreciable change in the EU's GNI international position.

As mentioned, what happens to EU GNI is vital for the EU as a member of the WTO. In this context, recall that the EU Commission has sole responsibility for conducting the EU's Common Commercial Policy[17]. This means that no single EU nation has any role to play in the WTO negotiations, deliberations or dispute settlement procedures: the Commission does all these on behalf of the entire EU. In this capacity, it should be apparent that the more economically powerful is the EU, the more strengthened would be its position in the WTO where the main players are the United States followed by Japan, with China edging ever so close. Since the EU enlargements have not impacted much on EU GNI, one can be justified in asserting that the enlargements have not resulted in any significant change in the EU's ability to exert influence within the WTO. In terms of the future however the picture may seem 'rosier' given the high growth rates of GNI in the enlargement countries shown in Table 4 for 2000-2005, especially as compared to those for the period 1990-2000 for all except Poland. Nevertheless, one cannot be referring to the medium-term, let alone the immediate future, since the present levels of GNI in the enlargement countries are very low indeed. Increasing one's racing speed when one has been taking an hour to cover a mile does not mean that one would be in contention for a place in the Beijing Olympics during the Summer of 2008! Needless to add, the rosier outlook would be greatly enhanced if one were to allow for 'older Europe' regaining its glowing economic growth rates of the heydays of the 1970s.

Of course, the absolute level of GNI should not be the be all and end all: as Table 1 clearly shows, in terms PPP GNI China is now the second largest economy in the world after the US, yet it ranks 107 in terms of per capita GNI (128 using market exchange rates). It is therefore the impact of the recent enlargements on per capita GNI that really matters since it reflects true economic prowess. As the information in Tables 1 and 4 shows, the per capita PPP GNI ranking of the EU member nations has been completely transformed from a range of 1-50 to one of 1-85. What is interesting is that if one were to ignore Portugal, the pre-enlargement ranking range was from 1 to 41 with the 41st on a per capita PPP GNI of $23,620 and the enlargements have brought in 12 countries in the range of 43-85, with the leader on $22,230 and the tail-ender on $8,940; the picture is not that different using straight exchange rate comparisons. Thus ignoring Portugal, as Figure 1 (based on the data in Table 4, the second column of which simply rearranges the EU member nations as given in Table 1 but in terms of

---

17   See, inter alia, Brülhart and Matthews (2007) for a detailed exposition.

per capita GNI ranking) makes more evident, one can categorically state that the enlargements have added members with per capita GNIs below the lowest in the EU15. To put it differently, using Eurostat data[18], if one were to assign an index of 100 to represent EU 25 then that for EU 15 would stand at 107.8 and 107.4 for 2006 and 2007 respectively, i.e. the enlargement to 25 eroded the average per capita GNI for EU 25. That for EU 27 would be 96.2 and 98.6 respectively, i.e. adding Bulgaria and Romania has lowered the average EU per capita GNI even more.

Table 4 EU nations' per capita GNI ranking and growth, inflation and unemployment rates					
EU member nation	per capita GNI $	Growth rate of GDP		Inflation rate[1] 2005	Unemployment rate (%) 2005
		1990-2000	2000-2005		
Luxembourg	65,340	na	4.0	3.8	4.5
Ireland	34,720	7.5	5.2	2.2	4.3
Denmark	33,570	2.7	1.2	1.7	4.8
Austria	33,140	2.4	1.5	2.1	5.2
United Kingdom	32,690	2.7	2.4	2.1	4.7
Belgium	32,640	2.1	1.5	2.5	8.4
Netherlands	32,480	2.9	0.7	1.5	4.7
Sweden	31,420	2.1	2.3	0.8	7.8
Finland	31,170	2.5	2.4	0.8	8.4
France	30,540	1.9	1.5	1.9	9.7
Germany	29,210	1.8	0.8	1.9	9.5
Italy	28,840	1.5	0.6	2.2	7.7
Spain	25,820	2.7	3.1	3.4	9.2
Greece	23,620	2.2	2.4	3.5	9.8
Cyprus	22,230	na	3.7	2.0	5.3
Slovenia	22,160	2.7	3.4	2.5	6.5
Czech Republic	20,140	1.1	3.5	1.6	7.9
Portugal	19,730	2.8	0.5	2.1	7.6
Malta	18,960	na	2.5	2.5	7.3
Hungary	16,940	1.6	4.1	3.5	7.2
Slovakia	15,760	1.9	4.9	2.8	16.3
Estonia	15,420	0.2	7.5	4.1	7.9
Lithuania	14,220	Δ2.7	7.8	2.7	8.3
Poland	13,490	4.7	3.2	2.2	17.7
Latvia	13,480	Δ1.5	7.9	6.9	8.9
Romania	8,940	Δ0.6	5.8	9.1	7.7
Bulgaria	8,630	Δ1.8	5.0	5.0	10.1

Notes: Δ means minus; 1 % change compared with previous year, based on harmonised index of consumer prices (HICP).
Source: selected from Eurostat (2006-07).

---

18 See EU Commission (2007).

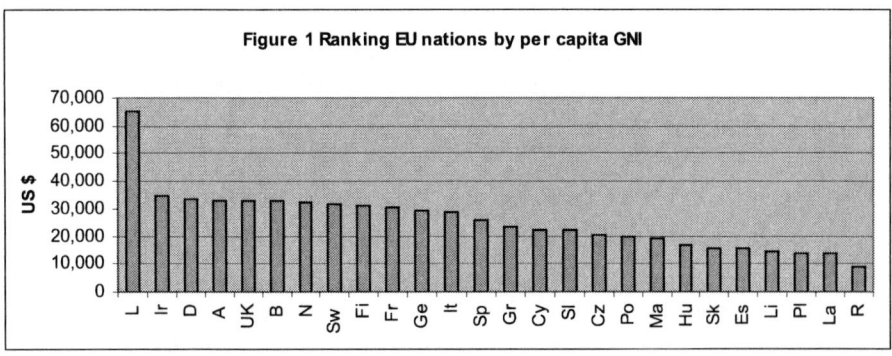

Figure 1 Ranking EU nations by per capita GNI

The situation regarding the EU within the context of the G8 (the four largest EU nations, Canada, Japan, Russia and the United States) differs from that of the EU within the WTO. This is because although the president of the EU Commission participates in the G8 meetings, the participation is in the nature of 'observing': it is the four largest EU nations that do so in their individual capacity. Hence, the enlargements have no impact on the EU's clout within the G8. What is intriguing is that the G8 is supposed to be the group of the eight richest nations in the world in terms of GNI. Yet, as Table 1 clearly shows, today neither Canada nor Russia meet this criterion since they rank 13th and 10th respectively (9th and 16th using market exchange rates) while China and India remain outside despite their 2nd and 5th respective ranking (5th and 10th respectively using market exchange rates, which would bring Spain in the picture with its 8th ranking). Confining membership to only the eight richest nations would mean replacing Canada and Russia with China and India (Spain instead of India using market exchange rates), which would mean that the EU nations will dominate the group by a ratio of five to three. But such a change would have nothing to do with the EU enlargements. If the membership of the G8 were to be extended to the 16 richest nations such that Russia can continue to stay in, then it would be not only a much diluted group, but also one that would find it more difficult to reach consensus, no matter how important or insignificant it might be. Moreover, some would then argue for replacing the G8 with the OECD since it is the long standing club of supposedly the world's 30 richest nations (EU 15 minus Ireland; Czech Republic; Hungary; Slovakia; NAFTA; EFTA minus Liechtenstein; Australia; Japan; New Zealand; South Korea; and Turkey); supposedly, because by today's data, they are not.

VI. Enlarged eurozone

Others would argue that with the enlargements bringing in 12 member nations committed to the adoption of the euro, i.e. they have no opt-outs as is the case with Denmark and the United Kingdom, then euro is set to be on par with the US dollar as the leading world currencies. Some would even venture that the euro would take over from the US dollar. If that were to happen, the EU would greatly improve it position as an international actor in the global financial markets. That may well prove to be so, but it would be far fetched to claim that the euro will take over from the US dollar any time soon. Not only that, but being 'committed' does not automatically guarantee eurozone membership since each country has individually to meet the criteria for joining[19] although they all hope to do so soon and the EU is helping them in their efforts in doing so. Indeed Slovenia quickly did, on 1 January 2007, and Cyprus and Malta will do likewise on 1 January 2008, but these are very small nations with a total population of 3.2 million (see Table 1). Moreover, as Table 4 makes clear, Bulgaria, Estonia, Hungary, Latvia and Romania with both high inflation and unemployment rates, necessitating budget deficit macroeconomic adjustments, which would make it difficult to pass the budget deficit criterion, are a very long distance from the cherished goal. Although the others have lower inflation rates, they suffer from high unemployment rates, hence are subject to the same fiscal problem and the consequent long wait in the queue. Nevertheless, here is where sheer numbers may count within our context: the more nations adopt the euro, the more the euro's global

---

19   These are the established conditions, by now almost common household knowledge (see, inter alia, Mayes and El-Agraa, 2007):
    Price stability. Membership requires 'a price performance that is sustainable and an average rate of inflation, observed over a period of one year before the examination, that does not exceed by more than [1.5] percentage points that of, at most, the three best performing' EC member countries. Inflation 'shall be measured by means of the consumer price index on a comparable basis, taking into account differences in national definitions'.
    Interest rates. Membership requires that, observed over a period of one year before the examination, a Member State has had an average nominal long-term interest rate that does not exceed by more than two percentage points that of, at most, the three best performing Member States in terms of price stability. Interest rates shall be measured on the basis of long-term government bonds or comparable securities, taking into account differences in national definitions.
    Budget deficits. Membership requires that a member country 'has achieved a government budgetary position without a deficit that is excessive' (Article 109j). However, what is to be considered excessive is determined in Article 104c(6) which simply states the Council shall decide after an overall assessment 'whether an excessive deficit exists'. The Protocol sets the criterion for an excessive deficit as being 3% of GDP. However, there are provisos if 'either the ratio has declined substantially and continuously and reached a level that comes close to the reference value; or . . . the excess over the reference value is only exceptional and temporary and the ratio remained close to the reference value.'
    Public debt. Here the requirement in the Protocol is that the ratio of government debt should not exceed 60% of GDP. But again there is an important proviso 'unless the ratio is sufficiently diminishing and approaching the reference value at a satisfactory pace.' Whether such an excessive deficit exists is open to interpretation and is decided by the Council under qualified majority voting (see Chapter 3). In helping the Council decide, the Commission is to look at the medium term and quite explicitly can have the opinion that there is an excessive deficit if there is risk, 'notwithstanding the fulfilment of the requirements under the criteria'.
    Currency stability. Membership requires that a member country has respected the normal fluctuation margin provided for by the exchange-rate mechanism of the [EMS] without severe tensions for at least two years before the examination. In particular, [it] shall not have devalued its currency's bilateral central rate against any other Member State's currency on its own initiative for the same period.

position is enhanced. If this may appear like a baffling statement, just think of how tourism will aid in this development. The enhancement would be reinforced if the United Kingdom were to join since it is both large and rich enough, absolutely and in per capita terms, to make a significant difference and its joining will most certainly entice Denmark into doing likewise, given its very long attachment to British sentiments in matters European. The enhancement would be reinforced because the euro is run by a single central bank, the European Central Bank, with guaranteed independence from the eurozone governments and its mandate is confined to only 'price stability'; hence its vision is clear and manageable[20].

Unfortunately, the chances of the United Kingdom opting out of the EU itself are more likely than of its joining the euro. The reasons for this would require a whole paper of its own, if not an entire book; hence I cannot go through them here[21]. I should however add that I am not referring to the United Kingdom's chances of someday passing the self-imposed Brown tests[22] (which Gordon Brown set in 1997 when British Chancellor of the Exchequer as conditions to be met before Britain took a decision on euro adoption), although that is not guaranteed, given the nature of the sixth test of a 'clear and unambiguous case' for euro adoption: how can one ever pass such a test on purely economic grounds when economics is not a pure science? I am referring rather to the British people voting 'yes' in a referendum on joining the euro after the tests have somehow been successfully and convincingly negotiated[23]: the 'pound' is not only deeply-rooted in British mentality, but also occupies a special place in British hearts.

VII. Conclusion

What can be concluded from this brief and cursory examination of these considerations is that the only items where the EU enlargements could impact on the EU as an international actor sometime in the future are the two where all or almost all of the EU

---

20 Mayes (2007b, p. 229) argues that limiting the ECB to a single policy is a great advantage because if a central bank has multiple objectives it would have difficulty explaining the balance between them.

21 See, inter alia, the final chapter of El-Agraa (2002), Mayes (2007a) and Young (1998).

22 When Chancellor Gordon Brown, now the British Prime Minister, first revealed the tests, these were: (a) that business cycles and economic structures should be compatible 'so that we and others could live comfortably with euro interest rates on a permanent basis'; (b) that there would be 'sufficient flexibility to deal with' any problems if they emerged; (c) that the adoption of the euro would 'create better conditions for firms making long-term decisions to invest in Britain'; (d) what the impact of the euro adoption would be 'on the competitiveness of the UK's financial services industry, particularly the City's wholesale markets'; and (e) whether the adoption of the euro would 'promote higher growth, stability and a lasting increase in jobs'. However, when Brown he formally announced the tests in October 1997, he added a sixth: (f) that the Treasury must decide that there is a 'clear and unambiguous' economic case for recommending British adoption of the euro. Recall that Britain failed these tests when the UK Treasury (2003) conducted them in 2003.

23 See, El-Agraa (2002) and Mayes and El-Agraa (2007).

nations have mandated a single person or sole institution to act on its behalf. The former refers to the EU Commissioner in charge of Trade, i.e. the person who conducts the EU's Common Commercial Policy, hence represents the EU in the WTO, although the occupier of this position always liaises closely with the authorities of the member states; hence does not have absolute autonomy. As mentioned before, presently it is Peter Mandelson from the United Kingdom, that enigmatic, energetic and some would say magnetic confidant of Tony Blair, himself now in the shadows of Prime Minister Gordon Brown, but not out of sight, given his new and more or less globally sponsored mission for the Middle East. The latter is the European Central Bank with its guaranteed absolute autonomy; its incumbent President is Jean-Claude Trichet of France, the much seasoned international banker who had a stint as governor of *Banque de France* starting in 1993.

It may be of interest to remind you that the EU had to fight very hard to get the outside world to understand and accept the EU Commission as the sole body responsible for its Common Commercial Policy. Witness the case of Japan which had to be subjected to the bizarre 1982 Poitier incident by France before it realised that it was not France it had to deal with in order to resolve the issue[24]. Ironically, in spite of the formal adoption by China of a policy for Europe, China is finding it difficult to deal directly with the Commission on related issues, but the reasons for this would take me another session to explain, so instead I refer those of you who are interested to my paper on the 'EU/China Relationship' in the *Asia Europe Journal* issue earlier this year[25].

The lesson to be drawn from this limited perspective is that if the EU would like to enhance its position as an international actor, enlargement would not be *the* answer. It is only by acting through a clearly defined single entity or as one solid bloc with clearly-specified policies that it would be able to do so. Unfortunately, given the state of play, there will be nothing of substance forthcoming from the EU in this direction for a long time to come, but time limitations prevent me from expanding on this.

---

24 In "1982, the French government did not know what to do in the face of the 'Japanese invasion' of the French VTR market, so they adopted the tactic of requiring all Japanese VTRs to go to Poitiers for customs inspection. Poitiers was a town almost completely lacking in staff trained in the procedures of customs inspection; hence a 'go slow' tactic had been adopted, ensuring that Japanese VTRs reached the consumer at a much reduced pace. This was a bizarre incident simply because the French knew very well that their tactic was clearly against the rules of GATT – human ingenuity in the creation of non-tariff trade barriers makes the mind boggle!..[W]hat is of significance is that before that incident, the Japanese government was adamant that it should deal with each member nation of the EC as a separate entity, but while the incident was taking place, the Japanese authorities approached the EC Commission and asked: 'What shall we do in order to solve this problem which is detrimental to our industry?' (Anouil, in an address to the Nihon EC Gakkai – Japan-EC Study Association – Conference held in Waseda University, Tokyo, in November 1984; reproduced in the Conference Proceedings in 1985)"(El-Agraa,1988, p. 6).

25 See, El-Agraa (2007a).

Enlargement has mainly to do with the reality that the EU must accept with open arms all those countries it deems to be 'European'[26].

But let me end on somewhat of a digression. In my presentation, I have stuck very closely to my decision to limit myself to the areas in which the EU acts as one bloc. I do however need to renege on this because there are some developments in which the EU does exert an increasing global influence merely by having become what it is, and the enlargements may somehow reinforce them. A simple example would be the changes in Granger causality for economic cycles, monetary policy, inflation, and so on and so forth. In the past, the US had been the clear leader in these matters even when the problem had been commodity shocks. That is slowly changing as the EU becomes more cohesive. There is now more feedback from the EU to the US: EU monetary policy shocks have an impact on the US economy. This also applies to economic and commercial standards where for example the US has been moving more towards EU accounting norms. In short, generally US hegemony seems to be declining, albeit slowly, and the euro is continuing to gain in popularity and not that slowly. This raises the pertinent and interesting question of who is waiting to take over: would it be the EU or would it be our host nation?

Appendix: the NATO Budgets

According to the US Congressional Budget Office (2007), NATO relies heavily on the 'national military capabilities' of its participating countries, which is tantamount to stating that NATO relies mainly on US military prowess. As one would expect, given the confidentiality, secrecy, vagueness (or whatever one wished to call it) surrounding the 'stocks' of military capabilities, no solid data is made available for public consumption on this dimension. We do however have data on the absolute value and percentage of GNI/GDP spent by each NATO nation on defence, but such data is of no direct relevance to what is argued in the main text of this paper. What we do have and is pertinent is data on the contributions made by each NATO member nation towards meeting the costs of running the alliance. These costs pay for maintaining a professional civilian staff, joint military headquarters and pipeline systems to ensure the distribution of petroleum products needed for military use at times of crisis or war. To meet these costs, NATO has three common budgets with specified shares for each member nation:

1. The civil budget covers the cost of the civil headquarters and personnel in Brussels.
2. The military budget pays for NATO's military headquarters and activities, including the Supreme Headquarters Allied Powers Europe in Mons, Belgium, as well as the NATO Airborne Early Warning and Control programme.

---

26 See, Mayes (2007b).

3. The infrastructure budget, known as the NATO Security Investment Programme (NSIP), which affords the alliance the underwriting of the cost of support facilities, including command, control, communications and intelligence facilities; transportation; and storage facilities.

NATO countries spend about $470 billion on defence each year. Hence the total of the three budgets, given in the final column of Table A1, represents about 2.24% of that expenditure; a minuscule percentage indeed. Note that these shares are determined, by NATO's senior resource board, on the basis of each member nation's GDP.

One may ask why the data in Table A1 stops in 1999 and the answer would be that one is unable to get the latest comprehensive set (below is provided the military budget approved for 2001) although the data provided in table A2 are fairly representative of the general picture. One is however able to compare the percentages provided here with previous ones. According to the Congressional Budget Office (2007), the civil budget cost shares have stayed about the same since 1955 and the military budget cost since 1966. However, those relating to NSIP have been reviewed over the years because the funds in consideration are used for specific construction projects.

Table A1 Allied contributions to NATO's common budgets in 1999 (million 1999 US $)			
	NSIP[1]	Military[2]	Civil	% of total
Belgium	21.1	15.5	4.4	3.7
Canada	16.1	29.0	8.6	4.8
Czech Republic	0.2	3.8	1.4	0.5
Denmark	16.9	9.2	2.4	2.6
France	34.3	29.3	24.7	7.9
Germany	108.0	85.5	25.0	19.6
Greece	4.2	2.1	0.6	0.6
Hungary	0.1	2.7	1.0	0.3
Iceland	0.0	0.2	0.1	0.0
Italy	36.1	32.9	9.3	7.0
Luxembourg	0.9	0.5	0.1	0.1
Netherlands	25.0	15.5	4.4	4.0
Norway	13.2	6.4	1.8	1.9
Poland	0.5	10.3	4.0	1.3
Portugal	1.5	3.5	1.0	0.5
Spain	6.5	19.5	5.6	2.8
Turkey	4.6	8.8	2.6	1.4
United Kingdom	53.6	91.3	27.9	15.5
United States	115.2	129.7	36.2	25.6
Total	**458.0**	**495.7**	**161.1**	**100.0**

Notes: 1. National Security Investment Programme.
2. Does not include contributions to NATO's Airborne Early Warning & Control Programme.
Source: US Congressional Budget Office (2007).

Table A2 Cost shares of NATO member countries' civil and military budgets (% of total)		Military budget			
	Civil budget	(headquarters, agencies and programmes)		(NATO Airborne Early Warning & Control Force)	
Belgium	2.76	2.80	3.30	2.5869	3.2821
Canada	5.35	5.33	5.95	7.1994	9.1343
Czech Republic	0.90	0.90	1.08	0.0000	0.0000
Denmark	1.47	1.68	1.94	1.5282	1.9389
France	15.35	15.25	0.00	0.0000	0.0000
Germany	15.54	15.54	18.20	21.4886	27.2638
Greece	0.38	0.38	0.46	0.4728	0.5999
Hungary	0.65	0.65	0.78	0.0000	0.0000
Iceland	0.05	0.04	0.05	0.0000	0.0000
Italy	5.75	5.91	7.08	5.5485	7.0397
Luxembourg	0.08	0.08	0.10	0.0825	0.1045
Netherlands	2.75	2.84	3.28	2.8625	3.6317
Norway	1.11	1.16	1.36	1.1146	1.4142
Poland	2.48	2.48	2.97	0.0000	0.0000
Portugal	0.63	0.63	0.75	0.5323	0.6754
Spain	3.50	3.50	4.19	2.7700	3.1000
Turkey	1.59	1.59	1.90	1.2419	1.5757
United Kingdom	17.25	16.09	19.12	20.8558	0.0000
United States	22.41	23.15	27.49	31.7160	40.2398
Total	100.00	100.00	100.00	100.0000	100.0000

Source: NATO (2007), *NATO Handbook*.

France does not partake in NATO's integrated military command; hence opts out of many activities funded by the common budgets. This means that the other member nations pay a prorated larger share of the military and NSIP budgets. Spain joined the integrated command in 1988 and now pays more towards the common budgets. Member countries can also negotiate changes in their budgetary shares as did Canada in 1994 when it persuaded several others to assume half of its NSIP share.

What is vital for the argument in the main text however is that the US share of the civil and military budgets has stayed around 25 per cent since the budgets were established in 1951. The addition of the Czech Republic, Hungary and Poland in 1999 reduced the share of the civil budget from 23.3 to 22.5 per cent; that of the military from 28 to 26.2 per cent; and that of the NSIP from 28.3 to 25.2 per cent. Hence, the US pays for a substantial proportion of these budgets even though there are miniscule relative to the county's overall military prowess as measured in terms of the stock of military capability. Note that the common costs of the 1999 enlargement, which NATO estimates at $1.5 billion over a decade, will be shared by the member nations through the military budget an NSIP. Of this total, $1.3 is for infrastructure improvements that are to be met by the NSIP. The share of the US will be about $400 million which is roughly one quarter of the total over the ten years.

Finally, note that currently the military budget also supports the operating costs of the NATO command structure for peace keeping activities (PSO) in Bosnia and Herzegovina and Kosovo. Also, that the total budget approved for 2001 amounted to about €746 million, including about €51 million designated for PSOs. At that time, the exchange rate between the US dollar and euro was on par, but falling fast for the euro; hence a comparison with the $495.7 million given in Table A1 suggests an increase in the military budget, but by how much one should not venture to specify, given the volatility of the euro at the time.

References:

Anouil, Gilles (1985) "EU-Japan relations at a turning point", *EC Studies in Japan*, No. 5, pp. 78-86.

Archer, Clive (2004) "The European Union as an international political actor", in Neill Nugent (ed.), *European Union Enlargement*, Palgrave: New York.

Ardy, Brian and El-Agraa, Ali M (2007) "The general budget", Chapter 19 of Ali M El-Agraa (2007b).

Armstrong, Harvey (2007) "Regional policy", Chapter 22 of Ali M El-Agraa (2007b).

Berkofsky, Axel (2003) "EU's policy towards the DPRK – engagement or standstill?". The European Institute for Asian Studies: Brussels.

Brülhart, Marius and Matthews, Alan (2007) "EU external trade policy", Chapter 24 of Ali M El-Agraa (2007b).

Council of the European Union (2007a), *Presidency Conclusions*, Brussels European Council 21/22 June.

Council of the European Union (2007b), *Presidency Conclusions*, Lisbon European Council 5 October.

El-Agraa, Ali M (2007a) "The EU/China Relationship: not seeing eye to eye?", *The Asia Europe Journal*, vol. 5, no. 2. pp. 193-215.

El-Agraa, Ali M (ed.) (2007b) *The European Union: Economics and Policies*. Cambridge University Press: Cambridge and New York. 8th edition of *The Economics of the European Community*, 1980.

El-Agraa, Ali M (ed.) (2002) "Will Britain adopt the euro?", Chapter 13 of Ali M El-Agraa (ed), *The Euro and Britain: Implications of Moving into the EMU*. Prentice Hall, Financial Times and Pearson Education: London and New York.

El-Agraa, Ali M (1988), *Japan's Trade Frictions: Realities or Misconceptions?* Macmillan: London; St. Martins Press: New York.

Elgström, O. and Smith, M. (eds.) (2006), *The European Union's Roles in International Politics: Concepts and Analysis*. Routledge: Lonon.

EU Commission (1997), *Agenda 2000: For a Stronger and wider Union*.

EU Commission (2000), *Agenda 2000: Setting the Scene for Reform*. 2 volumes: http://www.europa.eu.int/comm/agriculture/publi/review98/08_09_en.pdf

EU Commission (2003), *Convention for the Future of Europe*. http://european-convention.eu.int

EU Commission (2004), *Provisional Consolidated Version of the Draft Treaty establishing a Constitution for Europe*. EU Commission: Brussels.

EU Commission (2007) "GDP per capita in PPS", http://epp.eurostat.ec.europa.eu/

European Court of Auditors (various years), "Annual Report Concerning the Financial Year...", *Official Journal of the European Communities/Union*.

Eurostat (2007), *Europe in Figures: Eurostat Yearbook 2006-07*.

Laatikainen, K. V. and Smith, K. E. (2006), *The European Union and the United Nations: Intersecting Multilateralism*. Palgrave Macmillan: Basingstoke.

Lee, Moonsung (2007) "The EU's Korea relationship: enlargement effects", *The Asia Europe Journal*, vol. 5, no. 2. pp. 367-379.

Mayes, David G (2007a) "Enlargement", Chapter 26 of Ali M El-Agraa (2007b).

Mayes, David G (2007b) "The operation of EMU", Chapter 12 of Ali M El-Agraa (2007b).

Mayes, David G and El-Agraa, Ali M (2007) "The development of EU economic and monetary integration", Chapter 11 of Ali M El-Agraa (2007b).

NATO (2007), *NATO Handbook*. http://www.nato.int/doc/handbook/2001/hb090801.htm

O'Brennan, J. (2006), *The Eastern Enlargement of the European Union*. Routledge: London.

Openeurope (2007), *A Guide to the Constitutional Treaty*. http://www.openeurope.org.uk

Reichard, M. (2006), *The EU-NATO Relationship: a Legal and Political Perspective*. Ashgate: Aldershot.

Sauter, W. and Langer, L. (2007) "Competition Policy", Chapter 13 of Ali M El-Agraa (2007b).

UK Treasury (2003), *UK Membership of the Single Currency: An assessment of the Five Economic Tests*. http://assessment.treasury.gov.uk

United Nations (2007), *Improving Lives: Results from the Partnership of the United Nations and the European Commission in 2006*. United Nations System in Brussels: Brussels.

US Congressional Budget Office (2007), *NATO Burden-sharing After Enlargement*. http://www.cbo.gov/ftpdoc.cfm?index=2976&type=0&sequence=4

Young, Hugo (1998) *This Blessed Plot: Britain and Europe: from Churchill to Blair*. Macmillan: London.

World Bank (2007), *World Development Indicators 2007*. The World Bank: Washington DC.

The Four Dilemmas of the European Union[1]

Toshiro Tanaka

1. Introduction

Year 2005 may be recorded in future as the European Union had turned a corner for departing from the age of Internal Market and revival of new dynamism in European integration to the age of inward-looking and "enhanced cooperation".

The previous year, 2004 was full of rosy pictures on the development of the European Union. On May 1, ten states, mostly former members of the Warsaw Pact and the COMECON, formally joined the European Union, symbolising the end of the divided Europe and new unity of Europe. On October 29, the Head of State or Governments of the member states of the European Union had signed Treaty and the Final Act establishing a Constitution for Europe in Rome[2].

But, seven months later, on 29 May 2005, the French people rejected the Constitutional Treaty. 69.34% of the French voters went to polling stations for the ratification of the Constitutional Treaty and 54.9% were opposed to it (45.1% in favour). The result was far more decisive than the result of referendum in 1992 on Maastricht Treaty. Three days later, on June 1st, 62. 8% of Dutch voters went to vote and 61.7% of voters were opposed to it (38.3% in favour). It was an overwhelming and a landslide victory for "no" groups.

At the European Council held at Brussels on June 16-17, 2005, the European leaders issued declaration that read "the ratification process will continue, but the timetable for the ratification in different member states will be altered if necessary". They had agreed to set a period of reflection, clarification and discussion within Member States and they would come back to this matter in the first half of 2006"under Austrian Presidency. Therefore, November 1st 2006, the target date for the Treaty to come in force written in the Treaty, had been virtually abandoned. At least, the European summit had prevented the "Domino of Noes" by setting a period of reflection to salvage the Treaty.

The period of reflection was extended for another year at the Brussels summit one year later on 15-16 June 2006. The European leaders asked "the Presidency (Germany) to present a report during the first semester of 2007 and....it being understood that the

---

1   This paper was originally presented as "The State of the Union of the European Union" at the 4th NESCA Workshop and 4th EUSA Asia Pacific Conference on "The Enlarged EU as an International Actor", 11-13 October 2007, Fudan University, Shanghai, PRC. The new title has received a hint by Giandomenico Majone, *Dilemmas of European Integration: The Ambiguities & Pitfalls of Integration by Stealth,* Oxford, Oxford University Press, 2005.

2   For details see Toshiro Tanaka, "From Convention through the IGC to the European Constitution", *EU Studies in Japan,* No.25, 2005.

necessary steps to that effect will have been taken during the second semester of 2008 at the latest (France)"[3]. European leaders met again in Berlin and concluded "Declaration on the occasion of the fiftieth anniversary of the signature of the Treaties of Rome" by proclaiming that "we are united in our aim of placing the European Union on a renewed common basis before the European Parliament elections in 2009"[4] without any reference to the constitution.

Then, with strong leadership of German Presidency with Chancellor Angela Merkel and her SPD Foreign Minister, Frank-Walter Steinmeier, European Council on 21-22 June 2007 finally agreed to reset European Constitutional Treaty and to convene the IGC-2007 to draw up the Reform Treaty with precise mandate[5]. The IGC-2007 has convened by Portugal on June 23 and representatives from the Member States, European Commission and European Parliament had been engaged in process of drawing up a text with support of Secretariat of the Council.

On 2 October, the Portuguese Presidency made it known that legal experts had "found agreement" on the reform of the EU institutions, stating the "Treaty is ready"[6]. The provisional draft version of the EU's Reform Treaty was sent to European Heads of State and Governments to discuss over political issues when they met at informal summit in Lisbon on 18-19 October. The European Leaders then agreed and decided to sign on "Lisbon Treaty" on 13 December 2007.

All these events show that there are four dilemmas which the European Union is now facing: (1) The dilemma between 'neo-liberal Europe' and 'social Europe', (2) The dilemma of enlargement, (3) The dilemma of democracy, and (4) The dilemma between 'maximalists' and 'minimalists'.

2. Why did the French and Dutch voters reject the Constitutional Treaty?

It was not rivalry between Europe and France as in 1992 on Maastricht Treaty, but it was battle between 'neo-liberal Europe' and 'social Europe' in France. The 'no' groups succeeded to collect people who had vague fears against how the European Union affects their daily lives. As the rumour of 'Polish plumbers' indicated, the majority of the voters feared on the cheap labours from new Member States, and they thought them as 'social dumping'. *Flash Eurobarometer,* No. 171 (The European Constitution:

---

3   Council of the European Union, Presidency Conclusions-15/16 June 2006, 10633/1/06 REV1 , Brussels, 17 July 2006, para, 47-48.

4   Germany 2007—Presidency of the European Union, "Declaration on the occasion of the fiftieth anniversary of the signature of the Treaties of Rome", 25.03.2007.

5   For the analysis of referendums and the reflection period, see Toshiro Tanaka, "Failure of the European Constitutional Treaty: Background and Prospect (in Japanese) ", *Kaigai Jijyo (Journal of World Affairs),* Vol. 54, No. 2, February 2006 and Toshiro Tanaka, "Prospect of a Treaty establishing a Constitution for Europe (in Japanese) ", *Kaigai Jijyo,* Vol. 55, No. 6, June 2007.

6   "Legal experts hand over draft EU Treaty for approval", *EurActive,* 3 October 2007.

34

Post-referendum)[7], confirmed that " 'No' voters gave as the reason for their vote the fact that in their opinion the Constitution would have negative effects on employment in France (31%), whose economic situation in terms of unemployment is already considered to be to high (26%)"(para. 2.3).

The French and Dutch 'noes' have damaged the credibility of the European Union and its 'neo-liberal' way of policy management. The most important message of the "White Paper on the completing Internal Market" of 1985 and "Single European Act" of 1986 was the "competition in a borderless Europe". The competition has revived European economy and has eventually revitalized the integration dynamics and process. However, the message of French voters and lesser extent in the case of Dutch voters was "no more social dumping with free movement of workers from less developed European countries" and more 'Social Europe'.

Nicholas Sarkozy, new French President, had surprised his European partners in Brussels and then has succeeded to delete the commitment "to free and distorted" competition, which was in the European Constitutional Treaty to explain internal market in the objectives of the Union, from the Reform Treaty, while 'full employment' and 'social progress' remained as objectives. He has succeeded to ally concerns in his country that the EU has become too 'Anglo-Saxon'[8]. Mario Monti, the former EU competition commissioner who crashed with Mr. Sarkozy over the French bail-out of the engineering giant Alstrum, said that the change would undermine the Commission's role as an antitrust watchdog, including taking on multinational giants, including ones based in the United States[9].

Europe may move back to be more inward-looking and less competition and less European measures. Paradoxically, Europe may lose the source of their dynamism in economy, which even 'non- voters' would not like to face.

3. The dilemma of enlargement

The European Union may become less eager for enlargement in future. To enlarge the area of peace, prosperity, stability and democracy to the rest of Europe will surely be good thing, but it will cost more for the existing members because rich countries like Switzerland and Norway stay away from the EU and possible candidates are relatively poorer. Bulgaria and Romania finally managed to become member on January 1 2007. But, further enlargement will be more delicate and cautious issue.

---

7   *Flash Eurobarometer,* No. 171 (The European Constitution: Post-referendum survey in France, Fieldwork: 30&31 May 2005.
8   George Parker, Tobias Buck and Bertrand Benoit, "Key clause dropped from the EU treaty", FT.com Europe, last updated: June 21 2007 22:21.
9   *Ibid.*

But, the most recent *Standard Eurobarometer,* No. 67/Spring 2007[10] indicates that public opinion has become somewhat more favourable towards further enlargement. Support for further increasing the numbers of Member States in the Union has risen from 46% to 49%, with a similar decrease in opposition from 42% to 39% (p.30). There is a difference in opinion on further enlargement with average support running at 68% in twelve new Member States and 43 % in the former EU15 countries (p.30). The highest support for enlargement is found in Poland (76%), followed by Lithuania (68%), Slovenia and Romania (both 67%). At end of the spectrum, majority is against enlargement, in Austria (64%), France (60%), Germany (59), Finland (56 %) and the UK (48%)(QA27.4).

As far as the candidate countries are concerned, 72% of respondents in Croatia support their membership in the EU, and only 19% are against. 50% in Turkey support their membership and 26% are against.

Croatia may likely to join before 2014. But, Turkey's accession may face severe setback in future, although the formal negotiations between the EU and Turkey had been started on October 3, 2005 by "stopping the clock", along with Croatia. The worst scenario is that Turkey successfully negotiates the entry conditions after 10 or even 15 years and the accession treaty with ten year transitional period before Turkey to become full member, then one Member States, possibly France or Austria, may reject Turkish entry by referendum, and Turkey will be excluded from Europe. In order for Turkey to become a full member of the European Union, Turkey has to win on three fronts. First front is at Brussels in negotiation and the second front is within Turkey to maintain the support for the accession. The third and most difficult front will be in all 27 Member States of the European to get recognition that Turkey is European and on their side.

The European Union has to close her curtain someday, although the prospect of enlargement has been most important motives for possible candidate countries to make reform and adapt to the EU norms and standards. And if the European Union could open her door to country with different culture and religion, it will prove itself that the European Union is an open community and seeks for United in Diversity as the slogan says.

4. The dilemma of democracy

Although it was the third time that France had referendum on European issue, it was the first time that the Netherlands went for referendum on European issue. The Dutch government went for referendum because "The Constitution is not just another treaty amendment, and therefore, more involvement of citizens is necessary". This is the

---

10 *Standard Eurobarometer,* No. 67/Spring 2007 (Fieldwork: April-May 2007, First Results, Publication: June 2007).

third dilemma that the EU is facing. The more direct democracy for citizens, the more risk for the political leaders. Then, the Dutch government lost the war. Referendum is very democratic mean to hear voice of the citizens on the certain issue directly. But, at the same time, referendum is very risky mean, because the voters do not necessarily vote on the pros and cons of the specific issue. The European issue may be fought on national issues.

The ratification of the European Constitutional Treaty required unanimity amongst 27 Member States. The more than half of Member States, 18, including Bulgaria and Romania had completed their ratification procedures. Even after the two 'noes', Latvia, Cyprus, Malta and later Finland completed their own ratification procedure through parliamentary votes. Luxembourg was the only country went for referendum after the two 'noes' on July 10, and more than 90% of voters went to polling stations and 56.52% supported the ratification with 43.48% voted for no. Sweden had postponed their parliamentary procedures after the June 2005 Brussels informal summit. And, those Member States, which had announced to go for referendums, had postponed the referendums to 2006 or even to 2007. Britain, which had quickly announced to freeze the ratification procedure indefinitely even before the June 2005 informal summit, had allies, namely Denmark, Poland, Portugal, Czech Republic and Ireland.

These institutional impasse and dead rock have killed the European Constitutional Treaty. The Reform Treaty will be signed on December 13 2007 at Lisbon and the "Lisbon Treaty" will be put on ratification process of 27 Member States. With the experience of the ratification process on the European Constitutional Treaty, the ratification of the Lisbon Treaty may not be easy. Therefore, French and Dutch leaders may not go for referendums on the Reform Treaty but ratify through parliamentary procedure. Nicholas Sarkozy had been speaking of a simplified reform treaty or a 'Mini-Treaty' through Parliamentary approval for many months even before the Presidential election and thought to have received the mandate by his election as President. Dutch Prime Minister, Jan Peter Balkenende had already announced on 21 September 2007 that his government would follow a non-binding opinion of the Council of State, which had ruled that a referendum is not necessary because the new European Treaty...will not affect the National Constitution[11]. Only Ireland will surely go for referendum by their Constitutional obligation. Demark may go for referendum if they could not have five sixth support in the Folketing. A new British Prime Minister Gorgon Brown has insisted that the document should be ratified through Parliament although there are calls for referendum from the Eurosceptic lobbies and the pro-referendum campaigners[12]. How will Czech Republic and Poland do?

---

11 "Dutch PM rules out EU Treaty referendum", *EurActive,* 24 September 2007.
12 Hugo Brady, "Yes to a referendum, but not on this treaty", Centre for European Reform *bulletin,* Issue 56, October/November 2007.

5. The dilemma between 'maximalists' and 'minimalists'

The Reform Treaty, as produced in the Brussels summit on June 20-21 2007, is a compromise between 'maximalists', the states which would like to integrate more towards federal system, and 'minimalists', the states which would like to keep their sovereign power as it has and reluctant to delegate more.

The maximalist states, which had already ratified the European Constitutional Treaty, and representatives from Ireland and Portugal, with Spanish and Luxembourgish initiative, had a meeting in Madrid on 26 January 2007, gave strong backing for 'Maxi-treaty'[13]. But, 'Minimalists' states strengthened their offensives, although they had once agreed and signed European Constitutional Treaty. After German Presidency had conducted a series of bilateral consultations with other Member States, Germany came up with the draft of the Reform Treaty, and has finally succeeded to get agreement at Brussels summit on 21-22 June 2007. At 4:30 am on Saturday 23 June, after 36 hours of wrangling, European leaders agreed on deal to revive parts of the failed EU Constitutional Treaty[14].

Katinka Barysch, Centre for European Reform, wrote that "Merkel delivered more than many people had expected. The official objective of the German presidency was to get a negotiating mandate for a new IGC: it was not strictly necessary for Merkel to get agreements on the minutiae of the new treaty....Merkel aimed to settle as many outstanding issues as possible. The resulting deal was so comprehensive that it surprised even the optimists"[15].

But even Merkel once threatened to press ahead with drafting the new treaty and propose to convene the IGC without Poland, when Lech Kaczynski, Polish President, repeatedly made references the second world war. Polish leader claimed that "Germany owed Poland the new voting system: if it had not been for the second world war, Poland's population today would be 66 million, instead of 38 million". With the help of Sarkozy, Tony Blair, Spain's Jose Zapatero and Lithuania's Valdas Adamkus, the Poles finally compromised. The EU will adopt the double majority voting system, not in 2009 but in 2014 with another three year transition period. Poland also secured clause on energy solidarity in the treaty and a clause that insulated Polish law-making on morality, family and religion from the Charter for fundamental rights[16].

Tony Blair, another minimalist champion, in his final summit as Prime Minister won concessions on the "red line" areas, covering national sovereignty in the areas of foreign policy, criminal law, labour law and social security. Especially, in a victory for

---

13 "'Friends of the Constitutions' wants 'Maxi-EU Treaty'", *EurActive,* 29 2007/updated: 20 April 2007.
14 Katinka Barysch, "What the summit says about the EU", *Blog Archive,* Centre for European Reform, June 26 2007.
15 Katinka Barysch, *Ibid.*
16 Bertrand Benoit, "Polish leader warms to Merkel's soft touch", FT. Com. Europe, June 22 2007, 22:51.

the Prime Minister, Britain obtained in full its desired opt-out from the Charter for fundamental rights to ensure the European Court of Justice would have no jurisdiction over British employment matters[17]. But, it seemed odd that Britain made last minutes demand to cut the powers and resources of the new foreign minister, given that Britain had been behind the initiatives to create EU Foreign Minister[18]. The damages created were not only the renaming of the name of Union Minister for Foreign Affairs to the High Representative of the Union for Foreign Affairs and Security Policy but to divide a single treaty document into two documents, the Treaty on the European Union (TEU) and the Treaty on the Functioning of the Union (TFEU). General provisions on the Union's External Action and the specific provisions on the Common Foreign and Security Policy (CFSP) will be inserted in the ETU. The specific provisions on the CFSP will be as follows: "The CFSP is subject to specific procedures. It shall be defined and implemented by the European Council and the Council acting unanimously, except where the Treaties provides otherwise. The adoption of legislative acts shall be excluded...[19]".

6. Conclusions

As a result, "the TEU and TFEU will not have a constitutional character....The Term "Constitution" will not be used...There will be no article in the amended Treaties mentioning the symbols of the EU such as the flag, the anthem or the motto"[20].

Although the Reform Treaty, now Lisbon Treaty, may not be as beautiful as European Constitutional Treaty, it may contain more than 90% of the articles already agreed in the European Constitutional Treaty. Especially, the new posts of "President" and "High Representative" would replace the rotating presidency as, respectively, chair of the European Council and chair of the Foreign Minister's meetings. The High Representative would become a single external spokesman for the EU and "European External Action Service" would be established by experts recruited from European Commission, Council and the Member States. The Delegations of the European Commission in almost all capitals of the world and two Representative Office of the Council in New York and Geneva will be merged as the Delegation of the European Union. Although the European Union still has and would have much of limits and restrictions, "the European Union is a global player, ready to share in the responsibility for global security and in building a better world" as clearly expressed in the Solana

---

17 James Blitz, "London confident 'red lines' will hold out", FT.Com. Europe, last up-dated 23 June 2007, 00:00.
18 Katinka Barysch, *Ibid.*
19 Council of the European Union, Presidency Conclusions-21/22 June 2007, 11177/1/07 REV1, CONCL 2, Brussels, 20 July 2007, Annex□, Amendments to the EU Treaty, p.27.
20 Presidency Conclusions-21/22 June 2007, *ibid.,* Annex□,Draft IGC Mandate, para. 3, p. 16.

paper[21]. Whether the enlarged European Union will be able to act as an important and effective international actor in global world entirely depends on how twenty seven Member States can form common guidelines and positions, speak in a single European voice and take joint actions.

---

21 Council of the European Union, "A Secure Europe in a Better World: European Security Strategy", Brussels, 12 December 2003, p. 1.

Supranational Power:
Approaching a Theoretical Dilemma

Andreas Vasilache

It goes without saying that the scientific community is well aware that the singularity of the EU originates particularly from its supranational aspects.[1] Nonetheless, given the quantity and the diversification of literature on European integration, it is quite remarkable that books or papers that explicitly deal with the idea and the conceptual framework of supranational integration (or have that term in their title) are quite rare. While European Integration Studies prefer to concentrate on the institutional outline and the actual working of European governance in practice (of course without neglecting the supranational character of the EU), political philosophy – when focusing on the question of supranationalism – does not show particular interest in the European integration, but rather concentrates its attention on the concept of the *Weltrepublik*[2] in which – from a systematic perspective – the tension between supranational integration on the one hand, and state sovereignty on the other hand is resolved by the liquidation of the state and the establishment of a greater or even global republic.

The tendency to postulate – either in an implicit or explicit manner – the supranational character of certain policy-fields of the EU on the one hand, but not discussing the concept of supranationalism on the other hand, and especially not clarifying where the superiority of a supranational power lies, may be due to the conceptual precariousness of the idea of supranational power within the theoretical framework of the state. From the perspective of state theory, supranational integration is a difficult concept. It consists in the claim to meta-sovereignty while the sovereignty of the nation state supposedly remains intact, since supranationalism indicates the superiority over the state. This implies the existence of two competing sovereigns, i.e. a reduplication or a division of the sovereign power into two parts – an idea that can hardly be maintained within the conceptual framework of the state. Nonetheless, I think there are good theoretical reasons to state the supranational aspects of the EU. But this demands, of necessity, a reformulation of what supranational power actually is and how supranational power as a concept could be constructed and sketched in a theoretically conclusive and analytically fruitful way – after having deconstructed it, or in more general terms, after having taken it apart.

---

1   See for example Schmalz 2004, p. 123, Meyers 2004, p. 499.
2   For this discussion see for instance Merkel/Wittmann (eds.) 1996, Lutz-Bachmann/Bohman (eds.) 2002, and of course Höffe 1999, Gosepath/Merle (eds.) 2002 and – with regard to the relationship between supranational coercive power and the state – in particular Horn 2002.

I. Is Supranational Power possible at all?

No Common Power: The Realist Perspective on State Theory and on Supranationalism

Going back to social contract theory as the only genuine theory of the sovereign state, realist and neo-realist thought stresses the conceptual impossibility of supranational integration. According to the (neo-) realist interpretation of social contract theory,[3] the main conceptual feature of state sovereignty is its legal and factual monopoly on the use of force.[4] As the *raison d'être* of the state consists in overcoming the anarchic and therefore belligerent state of nature in which every person has unrestrained freedom of action,[5] sovereignty follows from the free will of individuals in the state of nature to relinquish their boundless and anarchic liberty and to forgo their power and their natural right to everything (life and health of others included), submitting to one single superior authority.[6] As the inhospitality of the state of nature resulted from the chaotic rivalry of individual interests and from the reciprocal threat of violence it is essential to end this anarchic cacophony and to have one sole sovereign agent. From the moment of the individual relinquishment of power, only the sovereign has the right to declare generally binding laws and has the exclusive legitimacy and the means to the use of force in order to enforce the rule of law. Without an efficient monopoly on the use of force – united in one hand and indivisible – no law or regulation is conceivable, because – as Hobbes puts it – agreements [...] without the Sword, are but Words [...].[7] And for Locke it is obvious that there has to be a clear and indivisible centre of sovereign power because it is [...] ridiculous to imagine one can be tied ultimately to *obey* any *Power* in the Society, which is not *the Supreme*. [...][8] Hence, the existence of one single sovereign power – understood as the sovereign's ability to assert the monopoly on the use of force in a legal way – is a minimum requirement for every state.

Supranational power in a strict systematic sense implies the existence of a superior power that is able to impose its will on the state, thus a power that is more powerful than the single state and that disposes of superior means of violence. It is an obvious

---

3   See Morgenthau 1993, pp. 333ff and Waltz 1969, pp. 163-186.
4   See for example Hobbes 1985, pp. 227f.
5   Cf. Locke 1966, pp. 298ff, 344f, Hobbes 1985, pp. 184ff, 227f, 353ff and Rousseau 1964, pp. 176, 191, 361, 422f.
6   See Hobbes 1985, pp. 225ff, Locke 1966, pp. 341ff and Rousseau 1964, pp. 360ff and on the alienation of natural liberty and the setting-up of sovereign stateness Kersting 2002, pp. 58ff.
7   Hobbes 1985, p. 223.
8   Locke 1960, p. 375 (italics by J.L.). Regardless of the differences between their approaches – especially with regard to the democratic or absolutist organization of their versions of the contractarian state –, Hobbes, Locke, Rousseau and Kant agree on the absolute necessity of having one ultimate sovereign authority and a clear and undoubted monopoly on the use of force. See also the excellent remarks of Preuß 2007, pp. 313-335 on the idea of sovereignty with special attention to its changes and ongoing relevance in the international context.

feature of the international system[9] that there exists no such common supranational power with the actual ability to impose its will on the states, either inside or outside of the EU,[10] and, within the framework of (neo-) realist theory, it is easy to explain. As an efficient monopoly on the use of force is the core attribute of the sovereign power and a precondition of stateness the alienation of power from the sovereign state to a supranational authority would ipso facto mean the loss of sovereignty of the state and, thus, the end of the state itself. Therefore, a voluntary transfer of sovereignty from the state to a supranational power is hardly imaginable[11], since the renunciation of sovereignty would mean giving up both the state's raison d'être and its constitutive sine qua non. This ultimately implies that, even in the unlikely case of a transfer of sovereignty to a superior agency, this new sovereign power could hardly be considered to be a supranational one, but rather as a new and bigger state power, i.e. as a regional or even global *Leviathan* since the former state has ceased to exist.[12] Thus, from the (neo-) realist perspective, which, in this point, goes back to classic (contractarian) state theory in general (i.e. not only to the Hobbesian tradition),[13] the very idea of supranationalism has to be considered as an contradiction in terms.

The Idealist Challenge to Realism

Liberal, neo-liberal, institutionalist and neo-institutionalist approaches challenge the (neo-) realist strictness in the interpretation of state theory. This is also the case for the mainstream of European Studies, since the existence of this research field already presupposes the belief in institutions. These approaches are quite frequently subsumed under the term of idealist theories of International Relations (IR),[14] as, in opposition to (neo-) realist thought, they *firstly* stress the importance of values, societal interests, beliefs and progress for the civilization of international politics. From this follows, *secondly*, that these approaches underline the possibility of mastering international anarchy by durable and stable institutional cooperation and integration. They emphasize that it is indeed possible for states to bind their will and behavior to international institutions or even to partially alienate their sovereign power to a superior agency without giving up their own existence as sovereign entities. Because the question of supranational power refers to both the common conceptual ground of these theoretical directions within the idealist schools, and the systematic correspondences to (neo-) realist thought, in the following discussion, I will use the more general term of idealist

---

9   Cf. Lieber 1991, pp. 356f.
10 The relevance of neo-realist thinking with regard to Europe is underlined by Mearsheimer 1990.
11 See Waltz 1979, pp. 91f, 96.
12 See Waltz 1979, p. 92 who explicitly writes that states might [...] prefer amalgamation with other states to their own survival [...].
13 See Waltz 1969, pp. 163-186.
14 See Zangl/Zürn 2003, pp. 25-37 and Menzel 2001, pp. 20ff.

theories and will not focus on the differences between (neo-) liberal and (neo-) institutionalist approaches.[15]

Laubach-Hintermeier, for instance, emphasizes that the global Leviathan on the one hand, and the anarchic state of nature on the other hand, are not – as the (neo-) realist paradigm suggests – the only two alternatives, but instead the two ends of a broad continuum. In between those extremities, she discerns plenty of institutional possibilities in order to stabilize and to control state behavior.[16] From this perspective, states are able to commit themselves to inter-, trans-, and even supranational institution-building that are meant to be of long duration and not subject to the arbitrariness of the state's day-to-day politics. Critics of the (neo-) realist interpretation of state theory point out that states might well be advised to bind their behavior to international institutions (like the UN), to transnational institutions (as for instance the PISA consortium) or even to institutions that are seen as supranational (as the European Court of Justice or certain policy-fields of the EU). Regional and global governance and integration (in the broader sense) are perceived to be rational choices for the state in order to overcome the dangerous implications of the global anarchy of states. Institutionalized economic cooperation in this respect seems to be of particular importance, and the democratic constitution of the state is seen as very advantageous for regional or even global institution-building and in particular for conflict prevention and solution.[17]

These suggestions are highly plausible and empirically proven, but they remain within the classic theoretical framework of the sovereign state.[18] Idealist thinking in IR and European Studies approaches provides an anti-realist interpretation of state theory and goes back (among other sources) to enlightenment philosophy and, in particular, to Kant's famous treatise on perpetual peace.[19] Although within the idealist tradition it is possible to develop a changed perception of international and transnational governance, this is not the case in regard to supranational power, since idealist approaches do not substantially challenge the concept of state sovereignty. The idea of sovereignty understood as the monopoly on the use of force and as the self-contained decision-making power of the state is not contested; indeed, the sovereign state takes precedence over any kind of inter- and transnational institutions. Kant explicitly points out the logical inconsistency and systematic impossibility to shape a concept of supranationalism within state theory as this would [...] according to reason [...][20] necessarily imply the fusion of states to a world republic and, hence, the dissolution of the former states.[21] As states would not agree to their unification and amalgamation

---

15 Please note that the use of the superordinated term which is necessary here does not deny the distinctions between different (neo-) liberal/(neo-) institutionalist etc. approaches.

16 Cf. Laubach-Hintermeier 1998, p. 90.

17 On the theorem of democratic peace see still the very good reader of Brown et al. (eds.) 1996.

18 This is underlined also by Zangl/Zürn 2003, pp. 59f, 140, 147.

19 See Menzel 2001, pp. 29f.

20 Kant 2006, p. 81.

21 Cf. ibid., pp. 78, 81.

to one giant state Kant suggests trans- and international measures in order to overcome a situation of constant reciprocal threat in international politics: [...] But since they [the states, A.V.] do not [...] want the positive idea of a *world republic* at all [...], only the *negative* surrogate of a lasting and continually expanding *federation* that prevents war can curb the inclination to hostility and defiance of the law, though there is the constant threat of its breaking loose again [...].[22]

We discern that, although idealist theory provides very different outcomes than (neo-) realist thought, it still refers to the same classic concept of stateness and sovereignty. The analytical framework of its interpretation of global politics remains largely unchanged. Non-realist approaches come to very different results than (neo-) realist thought in regard to both the possibility of institution-building and integration beyond the state on the one hand, and the appeasing impact of economic cooperation, of value-based policies and of democratic structures on the other hand. But in regard to the question of supranationalism the differences between (neo-) realist theory and its critics are insignificant, as both traditions are based on the theory of the sovereign state. When it comes to the systematic and conceptual logic of supranational integration, the critics of (neo-) realist thought have to go back to the idea of the *Weltrepublik* as a global Leviathan and, thus, meet their (neo-) realist opponents. The theoretical framework of idealist approaches is the contractarian state. They might favor Kant over Hobbes, but Hobbes' presence can be denied neither beside nor within Kant. Hence, with regard to supranationalism idealist theory-building is caught in the same dilemma as realist theories are. On the one hand, supranational integration is politically quite improbable as it would mean the alienation of sovereignty and thus the dissolution and loss of what it means to be a state. On the other hand, the unlikely event of the alienation of sovereignty would simply lead to a new and bigger state that, from a theoretical perspective, is not supranational, as the subjects of supranational power (that is the states) are not existent any more.[23]

This systematic problem of the concept of supranationalism cannot be solved by bringing into play other criteria for defining supranational power. For instance, the intention alone of an inter- or transnational organization to influence national policies or laws can hardly account for supranational power, since virtually every organization claims to do so. Neither is it conclusive to consider as the distinctive mark for supranational power the responsibility of an inter- or transnational organization for particular policy-fields and its temporal precedence over the states in dealing with problems in these policy-fields, since every international regime (such as, for instance, OPEC) could then be seen as a supranational organization. The same is true for the suggestion that the handling of transnational problems in combination with a decision-

---

22 Ibid., p. 81 (italics by I.K.).
23 Horn 2002, pp. 153-164 ignores this logical dilemma when he claims the necessity of a global coercive power and (conclusively) denies the continued existence of single states – but still regards this world republic as a supranational entity.

taking process that does not require a consensus can account for supranationalism.[24] Apart from the fact that in globalized political frameworks virtually every political actor deals with problems of transnational relevance, many inter- and transnational organizations do not require consensual decisions for the very reason that, in the end, the states cannot be forced to implement the decisions anyway. However, from this perspective, even the UN General Assembly – an institution that was built in order to secure and protect national sovereignty – could be considered as a supranational institution. These criteria (or a combination of these criteria) do not provide any analytical gain as they do not allow us to draw a distinction between supranational organizations on the one hand and any other kind of international, transnational, multilateral institutions, organizations or regimes on the other hand.

Neither would it help us to solve our problem if we were to introduce a distinction between super- and supranational power, as this suggestion would not address the core question of in what respect supra- or supernational authorities are superior to the state. The distinction between super- and supranational power is hardly conclusive as long as we are not able to say what exactly the superiority of a supranational entity to the state consists of. Finally, the reference to the social construction of the ideas and perceptions that build the global political system can't provide an answer to our question on supranational power either because the highly plausible insight into the social construction of the concepts of state sovereignty and of global anarchy[25] does not undermine the theoretical and factual power of these conceptions and traditions. The constructivist perception denies the idea of the inevitability of social arrangements but this must not to be confused with the proof of implausibility of particular constructs, and is by no means to be misconceived as a confrontation of social constructs with an ideal of objective truth.[26] Hence, pointing out how particular concepts (such as, for instance, state sovereignty) have been produced by men does not per se overcome the need to work and to deal with theoretical frameworks that are socially constructed.

As we are interested here in the question of supranational power, we should take a brief look at the EU's claim to superiority. In so doing, we will ask whether, from the perspective of classic (contractarian) state theory (and its emphasis on the monopoly on the use of force), which provides the conceptual basis for both (neo-) realist theory and its idealist and European Studies critics, the EU can be considered to have any supranational power at all.

---

24 Zangl/Zürn 2003, p. 161ff consider organizations that deal with transnational issues and in which decisions are not based on consensus as supra-state and supranational institutions, like for instance the International Monetary Fund (IMF) and the World Trade Organization (WTO).

25 See for instance Biersteker/Weber (eds.) 1996 and Weller 2003.

26 I have dealt with constructivist thought for example in Vasilache 2003, 2007.

Conditional Superiority is no Superiority

It is sufficient to mention just one point in order to demonstrate that from the perception of contractarian state theory the EU can hardly be seen as a supranational entity. Thus, the essential question here is not whether European legislative initiatives have to be confirmed by the Council of Ministers, i.e. whether the intergovernmental aspect is a sine qua non of European law making, or whether European acts have to be passed (or not) by each member state in order to become national law, i.e. to come into force and to be implemented.[27] Similarly, it is not essential to demonstrate that the precedence of the European Court of Justice over national courts is a conditional one, and that, for instance, the German Constitutional Court has decided that the precedence of European courts ends at that point where their decisions contradict the German Basic Law.[28]

In order to show the unrestrained persistence of state sovereignty within the framework of the EU, it is enough to stress the simple fact that the member state can withdraw from the EU when it does not want to take up a subordinate role to the EU any more. Every member state of the EU can at any time abscond from the Union's laws, regulations, decrees and initiatives by leaving the European Union. Any kind of institutional influence of the Union on the single state is meaningless if the national parliament decides that the state will retreat from the Union. Thus, from the systematic state theory perspective, any kind of subordination of the state under the authority of the EU – including the payment of penalties – has in the end to be understood as an absolutely voluntary act. By subordinating itself to the EU's authority, the state recognizes that following the Union's decisions might be advantageous. But this is not to say that it represents the recognition of an irrecoverable and irreversible superiority of the EU over the sovereign state. The EU's precedence over the member state in defined policy-fields has to be (and in fact is) recognized by both national law and national courts of the member states over and over again – without renouncing in principle the primacy of national legislative sovereignty and without renouncing at all the national monopoly on the use of force. From this follows that the legislative precedence of the EU is conditional and can be revised by national law without challenging the rule of law itself, the separation of powers, the democratic structure or any core attribute of the sovereign state, hence, without any systematic risk of legal national disintegration. In the last instance, there is no restriction of national legislative

---

27 Even Art. 25 of the German Basic Law for example – stating that international law automatically builds an integral part of the German law – does in the end not limit the legislative sovereignty of the state as this article can be abolished by the national legislation process at any time. In spite of Art. 25, Art. 23 (concerning the European integration) and Art. 24 (concerning international organizations) of the German Basic Law, there is usually of course still the necessity to pass international agreements into law by the national parliamentarian legislation process. If it comes down to the systematic level we discern that the EU follows an intergovernmental logic of law-making in which the sovereign member state has the last word.

28 See the decisions known as the "Maastricht-Judgment" (file number: 2 BvR 2134, 2159/92, in: BVerfGE 89, p. 175) and the "As-Long-As-II-Judgment" (file number: 2 BvR 197/83, in: BVerfGE 73, p. 387).

and enforcing sovereignty as the state can at any time legally, i.e. by changing national laws,[29] decide to abolish European rule by retirement. Thus, from the conceptual logic of state theory, it is beyond question that the sovereign member state does not substantially renounce to its claim to self-contained policy- and law-making. At the end of the day, the sovereign state still takes absolute precedence over any decision in the EU within its own territory. The binding character of the European authorities for the single state is, in the end, just a result of a cost-benefit calculation of the sovereign state – that can be revised anytime. From a systematic perspective it is of course irrelevant that there is no formal way of resignation from the Union (as was planned in the Constitutional Treaty). There will be a legal way if such a case really occurs, since a contract is a special and particular agreement based on the free will of the contracting parties and, thus, necessarily conflicts with the idea of unconditional validity.[30] A contract that can never be canceled is a contradiction in terms.[31]

II. What is so special about the European Union?

It goes without saying that this outcome is quite disappointing and does not reflect the idea and vision of the EU as a substantially unique institutional framework with supranational power,[32] but demonstrates that the EU is – when the focus is on its conceptual and systematic logic – a purely inter-national institutional construct, albeit a highly complex one. And even though this outcome neither corresponds to the actual working nor to the incontestable achievements in regional integration of the EU, it cannot just be ignored, since, *firstly*, it results from the theoretical constitution of the state which provides the conceptual foundation of the main traditions of IR theory and of the mainstream European Integration Studies, and because, *secondly*, stateness and sovereignty (in theory and practice) still rely on the monopoly on the use of force that is not divisible, the constitutive idea of a monopoly being that it may not to be divided. Zangl and Zürn as well stress the embeddedness of both the (neo-) realist tradition and its opponents into the classic, and, from their perspective, nowadays analytically

---

29 National laws stating self-restrictions of sovereign rights can be changed.
30 This is why for example the idea of natural law has never been framed in contractarian terms.
31 The same is true with regard to an exclusion of a member state. Although there is no recorded regulation for excluding a member from the Union it is hardly imaginable that for instance a member state changing its political system to a dictatorship or declaring war on another member state would not be excluded. In case of a long-term, malevolent violation of fundamental EU standards that challenges the institutional integrity of the Union, exclusion would just be a quasi-automatic reaction as the EU is not bound to contracts that a member state has already suspended. Thus, the question is not if a state can be excluded, but how exclusion would take place formwise.
32 I follow Jachtenfuchs' 2001, pp. 71ff defense of the uniqueness of the EU. Although I agree with Abromeit's 2001, pp. 91f, 96 warning that stressing the sui generis-perception of the EU should not lead to an unwillingness to think about institutional alternatives and visions I do not think that this is an inevitable or even a probable consequence.

inappropriate theory of the sovereign state and therefore suggest an epistemic shift of scientific attention towards the study of what they call (with recourse to Habermas) the *post-national constellation.*[33] But, in regard to the question of supranational power, it is important to emphasize that Zangl's and Zürn's critique of the state-centrism of both (neo-) realist and idealist approaches does not intend and therefore is not able to provide a concept of supranationalism or to conclusively explain in what respect supranational authorities are superior to the state.[34] Rather, the question of supranational competence disappears since the logical counterpart to supranational power, i.e. the state, loses its outstanding analytic weight. Paradoxically, the conceptual framework of the post-national constellation[35] cannot lay stress on the question of supranational power, as the state is not seen as a special and outstanding analytic unity in the study of global politics anymore. Thus, the analytical focus is directed towards the complex and polyphonic system of interaction between very diverse agents in global politics and is not very much interested in establishing a hierarchy of different types of actors. This is a plausible and legitimate setting of analytic priorities and – as long as the power and impact of the state actor is not underestimated[36] – a very fruitful approach especially with regard to the interaction of different actors in domestic, trans- and international negation and decision-making processes.

Nonetheless, in regard to our question on supranationalism, this focus is not helpful. It is of course unnecessary to subscribe to a methodological nationalism in order to show how supranational power can be understood. However, we need to pay special attention to the state, as, *firstly*, it is the subject to supranational power, and therefore the constitutive element of supranationalism, and because, *secondly*, the logic of the European integration process itself follows the classic conceptual framework of state theory and therefore has, until now, not been able substantially and irreversibly to challenge or limit the sovereignty of its member states. Thus, in regard to the question of supranationalism we have to be aware of the dilemma that, on the one hand, it is necessary to dissociate from the conceptual logic of the sovereign state, since it does not allow the giving away of state sovereignty to a superior authority without dissolution of the state itself, while, on the other hand, it is also necessary to still perceive the state as the subject – and thus the precondition – of supranational power. We see that the very idea of supranationalism, on the one hand, depends on the state while, on the other hand, supranationalism is impossible to conceptualize within the theoretical logic of the sovereign state. Hence, the most conclusive way of dealing with this dilemma seems to be to abandon the idea of supranationalism once and for all.

---

33 Cf. Zangl/Zürn 2003, pp. 59f, 140, 147 and Habermas 1998.
34 Cf. Zangl/Zürn 2003, pp. 161ff.
35 Cf. ibid., pp. 152-171.
36 See for an overhasty abandonment of the state for example Hardt/Negri 2001 and Beck 2002.

But because our brief contractarian reflection on the EU's missing supranationalism – although theoretically conclusive – does not provide any basis for understanding the unquestionable integrative success and the actual workings of the Union we maybe should be careful with entirely giving up the concept of supranationalism. Instead, we should take a look at some features of the EU that substantially counteract the classic perception of sovereignty. Thus, we have to draw the distinction between the conceptual idea of sovereignty and the actual working of sovereign states in practice,[37] and focus on the latter. But, in so doing, we have to remain within the conceptual and theoretical framework of contractarian state and sovereignty theory. We have to hold to its terms, as, *firstly*, we intend to discern deviations from state and sovereignty theory and because, *secondly*, supranational power is dependent on the notion of the state as its logical sine qua non.

Looking at the EU with special attention to the state's voluntary restrictions of both domestic (1) and external (2) sovereignty,[38] we discern that, from the perception of classic state theory, these restrictions are the most remarkable trait of the Union.

1) One of the most notable and unique features of the European integration process is that it has to a large extent pushed back the dogma of non-interference with domestic affairs of its member states, and thus challenges the concept of *internal and domestic sovereignty*. Instead, the European integration process has emerged as a multilayered framework of permanent interference with the policy of its member states. Every political initiative within the EU is an attempt to directly influence national policies – regardless if this attempt comes from the Commission, from a single member state or from a group of member states, and not dependent on whether the attempt comes from within the institutional framework of the Union or from the bi- and multilateral networks that member states maintain and that run parallel and/or in conjunction with the Union's institutional framework.[39] Thus, in the terms of classic state theory, the European integration process has produced a system in which both the European institutions and every single member state permanently interfere with the national policies of the other member states.

   a) Moreover, the member states do not hide their attempts to exercise influence on other member's domestic policies but even express the claim to do so openly. A German, French, British, Belgian, etc. initiative in the Council of Ministers or an initiative of the Commission necessarily is an open claim to change the law in other states.

   b) The possible reactions to unwelcome attempts to influence national policies are extremely heterogeneous and can vary from trying to substantially change or stop the initiative to even stating that the policy-field in question should be

---

37 For a very good systematic discussion on these two main possibilities of looking at the fundaments and changes of the notion of sovereignty see still Camilleri/Falk 1992, in particular ch.2.

38 Cf. for a discussion of this distinction Seidelmann 1995, pp. 566-569.

39 On these two simultaneous ways of policy-making in the EU cf. Jachtenfuchs/Kohler-Koch 2004, pp. 84f, 94.

regulated not on the European but on the state level. However, even the latter reaction has not to be confused with the reference to the dogma of non-interference with domestic affairs, which is very persistent on the global level and still dominates international law.

c) This framework of continuous interference with national policies in which the member states are open and self-confident subjects and objects of interference is institutionalized and legalized, and this to such a degree that actually there are types of European regulations that do not even need the approval of the member states but that come directly into effect as national law.[40] Hence, states abstain from making every European regulation subject to the national legislation process (with all the democratic deficiencies that are linked to this[41]).

d) Although in regard to the degree of integration, there are huge differences between different policy-fields the claim to common policy-making, i.e. the claim to and the acceptance of interference, is quite extensive.

e) Finally, deviations of member states from European regulations result in penalties. Although contractual penalties are nothing new or extraordinary in international law, the continuous willingness, at least in principle, of the states to accept penalties and subsequently to meet the European demands without being subordinated to any coercive power or to any means of violence is a unique feature of the EU. Obviously, member states can indeed be forced to meet European policies without the existence of any means of violence.

2) Apart from challenging the domestic side of state sovereignty, the EU also successfully defies in particular issues *the external side of state sovereignty* of its member states.

a) Especially the legal and factual possibility of every European citizen to directly address the Commission, the European Parliament or European courts without being represented by its national government, without the necessity of a governmental intermediation, demonstrates that EU member states abstain from their monopoly on the external representation of their citizens[42], which is – in classic conceptual terms of state theory – one core attribute of external sovereignty of the state.[43]

b) Especially in those policy-fields that are highly integrated, the behavior of member states towards each other is subject to legal control, and can – in case of non-compliance with the Union's law – result in penalties.

---

40 Cf. Jachtenfuchs/Kohler-Koch 2004, p. 87.
41 On the question of democracy beyond the state with special attention to Europe cf. Greven/Pauly (eds.) 2000.
42 I am grateful to Frederik Ponjaert for directing my attention to this point.
43 For a discussion of the political and methodological idea of the representation of the individuals by the state see Vasilache 2007, pp. 105ff, 141ff.

c) Until now, neither the CFSP in general nor the ESDP in particular can be considered to have led to a substantial restriction of external sovereignty of the states, which contrasts with the examples just mentioned. However, these attempts show that the Union's claim to the restriction of external sovereignty seems to be quite expansive.[44]

No other inter- or transnational organization has gone so far and was so successful in pushing back substantial attributes of the sovereignty of its member states. What indeed is remarkable and unique about the European integration is, *firstly*, that in fact the state voluntarily approves a permanent and institutionalized system of external interference with its domestic policy and regards it as being legitimate. *Secondly*, it is remarkable that the state partially binds its external behavior to European regulations, and in specific cases even abstains from its claim to absolute external representation of its citizens by tolerating the competing concept of European citizenship. These voluntary – and reversible – restrictions of domestic and external sovereignty lead to a conceptual blurring of domestic and external affairs and policies, i.e. to a blurring of a boundary that is constitutive for the classic concept of state sovereignty. This fading of the [...] Domestic-Foreign Frontier [...][45] within the EU has to be distinguished from the factual loss of relevance of the distinction between internal and external affairs due to the transnationalization of political problems that – as for example Habermas rightly emphasizes[46] – is a characteristic trait of the post-modern political situation. *Firstly*, the blurring of internal and external affairs and competences in the EU is – from a quantitative perspective – far more intense and deep than in any other international organization or than can be perceived in the global system in general. *Secondly*, and more importantly, the fading of domestic and foreign policies and competences in the EU is not just a factual consequence of or an answer to the transnationalization of political problems but is a conceptual and normative decision. From a theoretical perspective, this highly astonishing phenomenon of continuous voluntary sovereignty restriction of the member states and of the blurring of the state's systematic and territorial boundaries makes it necessary to reintroduce the notion of supranationalism, albeit in a light, weaker and conditional sense.

III. A light Notion of Supranationalism

It is neither surprising nor theoretically remarkable that the single state, at the end of the day, on principle, sticks to its unconditional sovereign power and to its monopoly on the use of force – reflected in the possibility of withdrawing from the EU at any time. The uniqueness of the EU consists in the fact that its institutional framework of

---

44 For the CFSP, the ESDP and the actor-quality of the EU in the international context see in particular the contributions in Telò (ed.) 2007.
45 Rosenau 1997.
46 See Habermas 1998, pp. 107f.

continuous domestic interference and the partial subordination of foreign behavior to general regulations do indeed work – while the sovereignty of the member state with its untouched monopoly on the use of force and the permanent right to leave the Union is still intact.[47] The remarkable and indeed unique feature of the Union is that the member states are willing – again and again – to take a subordinate role to common policies and abstain from simply asserting their anarchic freedom to self-contained policies. This is remarkable not because sovereign power has been given up, but precisely because it has not, and precisely because the EU is not a state itself and from a systematic perspective has no sovereign power at all.

It remains impossible to solve the principle dilemma that supranational power – understood in a narrow and systematic sense – is a contradiction in terms because the achievement of a systematically perfect supranationalism dissolves the states, and thus the logical precondition of supranationalism itself. But a weaker or lighter understanding of supranationalism is necessary and possible, because one can solve the dilemma of supranational power in the strict sense needing the sovereign state while at the same time claiming to go beyond the state by breaking it. Hence, in order to have an analytically conclusive concept of supranationalism I would suggest restricting the term to those organizations that 1) challenge core attributes of state sovereignty, i.e. that defy fundamental and substantial characteristics of state sovereignty, that are 2) based on voluntary membership of the states, that are 3) institutionalized and legally regulated, that are 4) meant to be durable, not only situational, and that 5) finally are successful, i.e. really do work in practice – especially in cases in which the institution has to assert a particular decision against the political will of a member state.

A detailed and complete list of the core attributes of state sovereignty, and thus the perception of what a substantial and fundamental deviation from the concept of state sovereignty actually is, might well vary with different interpretations of state theory. I have suggested that one can regard as deviations from substantial and fundamental core attributes of the state's sovereignty a state's (partial) rejection of the dogma of non-interference with domestic affairs, its general willingness to comply with the instructions of non-state institutions and courts (for example with regard to penalties), its abstinence from the claim to absolute representation of the citizens in international affairs and its willingness to bind (partially but permanently) its own external behavior to general regulations and rules. Other phenomena could be added depending on what one considers to be core attributes of sovereign power. However, given the conceptual tightness and strictness of the classic concept of sovereignty it can be assumed that a list of core attributes of sovereignty – and thus a list of possible deviations from these attributes – should not be too extensive.

---

47 Habermas 1998, p. 107 rightly stresses that state sovereignty and the monopoly on the use of force are *formally* intact also in the context of the post-national constellation. However, it has to be added that this necessarily implies that self-contained policy-making of the state – although anachronistic and nowadays inappropriate – could still be implemented and pushed through in practice, too.

The notion of supranationalism in a light, weak and conditional sense relies on the necessary concept of the state while at the same time focusing on those attributes that are contradictory to the very core of the state's sovereignty – for instance, the dogma of non-interference or the partial 'individualization of foreign relations' by transnational citizenship. A weak or light notion of supranationalism is the only way to stick to the concept of supranational power at all, because it allows one to conceptualize the idea of superiority over the state within the theoretical framework of sovereign stateness. To characterize this notion of supranationalism as a weak, light and conditional concept (subject to the will of the sovereign state to stick to its voluntary sovereignty restrictions) bears in mind, *firstly*, that a systematically strict notion of supranationalism is not possible since it dissolves the state as its own precondition, and that therefore the sovereign state is still in the game and can revoke its voluntary sovereignty restrictions. *Secondly*, a light notion of supranationalism takes into account that it is necessary to have a concept of supranational power in order to be able to classify and to understand institutional arrangements that go beyond classic inter- or transnational frameworks by being able to successfully assert themselves against sovereign states in particular issues. In regard to European Studies, introducing a light understanding of supranational power makes it possible to classify theoretically those features of the EU that substantially distinguish the Union's institutional framework and political functioning from other institutional frameworks in which the claim to unrestricted sovereignty of the state is not only put forward in conceptual terms, but determines the actual working of those organizations. *Thirdly*, a light notion of supranationalism makes it possible to name and classify the highly astonishing fact that states are willing to permanently take a subordinate position to an institution without being forced to do so by superior means of violence – i.e. the remarkable phenomenon that while states have the right to withdraw from such an institution at any time, they in fact remain allegiant.

Hence, what allows us to indeed speak about weak or light supranationalism is exactly the fact that the state – in a strict systematic sense – is not deprived of sovereign power, that in conceptual terms its sovereign power of independent policy-making remains untouched, and that the state stays in the game as an important entity. The reason that prevents us from talking about strong supranationalism, i.e. about supranational power in a theoretically strict sense, enables us to elucidate a weak, a light and conditional notion of supranational power which allows us to handle the systematically and theoretically complicated and delicate question of superiority over the sovereign state, thus, the question of superiority over a supreme power.

References:

Abromeit, Heidrun 2001. Jenseits des "sui generis". Kommentar zu Markus Jachtenfuchs' Beitrag. In: Landfried, Christine (ed.). Politik in einer entgrenzten Welt. 21. Wissenschaftlicher Kongreß der Deutschen Vereinigung für Politische Wissenschaft. Köln: Verlag Wissenschaft und Politik, pp. 91-98.

Beck, Ulrich 2002. Macht und Gegenmacht im globalen Zeitalter. Neue weltpolitische Ökonomie. Frankfurt am Main: Suhrkamp.

Biersteker, Thomas J./Weber, Cynthia (eds.) 1996. State Sovereignty as Social Construct. Cambridge: Cambridge University Press.

Brown, Michael E./Lynn-Jones, Sean M./Miller, Steven E. (eds.) 1996. Debating the Democratic Peace. An International Security Reader. Cambridge: The MIT Press.

Camilleri, Josph A./Falk, Jim 1992. The End of Sovereignty? The Politics of a Shrinking and Fragmenting World. Aldershot: Elgar.

Entscheidungen des Bundesverfassungsgerichts (BVerfGE) 1986. Vol. 73, Tübingen: Mohr Siebeck, pp. 339-388.

Entscheidungen des Bundesverfassungsgerichts (BVerfGE) 1993. Vol. 89, Tübingen: Mohr Siebeck, pp. 155-213.

Gosepath, Stefan/Merle, Jean-Christophe (eds.) 2002. Weltrepublik. Globalisierung und Demokratie. München: C.H. Beck.

Greven, Michael Th./Pauly, Louis W. (eds.) 2000. Democracy beyond the State? The European Dilemma and the Emerging Global Order. Lanham et al.: Rowman&Littlefield.

Grundgesetz für die Bundesrepublik Deutschland. Textausgabe. Stand: August 2006. Bonn: BpB.

Habermas, Jürgen 1998. Die postnationale Konstellation. Politische Essays. Frankfurt am Main: Suhrkamp.

Hardt, Michael/Negri, Antonio 2001. Empire. Cambridge/London: Harvard University Press.

Hobbes, Thomas 1985. Leviathan. Ed. with an introd. by C.B. Macpherson. London: Penguin Classics.

Höffe, Otfried 1999. Demokratie im Zeitalter der Globalisierung. München: C.H. Beck.

Horn, Christoph 2002. Kann man eine supranationale Zwangsgewalt befürworten, ohne auf selbständige Einzelstaaten zu verzichten? In: Gosepath, Stefan/Merle, Jean-Christophe (eds.). Weltrepublik. Globalisierung und Demokratie. München: C.H. Beck, pp. 153-164.

Jachtenfuchs, Markus 2001. Verfassung, Parlamentarismus, Deliberation. Legitimation und politischer Konflikt in der Europäischen Union. In: Landfried, Christine (ed.). Politik in einer entgrenzten Welt. 21. Wissenschaftlicher Kongreß der Deutschen Vereinigung für Politische Wissenschaft. Köln: Verlag Wissenschaft und Politik, pp. 71-90.

Jachtenfuchs, Markus/Kohler-Koch, Beate 2004. Governance in der Europäischen Union. In: Benz, Arthur (ed.). Governance – Regieren in komplexen Regelsystemen. Eine Einführung. Wiesbaden: VS Verlag für Sozialwissenschaften, pp. 77-101.

Kant, Immanuel 2006. Toward Perpetual Peace. A Philosophical Sketch. In: Kant, Immanuel. Toward Perpetual Peace and Other Writings on Politics, Peace, and History. Ed. and with an introd. by Pauline Kleingeld, translated by David L. Colclasure. New Haven/London: Yale University Press, pp. 67-109.

Kersting, Wolfgang 2002. Jean-Jacques Rousseaus "Gesellschaftsvertrag". Darmstadt: Wissenschaftliche Buchgesellschaft.

Laubach-Hintermeier, Sonja 1998. Kritik des Realismus. In: Chwaszcza, Christine/Kersting, Wolfgang (eds.). Politische Philosophie der internationalen Beziehungen. Frankfurt am Main: Suhrkamp, pp. 73-95.

Lieber, Robert J. 1991. No Common Power. Understanding International Relations. New York: HarperCollins.

Locke, John 1966. Two Treatises of Government. A critical ed. with an introd. and apparatus criticus by Peter Laslett. Cambridge: Cambridge University Press.

Lutz-Bachmann, Matthias/Bohman, James (eds.) 2002. Weltstaat oder Staatenwelt? Für und wider die Idee einer Weltrepublik. Frankfurt am Main: Suhrkamp.

Mearsheimer, John J. 1990. Back to the Future. Instability in Europe After the Cold War. In: International Security. Vol. 15, No. 1, pp. 5-56.

Menzel, Ulrich 2001. Zwischen Idealismus und Realismus. Die Lehre von den Internationalen Beziehungen. Frankfurt am Main: Suhrkamp.

Merkel, Reinhard/Wittmann, Roland (eds.) 1996. "Zum ewigen Frieden". Grundlagen, Aktualität und Aussichten einer Idee von Immanuel Kant. Frankfurt am Main: Suhrkamp.

Meyers, Reinhard 2004. Theorien internationaler Kooperation und Verflechtung. In: Woyke, Wichard (ed.). Handwörterbuch Internationale Politik. 9th ed. Wiesbaden: VL Verlag für Sozialwissenschaften, pp. 482-515.

Morgenthau, Hans J. 1993. Politics among Nations. The Struggle for Power and Peace. Boston et al.: McGraw-Hill.

Preuß, Ulrich K. 2007. Souveränität – Zwischenbemerkungen zu einem Schlüsselbegriff des Politischen. In: Stein, Tine/Buchstein, Hubertus/Offe, Claus (eds.) 2007. Souveränität, Recht, Moral. Die Grundlagen politischer Gemeinschaft. Frankfurt am Main/New York: Campus, pp. 313-335.

Rosenau, James N. 1997. Along the Domestic-Foreign Frontier. Exploring Governance in a Turbulent World. Cambridge: Cambridge University Press.

Rousseau, Jean-Jacques 1964. Œuvres complètes. Ed. by Bernard Gagnebin and Marcel Raymond. (Bibliothèque de la Pléiade.) Vol. III. Du contrat social. Écrits politiques. Paris: Gallimard.

Schmalz, Uwe 2004. Europäische Union als internationaler Akteur. In: Woyke, Wichard (ed.). Handwörterbuch Internationale Politik. 9th ed. Wiesbaden: VL Verlag für Sozialwissenschaften, pp. 121-152.

Seidelmann, Reimund 1995. Souveränität. In: Nohlen, Dieter (ed.). Lexikon der Politik. Vol. I. Politische Theorien. Ed. by Dieter Nohlen and Rainer-Olaf Schultze. München: Beck, pp. 566-569.

Telò,Mario (ed.) 2007. European Union and New Regionalism. Regional Actors and Global Governance in a Post-Hegemonic Era. Second Edition. Aldershot: Ashgate.

Vasilache, Andreas 2003. Interkulturelles Verstehen nach Gadamer und Foucault. Frankfurt am Main/New York: Campus.

Vasilache, Andreas 2007. Der Staat und seine Grenzen. Zur Logik politischer Ordnung. Frankfurt am Main/New York: Campus.

Waltz, Kenneth N. 1969. Man, the State, and War. A Theoretical Analysis. 7th printing. New York/London: Columbia University Press.

Waltz, Kenneth N. 1979. Theory of International Politics. Boston et al.: McGraw-Hill.

Weller, Christoph 2003. Internationale Politik und Konstruktivismus. Ein Beipackzettel. In: WeltTrends. Zeitschrift für internationale Politik und vergleichende Studien, No. 41, pp. 107-123.

Zangl, Bernhard/Zürn, Michael 2003. Frieden und Krieg. Sicherheit in der nationalen und postnationalen Konstellation. Frankfurt am Main: Suhrkamp.

The Essence of Transformation of European Governance Institutions after World War Two

Yang Na

From the Rome Treaty (1958) to the Single European Act (SEA, 1987), the Maastricht Treaty on EU (1993), and the Amsterdam Treaty (1999), with the EU changing treaty contents, the relations among its three supranational institutions- the Commission of the European Communities, the European Court of Justice and the European Parliament, the intergovernmental institution-the Council of European Union have been concerned.

Among the core institutions of European governance, the Council of European Union is the main decision-making and legislating institution; European Commission takes responsibility of the main administrative affairs; the function of European Parliament is co-legislation. The two dimensions of European governance institutions are like this as below:[1]

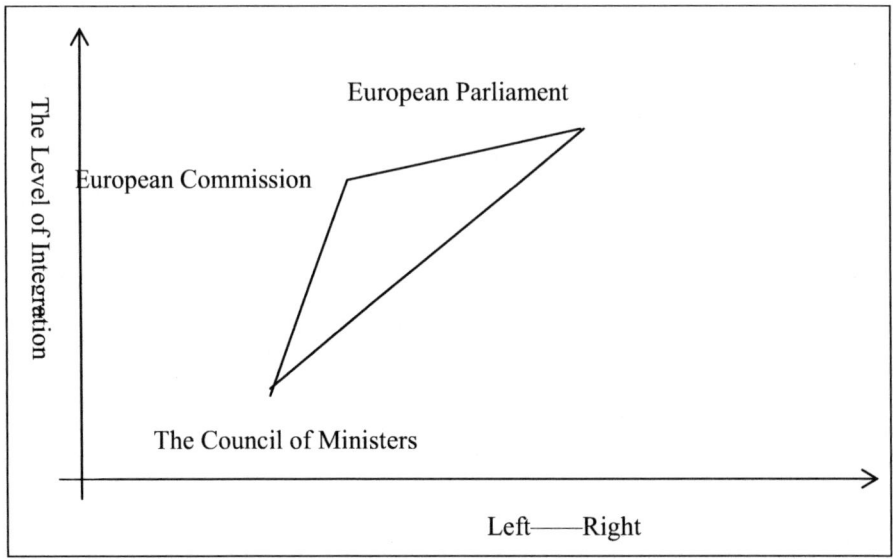

With the development of European integration, the institutions of European governance continue to adjust and reform. On the one hand, reform is aiming to adapt to the

---

1   George Tsebelis and Geoffrey Garrett, *The Institutional Foundations of Intergovernmentalism and Supranationalism in the European Union,* International Organization 55, 2, Spring 2001, p.377.

external environment of institution. On the other hand, it tries to solve problems which appear in the process of institutional development. And we have to concern that the balance of power among the four institutions has changed considerably since the signing of the Rome Treaty.[2]

In recent years, the role of the Council of European Union which presents intergovernmental nature has been strengthened; on the contrary, the position of European Commission which is supranational is weakened. The supranationalists are trying to strengthen the power of European Parliament which is also supranational to compensate for the inferior position in the process of competition between intergovernmentalism and supranationalism. Though some achievements, intergovernmentalists take advantage of "co-decision" process sharing with the European Parliament, make decisions steering clear of European Commission, the power of European Commission has been threatened to be nominal. In addition to the veto of European Constitution, supranationalists are encountering obstacles. European institutionalists are trying to develop complementary relationship between intergovernmentalism and supranationalism, however, in the practice of European integration, these two powers are mainly competitive, especially after the economic integration making great progress, in the context of the development of political and security integration, intergovernmentalism is predominate.

My thesis is on the basis of the history of European institutions. With the development of European integration, there are many problems and corresponding reforms which exist in the Council of European Union, the European Commission and the European Parliament, and the relationship between intergovernmental institutions and supranational ones changes after a series of reforms.

I try to answer some questions as follows. First of all, from the perspective of the history of European governance institutions, why these changes happened and what the essence of this kind of changes? What's the fundamental difference between intergovernmentalism and supranationalism? That is, in the process of European integration, which one is the leading power, the member states or supranational institutions?

The main theoretical divergence

Jeremy Richardson, proposes that there are "enormous diversity of theories of European integration, these approaches can be grouped into two broad school of thought: intergovernmentalism and supranationalism".[3]The main difference between the two theoretical schools can be summarized as below:

---

2   George Tsebelis and Geoffrey Garrett, *The Institutional Foundations of Intergovernmentalism and Supranationalism in the European Union,* International Organization 55, 2, Spring 2001, p.358.

3   Jeremy Richardson, *European Union: Power and Policy-making*, Routledge, 2006, p.76.

Intergovernmentalism:[4]

Level of abstraction	Dimensions of integration		
	Sectoral	Horizontal	Vertical
General assumption	Rationalist institutionalism in International Relations: states interact in an anarchical international system		
Explanatory theory	Bargaining theory	Club theory	Functional theory of institutions
Factors explaining integration	Exogenous preferences and relative bargaining power of governments		Governmental interests and control
	LI: sector-specific societal preferences and issue-area power		LI: monitoring and sanctioning of compliance
	RI: geopolitical preferences and overall power		RI: state autonomy and influence

Supranationalsim:[5]

Level of abstraction	Dimensions of integration		
	Sectoral	Vertical	Horizontal
General assumption	States and other actors interact in an institutionalized international environment RS: rationalist institutionalism CS: sociological institutionalism		
Explanatory theory	Dynamic theory of integration/institutionalization RS: historical institutionalism CS: theories of socialization		
Factors explaining integration	RS: intensity of transnational exchanges, autonomy of supranational actors, rule density, path dependence CS: identity, legitimacy, resonance		

"The central players in intergovernmental politics are the national executives of the member states, who bargain with each other to produce common policies".[6] "The supranational mode of governance is one in which centralized governmental structures (those organizations constituted at the supranational level) possess jurisdiction over specific policy domains within the territory comprised by the member states".[7]

---

4   Ibid, p.79.
5   Ibid, p.85.
6   Wayne Sandholtz and Alec Stone Sweet, *European Integration and Supranational Governance.* Journal of European Public Policy 4(3), p.302.
7   Wayne Sandholtz and Alec Stone Sweet, *European Integration and Supranational Governance.* Journal of European Public Policy 4(3), pp.302-303.

When it comes to the early theories about European governance institutions, one of the most effective theoretical schools is neo-functionalism which belongs to supranationalist "school of thought". The core content of neo-functionalism is that European integration develops from "low politics" (such as the field of economy and trade) "spillover" to "high politics" (such as the field of CFSP). Though researching on the process of preparation, construction and development of European governance institutions, we can see that the practitioners of European integration tried to build cooperative institutions in the area of economy and trade, and in the area of politics and security. However, the defensive alliance failed in the period of 1960s, the main reason is European member states had not prepared well to transmit sovereignty in the field of "high politics" to European level, it also proved that the "spillover effect" of neo-functionalism can not be practiced in the case of European integration. The judgment of common interests in the diplomatic and security field is much harder than that of economic field, thereby, it is very difficult to make a consensus even if supranational institutions exist. Moreover, the area of politics and security refers to fundamental national interests, self-determination right of governments and the problem of national identity, a country can not accept the situation which is out of control and without protection. The development of European integration can make progress as long as it accords with national interests of member states.

Besides the "spillover effect", the theory of neo-functionalism also focuses on creating supranational institutions. Therefore, in the early period of creating European governance institutions, there were contradicts between intergovernmentalism and neo-functionalism. The neofunctionalist-intergovernmentalist debate trys to pose two diametrically opposed scenarios for the European future: the EU as intergovernmental organization versus the EU as a putative supranational state.[8] Some scholars questioned that this dispute between them is a little bit extreme. For instance, it fails to pose all of the possible questions about contemporary European integration because it problematizes the EU integration in the preferred disciplinary terms of International Relations. And these two paradigms are unable to capture the complexity and dynamism of the emerging European polity, this debate marginalizes significant strands of international theory.[9] Neo-liberalists try to break the deadlock situation between intergovernmentalism and neo-functionalism, they accept the hypothesis of intergovernanmentalism, but eventually reach different conclusions. The theory of neo-liberalism concentrates on the complex decision-making system and institutions of European governance structure.[10] The neo-liberalists think that the institutions of European integration theory can be divided into two parts: formal and informal. The formal European institutions mean substantial ones, such as European

8 Ben Rosamond, *Theories of European Integration*, palgrave, 2000, p.105.
9 Ben Rosamond, *Theories of European Integration*, palgrave, 2000, p.105.
10 Wang Xueyu, *European integration: one process, various theories,* China Journal of European Studies, Vol. 2, 2001, p.16.

Council, European Parliament; the scope of informal European institutions is broad, such as idea, value and behavior. "The core content of Neo-liberalism theory is the interactive relationship between institutions and actors."[11] The historical institutionalists think that, "The structure of European institutions decide the behavior of member states."[12] The institutionalists encourage the creation and improvement of supranational institutions. They propose that the early stage of international institutions are instruments for which national states pursue common interests, but with the development and improvement of institutions, they gradually get rid of the control of national states, finally achieve independence[13.] The institutionalists support creating supranational institutions, promote to broaden the scope of supranational institutions power, and shift some problems from member states governments to the European level. Some scholars try to improve the theoretical framework of European integration. Alec Stone Sweet and Wayne Sandholtz develop a theory of supranational governance. They pitch the framework of supranationalism as a less state-centric and more supranational alternative to the theory of European integration. Alec Stone Sweet and Wayne Sandholtz deploy the image of demand and supply sides to integration. The role of transnational exchange is central to generate demands for regulation and governance capacity at the European level which supranational institutions can supply these things. They emphasize on transnational exchange and the development of social interaction between actors across borders.[14] They stress governance rather than integration as their dependent variable.

The opinion of realism is that "Institutions are the fundamental reflection of the distribution of power, they have no independent effects to the behavior of national states."[15] "The situation of market failure is not arose by deceptive behavior and lack of information, the main reason is distribution of power."[16] The international institutions are created by great powers, serve to national interests of great powers rather than international interests."[17] The theory of realism proposes that the development of

---

11 Wang Xuedong, *The Theoretical Review of New-liberalism on European Integration*, China Journal of European Studies, Vol. 5, 2003, p.85.
12 Wang Xuedong, *The Theoretical Review of New-liberalism on European Integration,* China Journal of European Studies, Vol. 5, 2003, p.86.
13 Paul Pierson, *The Path to European Integration: A Historical Institutionalist Analysis*, Comparative Political Studies, Vol.29, No.2, April 1996. P.A. Hall, R. Taylor, *Political Science and the Three New Institutionalisms*, Political Studies, Vol.44, No.5, 1996. Ronald L. Jeperson, *The Development and Application of Sociological Neoinstitutionalism*, EUI working paper 2001/5, Robert Schuman Centre, European University Institute (Florence, Italy).
14 Ben Rosamond, *Theories of European Integration*, palgrave, 2000, pp.126-127.
15 John J. Mearsheimer – *The False Promise of International Institutions* – International Security – Winter 1994/95, Vol. 19, No. 3, p.7.
16 Stephen Krasner, *Global Communications and National Power: Life on the Pareto Frontier*, Neorealism and Neoliberalism – New York: Columbia University Press, 1993.
17 Liu Jun, *From Realism to Constructionalism—The Evolution of the Idea of Security and the Rationality of the Existence of NATO after Cold War*, Social Science, Vol. 2, 2004, p.46.

European governance institutions cannot exceed the nature of intergovernmentalism, national states are still the main actors in the decision-making process of European institutions. "European politicians prefer intergovernmental cooperation just for pursuing common interests of national states."[18] Joseph Frieco identified four problems for neorealists on the assumptions of European integration. The first concerns is the core assumption of rationality among main actors. He poses that Maastricht negotiations are "irrational"; Secondly, the anarchy is not the main structural feature of international politics in the region of Europe; Thirdly, the upraise of Germany violates the balance of power. Finally, the influence of neorealism is threatened by functionalism, institutionalism and other eheretical starting points.[19]Until now, one of the most effective theories of creating European institutions is "liberal intergovernmentalism" by Andrew Moravcsik. "Liberal intergovernmentalism" is realism in essence, because Andrew Moravcsik sticks to the opinion that European institutions are not independent actors.[20] He proposes that the delegation of sovereignty to supranational institutions depends on the value they place on the issues and substantive outcomes in question: the higher the gains of a cooperative agreement for a government and the higher the risk of non-compliance by other governments, the higher its readiness to cede competences to the EU to prevent potential losers from revising the policy[21]. Moravcsik's work on European integration which adopts the two-level game approach draws on a sustained critique of neofunctionalism (or supranational institutionalism as he calls it).[22]

The Essence of the transformation of European governance institutions: intergovernmentalism versus supranationalism

The essence of the development and transformation of European governance institutions is the balance and competition between intergovernmentalism and supranationalism. The main divergence between intergovernmentalism and supranationalism is[23] that which is the most important thing in the process of European

---

18 Chen Yugang, *European Construction and European integration: Understanding International Relations*, China Journal of European Studies, Vol. 5, 2002, p.13.
19 Ben Rosamond, *Theories of European Integration*, palgrave, 2000, p.134..Grieco, J.M., The Maastricht Treaty , Economic and Monetary Union and the Neo-Realist Research Programme, Review of International Studies 21(1), p.28.
20 Chen Yugang, *Nations and Supra-nations—the Comparative Research on the Theory of European Integration*, Shanghai: Shanghai People Press, 2001, pp.63-70.
21 A. Moravcsik, *The Choice for Europe: Social Purpose and State Power from Messina to Maastricht,* Ithaca: Cornell University Press; published in the UK by UCL Press, London, December 1998, pp.486-7.
22 Ben Rosamond, *Theories of European Integration*, palgrave, 2000, p.142.
23 Am p. Branch and Jakob C. Ohrgaard, *Trapped in the supranational-intergovernmental dichotomy: a response to Stone Sweet and Sandholtz*, Journal of European Public Policy, London: Routledge March 1999; Wayne Sandholtz and Alec Stone Sweet, *European integration and suprana-*

integration, the European institutions or the nation states? There exists an argument that European integration is driven by either supranational institutions or national governments.[24] Jeremy Richardson makes a more clear distinction about the innate character of the two. He thinks that "The key distinction between intergovernmentalism and supranationalism can be found in their different answers to the question whether or not the process of integration can be seen as a transformative, self-reinforcing process."[25] Intergovernmentalists hold the opinion that member states have the capability to control the direction of development of European integration, and they view the EU's institutional structure as the dependent variable; supranationalists insist that institutions can be out of member states' control and make independent impact on the development of European integration; they view the EU's institutions as actors rather than dependent variables. Jeremy Richardson proposes that "Even though the beginning of integration project may well reflect the interests of the most powerful states, further integration has been largely the result of a self-reinforcing dynamic that was and is beyond the control of the member states."[26] Supranationalism and Intergovernmentalism differ not only in the importance they attach to member governments in the process of integration but also in how they treat the EU's institutions.[27]The original intention of creating European institutions is to maintain the balance between intergovernmentalism and supranationalism: the European Council has the function of decision-making, the European Council and the European Parliament bind each other. The way of decision-making of European Council decides that the final decision power is still held by member states. Due to the development of supranational institutions which is able to deal with problems which cannot be solved by a member state, it is better for member states to protect their national interests, and this is why member states allow supranational institutions playing roles independently in some specific fields. With the process of European integration back to the track, developing gradually and improving various institutions step by step. Both European Commission and European Parliament are "supranational institutions", one of the main aims of creating these kinds of institutions is to give them strong power, enable them to influence on the various cooperative areas even make decisions. However, from the Luxembourg compromise period (1958-87) to the period of SEA was ratified, the Council developed from an ineffective collective institutions to a more effective

tional governance revisited: rejoinder to Branch and Ohrgaard, Journal of European Public Policy, London: Routledge, March 1999.

24 Am p. Branch and Jakob C. Ohrgaard, *Trapped in the supranational-intergovernmental dichotomy: a response to Stone Sweet and Sandholtz,* Journal of European Public Policy, London: Routledge March 1999, p.123.

25 Jeremy Richardson, *European Union: Power and Policy-making,* Routledge, 2006, p.77-78.

26 Ibid., p.84.

27 George Tsebelis and Geoffrey Garrett, *The Institutional Foundations of Intergovernmentalism and Supranationalism in the European Union,* International Organization 55, 2, Spring 2001, p.385.

legislative institution.[28] So as Andrew Moravcsik said, the EU's changing treaty base has had a marked impact on the process of European integration.[29] With the development of European integration, the position of European Council which is intergovernmental is upgraded, the power of European Council is strengthened, and European Council can make decision regarding many European issues. This proves the realistic opinion about the development of European integration. With the broader scope of power of European Council, the supranational side considers this situation, and upgrades the position of European Parliament in order to balance the extension of power of European Council through the way of treaty reform. After the Maastricht Treaty and Amsterdam Treaty, the Parliament is a powerful legislator, coequal with the Council under the reformed codecision procedure.[30] Under the initial form of codecision, agenda control was given to the Council and was eliminated in the Amsterdam Treaty.[31] In the process of co-decision, the Council submits proposals to European Parliament; European Parliament has the power to veto proposals. In the process of co-opration, according to the rule of "conditional agenda-setting", new law can be sanctioned on the condition that both Qualified Majority Voting in European Parliament and Majority Voting in the Council. This rule endows more legislation power to European Parliament. Because the rule allows European Parliament to choose the proposals which it prefers. Compared with the veto power in the process of co-decision, European Parliament is more active in the process of co-opration. The power of European Parliament is more effective in the process of co-opration than that in the process of co-decision.[32] The power of European Parliament is an effective measure to balance that of the Council. However, with the introduction of co-opration process and co-decision process, the position of the Council has been threatened by the power of European Parliament. "The Council is locked in a complex relationship of cooperation and contestation with the two other institutions (Commission and Parliament).[33] The ambition of supranational institutions which expects to be the core decision-making institutions has threatened the fundamental national interests of member states. The uncertainty of institutions creation has emerged------the direction of the development of institutions is not the expectations of nation states, so adjustment is needed at once.

28 Ibid, pp.358-359.
29 Moravcsik, A., *The Choice for Europe: Social Purpose and State Power from Messina to Maastrcht,* London: UCL Press, 1998.
30 George Tsebelis and Geoffrey Garrett, *The Institutional Foundations of Intergovernmentalism and Supranationalism in the European Union,* International Organization 55, 2, Spring 2001, p.359.
31 Ibid, p.375.
32 Ibid, pp.374-375.
33 Marks, Gary, Liesbet Hooghe, and Kermit lank, *European Integration from the 1980s: State-Centric Versus Multi-level Governance.* Journal of Common Market Studies 34 (3), p.358.

The intergovernmentalists try to find a way to weaken the supranational power in the European institutions. "The treaty of European Union" regulates the agenda-setting power belongs to the Council; the Council is compelled to share decision-making power with European Parliament in the process of co-decision; it seems that European Parliament is on the equal footing as the Council. However, if the proposals are sanctioned through QMV in the Council and European Parliament, the position of European Commission decreases, some proposals which may be vetoed in the European Commission can pass easily in the Council. Therefore, the power of the Council is also strengthened in the process of treaty reform. The European Council and European Parliament make co-decisions in the process of co-operation and co-decision, the Council will not give up the leading role in the decision-making process. The main idea of European constitution endows more power to supranational institutions, but in practice, it is suffered from strongly rejection among member states, the veto of European constitution which led to the supranational power hurt heavily. Supranational power will not replace intergovernmental one as the developing direction of European governance institutions though there are full of competition and compromise between intergovernmentalism and supranationalism, especially when European member states have not agreed to transmit their main power to the European level, and great powers still dominate the future of Europe.

Conclusion

Because European institutions are the products of compromise of great powers to large extent, it manifests the power decides the practice of international politics. Power can decide who has the chance to participate in the international institutions and the rule of game, and the more powerful side can deprive of attending chances of the less powerful side or set barriers to prevent less powerful side from attending institutions. The crisis of European constitution is an appropriate reflection of realism. Once the European constitution is passed, it will be a great progress for European integration, but France and Netherlands vetoed it, which was a heavy blow to the process of European integration. Some voting approaches in the European constitution are not conform to national interests of small countries, such as Netherlands, and many EU institutions exhibit bargaining among great powers, so it is hard for small countries to achieve their aims, and this kind of situation may lead to imbalance among institutions. In conclusion, to large degree, the reforms of European institutions are competition and compromise among great powers about the distribution of power.

References:

Bache, Ian and Matthew Flinders – Multi-level Governance – London: Oxford University Press – 2003

Ben Rosamond, Theories of European Integration, palgrave, 2000

Bernard, Nick – Multilevel Governance in the European Union – London: Kluwer Law International – 2002

Bertelsmann Foundation and Center for Applied Policy Research (eds.), Bridging the Leadership Gap. A Strategy for Improving Political Leadership in the EU by the Thinking Enlarged Group, Gütersloh: Bertelsmann Foundation Publishers, December 2002

Biersteker, Thomas J. and Cynthia Weber – State Sovereignty as Social Construct – London: Cambridge University Press – 1996

Borrás, Susana – The Innovation Policy of the EU: From Government to Governance – London: Edward Elgar Publishing – 2003

Branch, Am p. and Jakob C. Ohrgaard, Trapped in the supranational-intergovernmental dichotomy: a response to Stone Sweet and Sandholtz, Journal of European Public Policy, Routledge, March 1999

Burkhard, Eberlein, and Kerwer Dieter – New Governance in the European Union: A Theoretical Perspective – Journal of Common Market Studies 42 – 2004

Corbet, R., Jachbs E, Shackleton M., The European Parliament, 4th edition, London: John Harper Publishing, 2000

Dermot, Hodson and Imelda Maher – The Open Method as a New Mode of Governance – Journal of Common Market Studies – Volume 39, Number 4, November 2001

Eberlein, Burkard and Abraham Newman – Innovating EU Governance Modes: The rise of incorporated transgovernmental networks – 2006 , www.councilforeuropeanstudies.org/conf/papers/EberleinNewman.pdf

Ekengren, Magnus – The Time of European Governance – Manchester: Manchester University Press – 2002

European Governance, A White Paper – Commission of The European Communities, Brussels, 21.11.2001

Frohlich, Stefan, The Difficulties of EU Governance: What way forward for the EU Institutions?, Frankfurt: Peter Lang, 2004

Fukuda, Koji – European Governance After Nice – London: Routledge – 2003

Grande, Edgar and Louis W. Panly – Complex Sovereignty – Toronto: University of Toronto Press – 2005

Hall, P.A. and Taylor R., Political Science and the Three New Institutionalisms, Political Studies, Vol.44, No.5, 1996

Hanop, Jeffrey – The Political Economy of Integration In the European Union – MA: Edward Elgar Publishing, 2000

Hashmi, Sohail H., State Sovereignty: Change and Persistence in International Relations – Bradenton: Penn State Press – 1997

Hofmann, Herwig C.H. and Alexander H. Turk, EU Administrative Governance, MA: Edward Elgar Publishing, 2006

Hooghe, Liesbet and Gary Marks – Multi-level Governance and European Integration – Lanham: Rowman & Littlefield Publishers – 2001

Horeth, Marcus – The Trilemma of Legitimacy-Multilevel Governance in the EU and the Problem of Democracy – Discussion Paper – C11 – 1998

Jachtenfuchs, Markus – The Governance Approach to European Integration – Journal of Common Market Studies – Vol. 39, Issue 2, 2001

Jens, Bartelson – A genealogy of sovereignty – New York: Cambridge University Press – 1995

Jeperson, Ronald L., The Development and Application of Sociological Neoinstitutionalism, EU working paper 2001/5, Robert Schuman Centre, European University Institute (Florence, Italy)

John, Campbell L. and Ove K. Pedersen (ed.), The Rise of Neoliberalism and Institutional Analysis, Princeton, NJ: Princeton University Press, 2001

Jorgensen, Knud Erik, Reflective Approaches to European Governance, NY: St.Martin's Press, 1997

Jupille, Joseph, James A. Caporaso and Jeffrey T. Checkel, Integrating Institutions: Theory, Method, and Study of the European Union, ARENA Working Papers, Series: 27/2002, http://www.arena.uio.no/publications/working-papers2002/papers/02_27.xml

Kees, Kersbergen van and Frans van Waarden – "Governance" as a Bridge between Disciplines: Cross-Disciplinary Inspiration Regarding Shifts in Governance and Problems of Governability, Accountability and Legitimacy – European Journal of Political Research – 2004

Krasner, Stephen D. – Sovereignty: Organized Hypocrisy – Princeton: Princeton University Press – 1999

Kohler-Koch, Beate – Network Governance within and beyond an Enlarging EU, paper presented at the ECSA-Canada Conference – Quebec, 2000

Kohler-Koch, Beate and Berthold Rittberger – The "Governance" Turn in EU Studies – ARENA Seminar 2006 – http://www.arena.uio.no/events/seminarpapers/2006/KohlerKoch_May06.pdf

Kohler-Koch, Beate – European governance and system integration – European Governance Papers – 2005 – Http://www.connex-network.org/eurogov/pdf/egp-connex-C-05-01.pdf

Kohler-Koch, Beate and Rainer Eising, The Transformation of governance in the European Union – London: Routledge – 1999

Kohler-Koch, Beate (ed.) – Linking EU and National Governance – London: Oxford University Press – 2003

Lansing, Robert – Notes on Sovereignty: From the Standpoint of the State and the World – NY: International Law and Taxation Publishers – 2005

Marks, Gary – Fritz W. Scharpf – Phillippe C. Schmitter – Wolfgang Streeck – Governance in the EU – London: Sage Publications Inc, 1996

Mearsheimer, John J. – The False Promise of International Institutions – International Security – Vol. 19 – No. 3, Winter 1994/95

Moravcsik, A., Prefernces and Power in the European Community: A Liberal Intergovernmentalist Approach, Journal of Common Market Studies, 31/4, 1993

Mouritzen, Hans – Review – State Sovereignty – Change and Persistence in International Relations – International Affairs – Vol.74 – No.4, 1997

Nugent, Neil, The Government and Politics of the European Union – London: Macmillan Press – 1999

Pegg, Carl H. – Evolution of the European Idea 1914-1932 – London: The University of North Carolina Press – 1983

Peterson, John and Michael Shackleton, European institutions of the European Union, London: Oxford University Press, 2006

Philpott, Daniel – Revolutions in Sovereignty: How Ideas Shaped Modern International Relations – Princeton – NJ: Princeton University Press – 2001

Philpott, Dan – Sovereignty – Http://plato.stanford.edu/entries/sovereignty/, 2003

Pierre, Jon – Debating Governance: Authority – Steering and Democracy – London: Oxford University Press – 2000

Pierson, Paul, The Path to European Integration: A Historical Institutionalist Analysis, Comparative Political Studies, Vol.29, No.2, April 1996

Richardson, Jeremy, European Union: Power and policy-making, London: Routledge, 2006

Robin, Sir – Improving Management in Government: The Next Steps. London: HMSO – 1998

Rosenau, James and Ernst-Otto Czempiel (eds.) – Governance without Government: Order and Change in World Politics – London: Cambridge University Press – 1992

Rougemont, Denis – The Idea of Europe – New York: Macmillan – 1966

Sandholtz – Wayne – and Alec Stone Sweet (eds.) – European Integration and Supranational Governance – London: Oxford University Press – 1998

Sandholtz, Wayne and Alec Stone Sweet, European integration and supranational governance revisited: rejoinder to Branch and Ohrgaard, Journal of European Public Policy, Routledge March 1999

Sbragia, Alberta M., The Treaty of Nice, Institutional Balance, and Uncertainty, Governance, Vol. 15, No. 3, 2002

Schaefer, G.F. (ed.), Governance by Committee, the Role of Committees in European Policy-Making and Policy Implementation (Final Report for the European Commission), EIPA, May 2000

Scharpf, Fritz W. – Governing in Europe: Effective and Democratic? London: Oxford University Press – 1999

Simon, Hix – The study of the European Union: The 'new governance' agenda and its rivals – Journal of European Public Policy – Vol. 5, No. 1, 1998

Tallberg, Jonas – European Governance and Supranational Institutions: Making states comply – London: Routledge – 2003

Tokár, Adrián – Something Happened. Sovereignty and European Integration – Extraordinary Times – IWM Junior Visiting Fellows Conferences – Vol. 11, Vienna, 2001

Tsebelis, George and Geoffrey Garrett, The Institutional Foundations of Intergovernmentalism and Supranationalism in the European Union, International Organization 55, 2, Spring 2001

Wallace, Helen and William Wallace – Policy-making in the European Union – London: Oxford University Press, 2000

Warleigh, Alex – Conceptual Combinations: Multilevel Governance and Policy Networks – In Michelle Cini and Angela Bourne – Palgrave Advances in European Union Studies – New York: Palgrave Macmillan – 2006

Warleigh, Alex, Understanding European Union Institutions – London: Routledge – 2002

Wilson, K. and Boer P. (eds.) – The History of the Idea of Europe – London: Routledge – 1995

Wincott, Daniel – Looking Forward or Harking Back? The Commission and the Reform of Governance in the European Union – Journal of Common Market Studies, Vol. 39, Issue 5, 2001

Part II:

Internal Effects

EU's Enlargement to the East:
Patterns, Causes, and Problems

Reimund Seidelmann

EU's enlargement policies in general and EU's enlargement policies towards the East have to be understood not as a unique process but as an important element of both the European integration and peace-building process. While the rounds of enlargement until the early 90's can be considered as the logical consequence of an integration process, which attracted other Western European countries to join, after and with the end of the East-West conflict the Eastern enlargements constitute a fundamental change in the architecture of Europe and are based on parallel policies of the post-Maastricht EU and NATO as the two driving actors. Thus Eastern enlargement rounds show both patterns of the past enlargement policies and mark at the same time a fundamental change in both national political and economic orders as well as the construction of the European regional system.

But while enlargement in general and enlargement to the East in particular reorganised the European regional system, it reflected, repeated, and revitalised traditional patterns, dilemmas, and problems of the integration process. In sum and in contrast to many hopes, enlargement neither caused structural change and improvement nor a stand-still of the integration process in qualitative terms. Both the idea that widening could linked to deepening and that enlargement would strengthen intergovernmentalism within the EU did not realise. But while enlargement did not change the character, nature, or dynamic of the integration process it nevertheless complicated decision-making. The tremendous increase of membership from the early six to the current twenty-six plus the slow adaptation to the "esprit de corps" of the EU – i.e. the informal patterns, modes, and rules of common decision-making - had a significant impact on the joint will-building and together-acting or the effectiveness of the EU as a willing and able actor.

1. The patterns of enlargement

To understand pattern, mode, and dynamics of EU's Eastern enlargement, one can argue in three interrelated steps: first to define Eastern enlargement by patterns of the integration process in general, second to define Eastern enlargement by patterns of the general enlargement process, and third to define Eastern enlargement by its specific patterns.

In general, the European integration shows three basic patterns:

The **first pattern** of the general integration process is the combination of the utopia of the "New United Europe" on the one side with a historic mission, common values and interests, and the understanding that subscribing to supra-nationalism creates significant advantages both to the inside and the outside and on the other side with member states, which try to preserve national power and competence and seek advantages of integration at the same time. This co-existence of an utopian vision and pragmatism has been understood by pro-integrationalists as a dialectic relation, which leads to continued progress to a more united and more powerful supra- (and sometimes) supernational EU-Europe, and by inter-governmentalists as an unrelated parallelism.

In the case of Eastern enlargement, however, the utopian or historic-change-oriented idea of Europe, played an important role both for the domestic transformation process as well as the re-orientation of foreign and security policies after the end of the East-West conflict. EU-membership was considered as the historic return to Europe as well as an external legitimisation for economic transformation processes with significant social costs; NATO-membership was sought to became part of the "West" including the U.S. and its global power – and security – projection capability. It was logical that the new Eastern members supported a parallel interpretation of the utopian and the pragmatic Europe and did not support policies, which sought to operationalise the utopia into a comprehensive concept of gradual but continued deepening of the integration process. First, their newly acquired national souvereignty together with nation-building in the newly independent Eastern countries such as the Baltic States conflicted with the supranational notion of transfer of national souvereignty towards the EU (or a re-organised NATO), which resulted in a policy of restraining the idea of continued unification to an utopian rethoric. Second, the maximising national benefits from both memberships did not allow to accept or even support too much additional integration in general and particular in the security and defense dimension, where Europeanised EU and U.S.-dominated NATO competed for transfer of competences, resources, and legitimisation of national security and defense capabilities.

The **second pattern** of the general integration process is its stop-and-go dynamic, based not on a longterm and comprehensive masterplan to build the new Europe but on the sometimes reactive and sometimes pro-active exploitation of constellations, coalitions of the political willing, and making use of windows-of-opportunities – in sum a sort of pragmatic exploitation of upcoming opportunities. In contrast to hopes of functionalism of a quasi-automatic dynamic after an initial start-up but in contrast to inter-governmentalists the European integration process is marked by break-throughs, stagnation, and even regression, which result from actual constellations of objective and subjective factors. Thus, steps in integration depend on the cumulation and consequent coalition-building of political will primarily of member states and both of internal and external conditioning factors, which altogether create a constellation of progressive forces able to overcome stagnative and regressive tendencies.

For Eastern European countries seeking membership, both the Maastricht Treaties and their implementation in the post-Maastricht period constituted an illustrative lesson of such a pattern of will-building and will-blocking. While the establishment of EWU served as the example of the advantages of uncompromised integration policies and politics as well as a proof that consequent integration means significant increase in relative and absolute power of the EU as global actor, the slow and restrained development of CFSP, ESDP, and the EU Crisis Intervention Force demonstrated that intergovernmentalistic models, compromise-on-the-lowest-possible denominator ways, and even decision-making-blocking tactics constitute feasible options after membership. Torn between new sovereignty - and in some cases revitalised nationalism – and transfer of sovereignty towards the EU and resulting from competing political orientations – i.e. Europeanised EU and U.S.-dominated NATO – the new Eastern members referred less to EMU's pro-integrationism but more to national advantages through inter-governmentalism or even blocking, delaying, and re-nationalisation tactics. Thus, the policies of new Eastern members in the cases of the Second Iraq War, of improving ESDP and the European Intervention Force, and of the Constitution was not a new pattern but a reference to the long-existing duality between pro-integrationism and inter-governmentalism.

The **third pattern** of the general integration process – and the basis for integration progress – relates to the specifics of the decision-making process within the EU. Concrete will- and consensus-building in the EU result mainly from member states' governments cost-benefit-calculations, multiple coalition-building between member governments, and package-deal-tactics, which traditionally involves financial benefits to buy consensus and support. Reaching and implementing unified supranationalism was less a matter of leadership such in the case of NATO but in creating a win-win-situation for all members involved primarily through financial advantages.

Again, forthcoming Eastern EU member-states adapted quickly to this pattern. In particularly, they learnt from the own case of becoming members both in positive as well as negative ways. First, they understood clearly the logic of the establishment of the Cohesion Fund as nothing else than a financial compensation of member-states for accepting and agreeing to the first round of Eastern enlargement. Consequently, they followed the same pattern, when as new member-states they had to decide on further enlargements. Second, they quickly understood and adapted the principle of national cost-benefit rationality. Political learning based on such a national cost-benefit calculations mark for example the case of Slovak EU membership. In the beginning of Eastern enlargement, the Slovak Republic was rejected as candidate for the first round or membership because of its domestic and foreign policy. Regarding EU-membership as a major net advantage and less risky than staying between the EU and the new Russian-dominated East, the Slovak Republic initiated a political turn-around, which then led consequently to membership in the second round. Again, the Second Iraq War case demonstrated the dominance of national – and only national – calculations for decision-making within the EU. In reference to the general pattern of cost-benefit calculations based on a national cost-risk-benefit calculation a number of new Eastern members viewed their individual interests in supporting the U.S. positions and actions superior to the idea of a unified or "common" foreign policy of the EU.

Following such general patterns of integration, the general enlargement process from a community of six to a community of twenty-seven plus-x showed the following particularities:

First, it was less a strategically planned and systematically prepared widening of membership in the pursuit of the formula that EEC/EC/EU should be not an but the European actor but an exploitation of economic and political constellations both within EEC/EC/EU as well as in the potential member-states. British membership resulted primarily from the economic failure of EFTA vis-à-vis the economic success of EEC/EC plus a change in French attitudes to this particular case. Spanish membership happened in the political transition after the death of dictator Franco, when the EU seized the political opportunity to attract Spain through political and economic advantages of membership and when influential member-states' governments viewed EU membership as a mean to support democratisation plus the new Spanish Socialist government. Membership for former neutral and non-aligned countries like Sweden, Finland, and Austria followed a constellation after the end of the East-West conflict, when neutrality had lost relevance and economic modernisation through EU membership seemed attractive both for the EU and the membership candidates. Finally, the end of the East-West conflict was less an outcome of a systematic and coherent strategy of the EU to end military confrontation and overcome the political-economic East-West division but an opportunity for EU member-states such as Germany to promote EU enlargement because this served German economic, military, and political interests in a political stable, military secure, and economically high-absorbing Eastern neighbourhood.

The decision about the Copenhagen Criteria for enlargement underline, how much the EU exploited opportunities and how less it followed a masterplan for systematic widening. First, a masterplan rationality would have demanded that criteria would have been established much earlier – i.e. before the first enlargement – and that a continued updating would have been introduced. Second, the Copenhagen Criteria are not comprehensive but a minimum base without specifying either the final identity of the EU nor in-/outruling future memberships towards the East, the Balkan, and Turkey. Third, they did not solve the political-versus-economical argument for and against widening. Fourth, they ignored EU's widening-and/or-deepening dilemma, which came apparent in the debate about the Constitution. And finally – and in full discrepancy to all enlargement experiences of the past – Copenhagen did not deal with the necessity of ensuring that the new Eastern members with their far-reaching lack of familiarity with the formal and informal ways, modes, and dynamics of EU-decision-making would accept, follow, and promote the long-established informal code of conducts in common decision-making In sum, the Copenhagen Criteria constitute pragmatic minimalism in order to exploit reactively the opportunities of a new constellation.

Second, EU enlargement policies are policies based primarily on political decisions without adequate preparation or follow-up. Both in economic as well as in political terms, both EU and candidate countries considered membership as a sort of big-bang effect, i.e. that with membership all domestic problems would be solved and that membership would create a win-win-game without loosers both within the new memberstate as well as within and between old members. Such a view was acceptable for the first round of enlargement, which included highly developed and competitive economies such as the one of the United Kingdom. But things changed fundamentally, when in the Mediterranean enlargement the Portugal, Spain, and Greece became members, which at that period had to be considered as less developed vis-à-vis the political and economic standards of the old member-states.

While in economic terms gradual accession to full membership aimed to soften the often painful socio-economic adaptation to the competitive and dynamic common market, enlargement policies followed the model of unrestrained economic liberalism and left the post-entry economic processes to the free market forces ignoring the social and economic costs of EU membership particularly for economically weaker und less developed countries. But such policies of ignoring the consequences of membership in economically less competitive new members was complemented by the ignorance of the EU as such vis-à-vis the effects of enlargement for its Common Agricultural Policy (CAP) in general and CAP's budgeting in particular. Although it was obvious already at the time of the first Southern enlargement that CAP had become anachronistic both towards the inside as well as the outside of EEC/EC, the decision of enlargement was decoupled from the necessary reform of CAP. And while such concerns could be marginalised in the hope that economically stronger member-states would rescue the EU budget from bancrupsy until the late 80's, this policy of ignorance continued vis-à-vis the Eastern enlargements, where both ability and capability of old member-states such as Germany to cover EU's deficits did not exist any more and where the calculated costs of a non-reformed CAP were much higher than in the case of former rounds of enlargement. Thus, enlargement policies not only follow the general pattern of pragmatism but combined this with ignorance and short-term muddling-through activities.

A similar pattern can be found in the political dimension of post-enlargement effects. Again, the first enlargements did not cause political problems neither concerning norms nor management of civil society and democracy. However, this changed, when countries with a non-democratic past – such as the three Mediterranean, the Eastern European, the Balkan, and the South-Eastern European countries joined the EU. In repetition of the muddling-through and ignorance syndrome, the EU as such disregarded the problems of democracy- and civil-society-building plus good governance in those countries and like in the economic dimension left the difficult task of political transformation and civilisation to the new member-states. In the case of the three Mediterranean countries such a non-policy could be legitimised in reference to the many programs and activities of other EU member-states, but instead of learning from the lessons of these developments the EU continued such policies towards the Eastern enlargements, when bilateral programs either did not exist or were too limited to induce necessary and sustainable change to the general norms and political models of the old EU. Although the lack of provisions of how to prevent de-democratisation or violations of basic norms marks the European integration from the very beginning, such pragmatism could be justified in referring to the stable and deep-rooted democratic ways, means, and structures in the early EEC/EC. But continuing such doctrines of optimistic belief in democratic stability and progress in enlargement policies after the

Balkan wars and decoupling enlargement and constitution-building again illustrates EU's deficits when it comes to coherent grand strategies. While this is already a problem in the economic dimension of EU policies – the traditional domain of European integration -, Maastricht's definition of the EU as political union based on common norms and an advanced and enhanced understanding of democracy made this strategic deficit even more obvious.

Third, EU enlargement policies follow a basically asymmetric pattern, in which the politically attractive, economically strong, and socio-economically advanced and dynamic EU negotiates – or better dictates in a more or less benevolent mode – conditions and timing for accession. This asymmetry can be found in membership negotiations procedures and substance. Traditionally, EEC/EC/EU has bilateralised membership negotiations, i.e. follows EU-to-candidate-country tactics even when the EU deals with groups of countries with high degree of homogenity. Such divide-and-rule-tactics complement EU's general line concerning the political substance of the membership negotiations, which in follows the line that enlargement means projection of economic-political norms, models, and dynamics as well as the current set of EU administrative rules into the new member-states. And the more enlargement policies have been successful and the more attractive EU membership is regarded, the less the EU is willing to compromise, to accept national specifics, and to accept longer transition and adaptation periods after granting membership. Both EU and candidates know that there is no alternative to membership in the EU particular in the economic-political dimension and that even limited influence as a member subject means more advantages and more power than staying outside and becoming an object of the EU. All attempts to create subregional groupings within the EU either before, during, and after membership negotiations – however they would improve the candidate's negotiation power and influence after becoming member -, failed both in the enlargement process in general as well as in the case of Eastern enlargement in particular. It is the EU, which dictates terms, conditions, timing etc. of membership – not the candidate countries.

Fourth, EU enlargement and NATO enlargement have to be regarded as complementary in objective but competitive in subjective terms. Although EU and NATO membership do not always overlap the conditions for membership show similar objectives: while in principle the acceptance of the normative standards and inofficial rules for cooperation, conflict management, and subscribing to the patterns of joint decision-making are the same the difference lies in the different nature of both. As primarily a defence- and security-projecting alliance NATO adds specific conditions concerning security, defence, and military policies of enlargement candidates and as a U.S.-dominated alliance NATO demands special attention towards U.S. interests and policies. Due to its basically economic-political nature EU put special emphasis on economics and politics but allows a much greater freedom for dissent than NATO because of its power structure based on shifting case-to-case, issue-to-issue, and dimension-to-dimension character.

2. The causes for enlargement

Summarising and systematisising enlargement on the base of the many existing analyses, country and case studies, and theoretical debates one can speak of four currently existing clusters of explanations: historical-normative identity, cost-effectiveness rationality, functional-institutional explanations, and realism.

The **first cluster** of explanations refers to normative understandings of enlargement as a historical necessary step in the building of the New Europe or the re-building of Europe after the end of the Second World War. It interrelates three understandings of the European integration process and necessarily is based on the vision not of a "limited"- but an "all"-European or "as-great-as-possible" Europe. Because of the reductionist tendency of current realism vis-à-vis the European integration process the most important points of this cluster will be re-introduced here:

1. The European identity is not limited to the original six but is understood as an open process of Europeanisation of all „European" societies, economies, and countries. This identity is based on traditions of enlightment and define European identity not only as an introvert but as an extrovert progressive process of all Europeans defining European identity as a combination of political-geographic, economic, socio-cultural dimensions as well as a community open to newcomers and designed to become a responsible regional and global actor.

2. Following such ideas of enlightment, European history in general is considered on the one side as an opportunity to progress by learning from past failures and mistakes and on the other side as a special historical responsibility both to the inside as well as to the outside. It is important to accept that such an understanding of European history as a process of progressive intra- and extra-civilising carries the notion and often the myth of grandeur. But the idea of "Europe can and will do better" has to be considered as an important instrument for legitimisation and enlargement of the integration and unification process.

3. The normative base of such an identity and historical responsibility can again be found in common European traditions, European political culture of democracy, and classical theory of democracy. Whether one starts with the Greek/Roman political thinking, the British or the French revolution or refers to the many democratisation and unification processes in Europe of the 19th and 20th century is less important than the common normative understanding that democratic norms and values cannot be limited to a national society or state because of their very universal character. Like in the case of the French revolution, universalism is considered not as a sort of a sudden global revolutionary act but of a gradual learning process in which more and more societies in the region - and later in the global system - understand these democratic basic norms and values as both universal and as the base for best global governance. Gradualism or the idea that democratisation as a process both to the inside as well as the outside – i.e. a matter of deepening and widening – has to be related to the idea of multi-level governance

from the local to the global democracy. In such an understanding both widening and deepening of the democratic normative catalogue was and is essential, while European integration is considered not as the but as a level of political organisation in a greater global community.

Particular in the case of Eastern enlargement such a combination of identity, history, and norms and values played an important role. The above-mentioned European identity with its liberalism, freedom-orientation, and civil-society-approach has always been attractive for Eastern Europe during the East-West conflict, which was often viewed as an un-natural division of Europe, as a Sovietisation and Russification of Eastern European societies, economies, and political systems, which belonged to Europe understood basically as Western Europe. European history – and the wish both to return to European history as well as to become an active part of it through EU-membership – was a way to map a political future in looking back to a glorious European past as well as towards an attractive and beneficial participation in the New Europe. And the normative and value-based understanding of the New Europe and particularly the new European Union was considered as an important stimulus, reason, and legitimisation for political, economic, and social transformation after the end of the East-West conflict. Once again – in this interrelated formula of identity, history, and norms – objective and subjective factors came together; the important role of EU-membership for the Eastern European countries was not only a sort of the return into the European "family" but as well the reference to the myth of old and new paradise through EU-membership, which was both necessary for public consumption as well as helpful in accepting the long negotiations for EU-membership including as the many concessions and the overall price for membership the Eastern European societies, economies, and political publics had to pay.

The **second cluster** of enlargement refers to the already mentioned cost-risk-benefit rationality of nation-states seeking membership as well as the European Union granting membership. While the first cluster is a matter of political ideas, the second is a matter of calculations. Such a rationale for seeking membership was based on the idea of cumulative net-advantage for membership, i.e. the questions, whether weighted individual advantages or benefits are significantly bigger than disadvantages or costs, whether positive perspectives surpass the expected risks, and whether in the very end such calculations lead to the assumption that membership has a major net-advantage compared to non-membership or associative status. Such a rationality results again from the combination of objective factors and their subjective perception; and in the subjective perception the many assumptions such as of paradise-through-membership, compensation domestic shortcomings through playing an "important" role in the community, and inflationary estimates of advantages of EU-membership translate common-good- into political rationality sometimes far away from objective reality. But if one considers misperceptions as collateral costs of such a rationality, one still can regard enlargement or agreements about EU-membership as a matter of rational choice or the complementary but different cost-benefit calculation between the candidate country and the EU or the collective decision-making within the EU.

In the case of Eastern enlargement there is broad agreement

- that both the absolute and the relative economic, political, socio-cultural advantages of membership for Eastern European countries were and are extremely high and that the costs of EU-membership and related modernisation could and can be effectively controlled,
- that the risks of EU-membership were and are low compared to the risks of the option to stay outside the EU,
- that the perspectives of EU- plus NATO-membership concerning political stabilisation, economic growth, and military-political security were and are extremely positive, and
- that concerning foreign orientation in terms of economy, security, and policy the Eastern European countries had no attractive alternative to EU-membership.

Equally and despite all calculations particular about the economic burdens of Eastern enlargement for the EU and its old member-states, there is broad agreement that the EU not only had and has to enlarge but that it is in their long-term economic, political, and military interest as well.

Although the general line of this argumention does not follow either functionalistic or institutionalistic explanations of integration in general and enlargement in particular, both approaches have to be considered as a **third cluster** of explanation of enlargement. Functionalism has to be considered not only as a matter of intra-EU deepening but logically of EU widening as well. And the logic of institutionalism points to enlargement particularly in terms of more and extended power, influence, and control of European institutions.

And if one finally turns to the **fourth cluster** - i.e. realism -, Eastern enlargement is an illustration of complementary power calculations in general: widening towards the East was and is not only a matter of economic, political, and military calculations but of a EU grand power strategy as well:

- For the EU widening meant and means that the community of the six as a European actor turned to the European actor; consequent enlargement meant and means a broader base of power, better control of Eastern Europe through integration, and more legitimacy for the EU as regional and global actor. Eastern enlargement carried an additional and important historical argument for the supporters of the New-Europe-vision: membership for Eastern countries underlined that the East-West divide not only came to an end but that it was the European Union, which benefited from the dissolution of the conflict in terms of power, in terms of norms and values, and in terms of foreign policy attractiveness.
- For the candidate/member states the loss of national decision-making power was and is by far compensated by the benefits of direct access to the much bigger EU power formula and to participate – even in marginal extent and intensity – in power-projection of the EU (as well as NATO). The power formula for the Eastern

candidate/member-states was simple and political convincing: either to continue as a politically marginalised nation-state between the EU and Russia and become the object of their policies or to join EU and NATO in order to get direct access to and influence in the decision-making of EU and NATO as a subject – even in a limited way.

In sum, enlargement in general and Eastern enlargement in particular can be considered less by a consistent, coherent, and longue-durée-oriented grand strategy of the EU but more by a more pragmatic strategy, which is based on a pattern of using windows of opportunities, by a highly reactive tactic of responding to stimuli and constellations, and finally by the quality and impact of lobbying and coalition-building of the candidate-countries. Candidates' and EU's calculations, perceptions, and objectives normally have been and are not identical; it is the critical mass of net-complementarity, which decides about membership in general and transition periods, special exemptions, and specific conditions for the future member country.

In sum, enlargement has to be explained by a multidimensional set of the above-listed four clusters; the weight of the different clusters against each other and of the factors within each cluster depend on the theoretical-systematic preferences of the analyst. But in addition to that, one has to remember the general law of all political processes in general and international politics in particular: objective factors, constellations, and dynamics are less relevant than their subjective perception and subjective perceptions depend on decision-making structures including the personality of the responsible actors. Thus European integration in general and enlargement in particular are not only processes based on objective interests and power calculation, but as well a matter of norms and values, of visions and myths, and of illusions and learning processes.

3. Problems of Eastern enlargement

As it has been discussed above, the main problem of enlargement policies in general and Eastern enlargement in particular is that both have reconfirmed but not improved the general problems, with which the integration process is plagued since its beginning:

- The tactical argument that widening would force the new EU into deepening, political re-organisation, and more effective will-building have proven invalid, the case of CAP illustrates both the lack of political will and institutional ability to introduce necessary reforms even in the case of an obvious necessity.
- The hopes that the new Eastern European members would develop into active integrationists thus reducing the relative power of the inter-governmentalists proved equally wrong.

But enlargement not only reconfirmed the old problems of the European integration process and the EU, but created a new double-problem for the process of political will-building as well as translating common political will into concrete and effective action. Will-building and will-implementing are essential conditions to become a regional and global actor – a particular objective of the EU after Maastricht.

The first aspect of this problem is that enlargement became a major problem for EU's grand agenda and dominated will-building to a great deal both due to the controversies between the old members of the EU as well as between the EU and the candidate countries. If one assumes that political organisations of such a complex architecture as the EU have limited capacity in agenda-managing, i.e. cannot deal with too many major issues at the same time in an efficient and successful way, and if one assumes that the Maastricht agenda – creating a Political Union, establishing EMU and CFSP, and transforming the EU into a capable global actor – was already overloaded, the additional issue of enlargement and further enlargement created an inflationary pressure, which the system as such could not manage.

The second aspect is that the overload problem is not only a matter of the agenda but of the concrete decision-making process as well. Being not based on a leadership but on a collective power formula, the will-building process relies on intense consensus-building procedures and processes. The simple expansion of numbers of formally equal will-builders from six to twenty-six results in a multiplication of consensus-building procedures including all obstacles because of intergovernmentalism, national egoism and egocentrism, and irrationality.

The third aspect – and this is particularly true for the Eastern enlargements – is that the newcomers in the will-building process were not equipped with the formal and informal preconditions for the traditional European will-building way. They often lacked the necessary civil-society- and multi-party-experiences in constructive compromising, they were not used to common-interest-building beyond national interest pursuit, and they were unfamiliar with the procedures, modes, and particularities of the complex interaction between member-states on the one side and European Commission, European Council, and European Parliament on the other side.

A comparison of the EMU and the CFSP project illustrates the scope of the problem and offers a solution. EMU as a truly integrationistic model carried the precondition for membership not only of a specific economic-monetary performance but as well of a fundamental pro-willing attitude. As such, it was based and reconfirmed an integration strategy based on the géometrie-variable-model with particular coalition of actors such as Germany, France, and the European Commission. All these three characteristics can be considered as necessary conditions for its success both towards the inside as well as to the outside – i.e. as a global actor. CFSP, however, was build on the principle of intergovernmentalism, replaced the "coalition-of-the-willing"-approach by a model, which involved all member-states – including the non-willing, less-willing, and ad-hoc-willing - fully and from the very beginning, and opened the decision-making process to obstruction, delay, unilateralism, etc. Accepting a parallel – and not integrated – process for EU- and NATO-membership for the Eastern European countries, further opened a window of opportunity for those new members, who hoped to gain advantages in NATO through block progress in CFSP, ESDP, and the build-up of the European Crisis Intervention Force.

While CSFP can be considered primarily a matter of building a common interest and a common power base, the efforts of establishing a European Constitution demonstrate that the problem of will-building is not limited to interests and power calculations but in addition to normative and value-setting as well. Again, Eastern European members not only actively joined the intergovernmentalists and the anti-Constitution-coalition but become their most outspoken protagonists. While it would have been logically that their experiences during the East-West conflict and in the Eastern bloc plus there will to return to Europe would have turned them into supporters of a European Constitution, which exactly secures their new freedoms and liberties, they revived and exploited their nationalistic traditions in delaying, blocking, and finally preventing the set-up of an effective European constitutional regime.

In sum, enlargement in general and Eastern enlargement in particular have not only reconfirmed the existing structural problems, dilemmas, and weaknesses of the European integration process but have further intensified them. In addition, the past and recent experiences with the new – and particular the new Eastern – members of the EU have made clear that the old informal and formal will-building process of EEC/EC cannot cope with the new situation both because of the increased membership as well as the increased agenda. Thus, the performance of most new Eastern European members in the common will-building process might lead to the opposite of what they looked for – instead of preserving and increasing their influence, leverage, and relative power status within the EU and through EU-membership the debate about the coalition-of-the-willing model or the return to the power formula of the coalition of the six-plus-Spain might limit, reduce, and even marginalise their influence within the New Europe and the EU.

References:

D. Bourantonis/M. Evriviades (Eds.), A United Nations for the Twenty-First Century, Dordrecht/ Netherlands 1996

Rene Cuperus/Johannes Kandel (Eds.), Transformation in Progress. European Social Democracy, Amsterdam 1998

Journal of European Integration No 2-3/1997, Special Issue on Problems of Eastern Europe

Klaus Dicke/Klaus-Michael Kodalle (Eds.), Republik und Bürgerrecht. Kantische Anregungen zur Theorie politischer Ordnung nach dem Ende des Ost-West-Konflikts, Weimar/Köln/Wien 1998

Janusz Golebiowski (Ed), Poland, Germany, Russia. Perspectives in Collaboration, Warschau 1995

Klaus Gottstein (Ed), Tomorrow's Europe. The Views of Those Concerned, Frankfurt 1995

Eric Remacle/Reimund Seidelmann (Eds.), Pan-European Security Redefined, Baden-Baden 1998

Reimund Seidelmann (Ed.), Crises Policies in Eastern Europe, Baden-Baden 1996

Reimund Seidelmann, Democracy-Building in the European Union. Conditions, Problems, and Options, in: Mario Telo (Ed.), Democratie et Construction Européenne, Bruxelles 1995, p. 73-89

Reimund Seidelmann, EU and Eastern European Security. In: Tomsk State University (Ed.), The future of European Union Relations with Eastern Europe, Tomsk 2003, p. 48-53

Reimund Seidelmann (Ed.), EU, NATO and the Relationship Between Transformation and External Behavior in Post-Socialist Eastern Europe. The Cases of the Slovak Republic, Bulgaria, Romania and Ukraine, Baden-Baden 2002

Reimund Seidelmann, European Union and Eastern Europe, in: Mario Telo (Ed.), European Union and New Regionalism. Regional Actors and Global Governance in a Post-Hegemonic Era, 2. edition, Aldershot 2007, p. 235-253

Reimund Seidelmann, Stichwort „Erweiterung und Vertiefung der Europäischen Union", in: Beate Kohler-Koch/Wichard Woyke (Eds.), Lexikon der Politik. Bd 5 Die Europäische Union, München 1996, p. 54-59

Mario Telo/Paul Magnette (Eds.), De Maastricht à Amsterdam. L'Europe et son nouveau traité, Bruxelles 1998

Mario Telo (Hrsg.), Vers une nouvelle Europe, Bruxelles 1992

Jan Zielonka/Alex Pravda (Eds.), Democratic Consolidation in Eastern Europe. Vol. 2. International and Transnational Factors, Oxford 1999

Challenges to the Policy–making Process in the Enlarged European Union

Frank Delmartino

Introduction

The EU's enlargement with 12 new member states can be regarded and assessed from different perspectives. The most striking feature is the *territorial expansion* of the Union. Presently the EU covers most of the European continent, with the notable exception of Russia and the countries in the Russian sphere of influence. Given the fact that the Western Balkans enjoy a kind of pre-accession status and that countries as Norway, Iceland and even Switzerland are actually closely associated with the EU, one can put forward that Northern-, Western-, Southern- and Central Europe are nowadays fully taking part in the European integration process. Nearly half a billion of inhabitants, most of them already now full EU citizens, are directly involved.

Next to the thoroughly redesigned map, however, one should pay attention to the *momentum* this enlargement represents in the self-definition of the Union and to its *perception* by the outside world. Moreover, the question arises to which extent an enlarged EU is still manageable with the institutional instruments that originally have been designed for a 'Common Market' with six member states. And, finally, what does the involvement of the Union means vis-à-vis 'young democracies' with a weak system of governance, confronted as they are with huge economic disparities compared to the EU-15 ? Is there no risk that the process of *'Europeanisation'* could imply a modelling on the aims, standards and procedures of the 'old' member states, thus fundamentally affecting the traditional notion of integration ? Therefore, and perhaps even more significantly than a quantitative leap forward, the recent enlargement may be weakening the Union's governance capacity and affecting its self-understanding as a system of cooperation, whose aim is to strengthen – and surely not to challenge – the internal political and societal order of the member states.

The events are, of course, too recent in view of any valid assessment of these rather provocative assumptions. Moreover, empirical research is incipient and scattered. This paper, nevertheless, aims at linking the apparent effects of the recent enlargement to the literature available on the ongoing processes of constitutionalisation and europeanisation.

The EU is indeed going through a crucial period of re-definition, *ad intra* and *ad extra*. Whereas most observers focus their attention on the EU's enhanced capacities as a global actor, questions can arise on the enlargement's impact on the internal political order and even the welfare state-model of (some of) its member states. In a couple of cases, this *malaise,* reinforced by the prospect of future enlargements, has contributed to the rejection of the Constitutional Treaty by the general public. In other words, the 'exercise' of enlargement is not a merely technical operation that can be isolated from its historical and institutional context.

Therefore, in a first point, a brief comment will be given on the political context of the enlargement to the Central- and East-European Countries (CEEC's). Linked to it, the notion of *europeanisation* will be clarified. Supported by this historical and conceptual framework, the present-day realities can be touched upon, focusing on the impact of the enlarged Union on its decision-making capacity. Finally, by way of conclusion, we would like to deal with the shift in the very notion of *integration* : what does it imply for the political, social and economic system of a country, to become a member of the Union ?

1. The historical – political context of enlargement

The sequence of events following the fall of the Berlin wall (1989) and the collapse of the Soviet-Union (1991) have been adequately described in many monographs and textbooks (1). Eighteen years after the CEEC's opened their borders, one should still be fully aware of the momentum of this turn from the 'East' to the 'West'. A new understanding of political democracy and individual freedom went along with a strong belief in market economy. In other words, the shift was not just a political one, but was deeply affecting societal life. The West-European countries, and the Western world as a whole, were seen as 'models', illustrating the way to political freedom and economic performance. Therefore, right from the beginning, for the CEEC's a form of reliance on, or association with the EU countries was self-evident.

It is well known that the implosion of the Communist regimes has taken the Western world by surprise. No scenario was readily available for dealing with the CEEC's, let alone integrating them in one way or another. Actually, several European leaders were not too enthusiast about the newly created situation, since it fundamentally challenged the balance of influence, even among the major EU member states. Germany, all of a sudden, was becoming predominant in size, thus disturbing the well-established equality among the 'Big Four'.

More importantly, the very *raison d'être* of the Union had to be reformulated. It was no secret that the initial readiness to 'integrate' the economies of the six founding member states in the midst of the cold war, had been part of a common strategy to cope with the (perceived) threat from the Soviet bloc. The end of that era of confrontation compelled the EU-12 to reposition themselves on the global chessboard, highlighting their political and economic motivations for further integration.

The Treaty on European Union (TEU), also known as the Maastricht Treaty, negotiated in 1991 and signed in 1992, should be seen in this perspective. It is far from coherent and not operational at all regarding the second and third 'pillars', resp. dealing with Foreign- and Security Policy and Justice and Home Affairs. The TEU has nevertheless contributed to the *deepening* of the integration process, since all member states agreed to ' *an ever closer Union* '. For sure, the shift from *Community* to *Union* and the introduction of the concept of citizenship largely belong to the domain of political symbolism, but they signal a renewed impetus after the unexpected events of 1989 – 1991.

The 'Fathers of the Treaties', however, having recalled " the historic importance of the ending of the division of the European continent and the need to create firm bases for the construction of the future Europe " (2), left the *modus operandi* in view of realizing that aim to a great extent in the dark. Therefore, in 1993 the well-known *Copenhagen criteria* for full accession to the EU of the Associated Countries (Europe Agreements) had to be established, specifying the requirements for the CEEC's. Next to the full acceptance of the political principles of liberal democracies, the candidates had to be successful in implementing a functioning market economy. In other words : they should have the capacity to cope with competitive pressure and market forces within the Union (3). The long accession process would last some ten more years, even twelve in the case of Bulgaria and Romania.

The 'long way to Europe', with its gradual absorption of the 'acquis communautaire' and the particular conditions set to each of the candidates, are well documented in the 'Progress reports' of the European Commission. In the final part of this paper, the impact of this 'conditionality' on the CEEC's will be discussed. Here we only want to stress that the oncoming enlargement process was already present in the shaping of the Maastricht Treaty. By anticipating on what had to come, the TEU was creating a political framework for the reformulated aims of the Union, for its broadened scope of policies and for some qualitative innovations such as the political principles and the values of the Union.

The *mental* enlargement of the Union, therefore, neither did take place in January 2004 / 2007, nor at the start of the negotiations with the CEEC's, but at the moment, back in 1990-1991, that the member states decided to embark on a fundamentally new treaty arrangement. Since that shift from Community to Union, the CEEC's have manifestly been in mind when the new design came into existence.

2. The concept of Europeanisation

When analyzing the 2004 and 2007 rounds of enlargement, West-Europeans tend to focus the attention to two precise moments in the process. On the one hand, they highlight the general preconditions for membership, crystallized in the Copenhagen criteria and the initial positive reaction to the application of the candidates. On the other hand, after years of negotiation, chapter by chapter, on all aspects of the *acquis* that have to be implemented, the final green light is (eventually) given and the date for accession fixed.

In recent years, policy analysts have drawn the attention on a less visible aspect of EU membership. The concept of *Europeanisation* has many fathers. Just to quote two of them, Héritier defines it as " the process of influence deriving from European decisions and impacting member states' policies and political and administrative structures " (4). So, all member states, even the long-standing members and the core actors, are affected by this phenomenon. A fortiori, it applies to the countries with a fundamentally different economic and political background that recently joined in.

A more elaborate definition is offered by Radaelli, drawn upon the publications of Ladrech, Green Cowles, Caporaso and Risse (5) : " a series of processes of construction, diffusion and institutionalisation of formal and informal rules, procedures, policy paradigms, styles, ways of doing things and shared beliefs and norms which are first defined and consolidated in the making of EU decisions and then incorporated in the logic of domestic discourse, identities, political structures and public policies ".

Joining the lively debate on this concept does not enter within the purpose of this paper. We are, however, convinced that the Europeanisation approach is a useful analytical tool for shedding more light on the *internal* processes the new member states have gone , and are still going, through. The 'conditionality' set by the EU-15 for the 10 CEEC's did not limit itself to the implementation of the *acquis* as such, but was extended to the national poltical and administrative structures and culture, considered to be a *conditio sine qua non* for *good governance*. Next to changes in legislation, the reform of the political decision-making process and the bureaucratic procedures were prominently present on the agenda of the negotiations and in the – still ongoing – monitoring exercises (6). Summarizing, the impact of the EU on the new member states has been – and still is – of a different magnitude and even nature than it has been in the past wave of enlargement. It would be worth examining the impact of this Europeanisation in the years to come.

Another comment on the current understanding of the concept of Europeanisation has to do with the one way – direction of influencing that is suggested by the definitions mentioned above. The formal and informal rules, policy paradigms, shared beliefs and norms in Radaelli's approach, are for sure not the monopoly of the Brussels bureaucracy, but have been inspired and influenced by the member states and the shifts in policy preferences that have taken place over the years. Lots of examples could be given in the 50 years since the Treaties of Rome. Let's just refer here to the remarkable strengthening of the principle of transparency and its legal implementation since Nordic countries as Sweden and Finland joined the Union in 1995. It will be interesting to assess in a few years the impact the 'newcomers' will have on, let's say the EU's policy style, just to use one of Radaelli's terms. By way of hypothesis, we would like to put forward a *two way* - Europeanisation process.

3. The impact of the enlarged EU on decision – making

It will be clear that the 2004 – 2007 wave of enlargement can by no means be compared to the previous one in 1995. If the latter was based on strict negotiations between three (originally four) 'welfare states' and the EU-12, in the latest round the political, economic and administrative 'conditionality' was pre-existent to the negotiations and to a certain extent imposed.

If one can thus assume that the CEEC's were in a weak position before accession, they nevertheless are full members since January 1st 2004, resp. 2007. Although quite some measures of transition are still in place and some temporary restrictions have been imposed, e.g. on the free movement of workers, the newcomers have taken their seats in all EU institutions. In this part of the paper we would like to discuss the consequences of the enlargement on the functioning of the decision-making bodies.

Starting at the highest level of political decision-making, the **Council** (of Ministers) and the **European Council** (of Heads of State and Government), one is first struck by the sheer number of partners around the table. Half a century ago, when the Treaties of Rome were negotiated within the walls of the Brussels castle of ' Val Duchesse ', six *fauteuils* around the open fire happened to offer the perfect setting for confidential talks. When one nowadays visits the meeting room for the European Council in the Lipsius Building in Brussels, the participants need screens for being able to adequately watch the speaker. The real negotiations, face to face, take mainly place in the 'coulisses', i.e. at lunch or dinner, unless the acting chairperson insists on a '*tête-à-tête*' with each of the participants, in what is known as the 'confessional' method.

As one can imagine, the number of actors inevitably plays a role when coalitions have to be formed in view of compromises or majority building. Even the sheer presentation of national positions at the very start of a ministerial meeting is extremely time consuming. After the traditional 'tour de table' the morning session has to be concluded for the lunch break.

Despite their superficial character, these features are not unimportant in real life. Much more relevant, however, are two dimensions of the proper decision-making process.

Firstly, there is the striking imbalance between the profile of the countries involved. Their size, their political weight and economic performance cannot be neglected in the policy-making process, especially when issues are at stake that involve budgetary implications. It's a delicate issue within a forum that pays tribute to the culture of consensus building. Therefore, in the past, votes were rarely taken at the Council and voting is unknown at the summit level of the European Council. Consensus is seen as the perfect outcome of a negotiation and is formally required for all matters of principle, first and foremost for all Treaty amendments.

However, right from the beginning, it was clear that some member states were a bit ' more equal than others '. In the mid-sixties a first major crisis had to do with the question if a member state (France in this case) could be 'overruled' by the others. The Luxembourg compromise (1966) did not really settle the issue, but all partners agreed on 'prolonged' negotiations in case major national interests were at stake. As we will see, forty years later, similar ideas are still alive and well.

In the meantime, especially since the Single European Act (1986) and in all subsequent treaties, qualified majority voting (QMV) has been introduced as the regular mode of decision-making in the Council. Over the years, more and more domains have been opened up for QMV and also in practice votes are more and more taken. Consequently, the way those votes are weighted is of utmost importance. We will not enter into detail, but it is well known that the Nice Treaty negotiations (2000) had to go through a ' long night ' on this matter and that the final agreement on the Constitutional Treaty was for some time blocked for this reason.

It's an old problem indeed, but the weighing of the votes of the CEEC's proved to be particularly difficult. Which criterion should be used for ranking the newcomers ? Their GDP, their economic potential, their political correctness, the geographical size or the number of inhabitants? The latter criterion happened to be the least controversial. So, already in Nice, Bulgaria was given the same weight as Austria and Sweden, Romania preceded the Netherlands and Poland joined Spain as a sub-top member state. Especially this last case created controversy at the occasion of the drafting of the Constitutional Treaty, where a new set of criteria was proposed. We will not embark on this issue since a compromise has been found in the recently signed 'Reform Treaty' (Treaty of Lisbon). The arguments Poland is advancing have a bit of *'déjà vu'* : no reform of the voting system that would weaken the status acquired in Nice, extended negotiation in case the country would be outvoted despite a significant minority was opposing the decision. "L'histoire se répète " : the larger member states have a problem with majority rule.

In the case of Poland the issue is most relevant since the country has particular views on quite a few subjects. Sometimes it is a matter of national interest, e.g. its export of meat to the Russian Federation. In other cases, it has to do with ethical considerations, for instance on family law. The situation becomes really embarrassing for the Union as a whole when Poland objects a strategic arrangement with Russia on the provision of energy, a 'deal' that requires unanimous support. No pressure and no 'compensation ' on other issues could convince the leadership in Warsaw. This atypical reaction to a controversial question is not welcomed at all by the European capitals, since it fundamentally weakens the position of the EU on the international scene. It reminds the European partners on the other major 'split', when Poland chose the side of the US on the war in Iraq, giving Donald Rumsfeld the occasion of distinguishing between the 'old' and the 'new' Europe. Nowadays, Poland is the most prominent new member state in the EU and it does not hesitate to use its prerogatives.

However, not all attention should be given to the top level of decision-making. Council and European Council are only the most visible part of the European iceberg. Day-to-day policymaking is in the hand of numerous working parties where national civil servants and experts meet with the officials of Council and Commission. Due to the expertise built up during the long negotiation process, number of national specialists from the new member states are actually ready to pick up their position, either in their permanent representation, or as a newly appointed official in the European institutions.

So, it is not that much the technical expertise that is lacking on the side of the CEEC's. The problem is parallel to what has been signalled with regard to the politicians : the culture of compromising by making 'package deals' is apparently less prominently present in Central- and Eastern Europe. One has to realize that those countries, despite their common past, are not that familiar with each other. Old prejudices survive and new rivalries emerge. In other words, the CEEC's are clearly Brussels-oriented since they expect a lot from their newly acquired membership, but this does not necessarily imply great solidarity among themselves. The well-known balancing of positions and interests, sometimes qualified as bargaining, that has been so characteristic for the relations at the level of the permanent representations of the EU-15 (the so-called Coreper), has sometimes difficulties in adapting to the new setting. This is important, since **Coreper** has always been the *antichambre* for political agreements, where prominent successes of Council decision-making have been duly prepared.

Another major subject of debate is the representation of the member states in the **European Commission**. Despite their solemn oath not to take any instruction from their capital city, Commissioners are mostly seen as the ultimate guarantors that national interests are being given the attention they deserve (7). Until now, all member states, large and small, are represented by a single Commissioner they can nominate to the president-elect of a newly starting Commission. After the assent of the European Parliament with the team as a whole, the Council will appoint the nominees.

It is crystal clear that an executive body with 27 members, in theory all equal, apart from the president, and deciding collectively, is actually unworkable. Moreover, there are no 27 meaningful domains in the Commission's policy portfolio. Internal consistency cannot be guaranteed in the given circumstances. The struggle for the key competences is legendary and the member states are not hesitating to intervene in favour of their *protégé*.

Newcomers as Romania have been given a marginal assignment, such as "promoting multilingualism".

Given the prospect of a few more accessions, especially in the Western Balkans, the system needed a fundamental overhaul. In Nice the EC Treaty was adapted as follows:

"When the Union consists of 27 member states…the number of members of the Commission shall be less than the number of member states. The members of the Commission shall be chosen according to a *rotation* system based on the principle of *equality*, the implementing arrangements for which shall be adopted by the Council, acting unanimously (8).

Since the rotation system had to be applied from 2009 on, a major debate was taking place on its modalities. The European Convention, the negotiators of the Constitutional Treaty and, nowadays, the Reform Treaty, have spent lively discussions on how to apply the quoted principle of equality. Understandably, the major actors cannot conceive a Commission without their presence, while the smaller countries and especially the newcomers want to avoid a kind of *Directory* (directoire in French) composed of the big players. Clearly enough, the EU is still an arrangement among member states and the Monnet idea of European interests to be defended by a trans-national group of technocrats is still far away. Nevertheless, the Reform Treaty has confirmed the rotation principle, however postponing it till 2014 (9).

The **European Parliament** (EP) has to be adapted as well to the new realities after enlargement. The maximum maximorum of 732 members (10) has been fixed by the EC Treaty, but is presently surpassed by the accession of Bulgaria and Romania during the parliamentary mandate 2005 – 2009. So, almost all member states have to give up a few seats (or a more significant number, as e.g. Germany) in order to achieve a fair representation with a guaranteed minimum for the smallest states. This consequence of the enlargement process is not always welcomed, since it implies a loss of influence of a particular country in the overall decision-making. Apparently, the EP is not only representing citizens but the states' interests as well.

4. Towards a new understanding of 'integration'

When discussing the most visible, almost tangible, implications of the recent enlargement wave on the institutional setting and functioning of the Union, at several occasions reference has been made to a more fundamental shift in the relations of the EU vis-à-vis its member states. Perhaps the most crucial implication of the accession of countries with a different political past and economic potential, is the role assigned to the EU in setting standards of political democracy and good governance far beyond the reach of its traditional involvement in internal state affairs.

In the previous wave (1995) the new member states had to 'absorb' the *acquis*, but their political institutions, judiciary, financial control mechanisms and bureaucracy were flexible enough for dealing with that challenge. In contrast, the CEEC's did not dispose of these institutional instruments given their different state tradition. So, the EU had to set operational targets for modernisation of institutions and procedures as well as to contribute to the training of officials. In more academic language, Grabbe has qualified these operations under the headings: *benchmarking*, *monitoring*, provision of legislative and institutional *templates* (11).

The EU was in a position to offer or even to impose these innovations thanks to its role as *gate keeper*. There was no perspective on accession without living up to the 'conditionality' set up by the EU. Via its progress reports the Commission was rather straightforward when assessing the improvements made and the deficiencies encountered in terms of structures or skills. Sometimes, when the process of modernisation in a particular country was nearly coming to a standstill, the Commission did not hesitate to openly report on the achievements of each and every 'student' in the class of enlargement. The sooner the 'homework' finished, the earlier the accession was granted.

Since every participant in the race wanted to reach the finish within a certain timeframe, less attention was given to the *legitimation* of the standards of good governance put forward by 'Brussels'. To a large extent these guidelines had never been formulated in operational terms and certainly not as benchmarks for Central- and East-European countries in transition. So, within a few years, a kind of doctrine has been developed on the organisation and management of state systems, a matter that normally is excluded from EU involvement. This remark should not be understood as a criticism. We rather refer to a paradoxical situation. In the pre-accession phase, the EU (both Commission and Member States) sees itself as a supervisor and even guarantor of legitimate and effective governance. However, once the candidate is promoted to a full member state, 'Brussels' should retreat to its traditional position as a broker, a planner, a coordinator and implementer of policies. Given the fact that a lot of supportive work has still to be done in the CEEC's, including close monitoring, and that several new candidates are queuing up for joining the Union, it would be meaningful, firstly, to recognize the EU's role in coaching the newcomers, and, secondly, to collect the explicit requirements and less formal recommendations in a *'Corpus of good governance'* that would apply to *all* member states. In any case, more transparency is needed in order to avoid total dependency on 'Brussels' during the process of accession.

It is in the interest of all member states and of the European integration process as a whole, to reflect on the very notion of integration, at a moment that all West-European countries (in the broadest sense) have joined in one way or another, and that new membership per definition has to be found in South-Eastern Europe (and beyond). Will the EU stand on its original design of promoting common policies among highly developed and strongly independent countries, or will it rather focus on setting a legal and procedural framework for practising good governance when implementing common policies ?

The recent enlargements and the enlargements to come are probably constituting a turning point in the process of integration. It is impossible to predict the outcome yet. Will *widening* actually weaken the *deepening* of the integration process? Or will it contribute to more 'steering' from the 'centre'? The signing of the Reform Treaty on 13 December 2007 in Lisbon, has proven in any case that consensus building with 27 Member States around the table is still possible. Moreover, some crucial decisions regarding the decision-making process have been taken from the failed Constitutional Treaty, showing continuity and an equal commitment as in the past to the strengthening of the Union.

By way of conclusion

Although this paper was mainly EU-inward looking, assessing the context of enlargement and its consequences, both in terms of operational capacity building and of self-definition of the very notion of integration, it is clear that on the long term the most striking impact of enlargement will probably be noticed with regard to the EU as a global actor. Therefore, it is not without relevance to quote the new article in the Treaty of Lisbon explicitly referring to the aims of the Union vis-à-vis the 'wider world': "The Union shall uphold and promote its values and interests. It shall contribute to peace, security, the sustainable development of the Earth, solidarity and mutual respect among peoples, free and fair trade, eradication of poverty and the protection of human rights…as well as to the strict observance and the development of international law, including the respect for the principles of the United Nations Charter..." (12).

This updated Treaty article provides the EU with a specific profile: not as a superpower but as a global actor in particular policy fields such as free trade, environmental concern, security and fair North-South relations. The EU is clearly more than an economic bloc, since it has an outspoken political dimension, but it is not a state in the making.

This *mission* statement reflects the views of all 27 partners, old and new, CEEC's and West-European countries. At least in the political discourse, the enlargement operation has not watered down the views and ambitions of the Treaty on European Union, formulated after the reunification of the continent. The EU has become more complex since its enlargement, but it is as determined as it was before 2004.

References:

1. Desmond Dinan, *Europe Recast*. A History of European Union. Palgrave, 2004, esp. pp. 265 – 279.
2. Preamble of the Treaty on European Union.
3. European Council, 1993.
4. A. Héritier, *Differential Europe*. The European Union Impact on National Policy-making. Lanham, Rowman & Littlefield, 2001, p.2
5. C. Radaelli, *Europeanization of Public Policy*, in: K. Featherstone & C. Radaelli (eds.), The Politics of Europeanisation. Oxford University Press, 2003, p.30.
6. Heather Grabbe, *European Union Conditionality and the Acquis Communautaire*. International Political Science Review, vol. 23, nr. 3, July 2002, pp. 249 – 268.
7. Art. 213 of the EC Treaty
8. Protocol nr. 10 on the enlargement of the European Union (2001), art. 4.2
9. New art. 9 d (ad 5) of the Treaty on European Union (Reform Treaty).
10. Art. 189 of the EC Treaty
11. H. Grabbe, *Europeanization goes East* : Power and Uncertainty in the EU Accession Process, in : K. Featherstone and C. Radaelli (eds.), op.cit., pp. 303 – 327
12. New art. 3 (ad 5) of the Treaty on European Union (Reform Treaty).

The European Union after Enlargement: A Polish View

Iwona Anna Hanska

Introduction

Within the Eastern enlargement process, Polish membership in the EU is of particular relevance. Poland was not only the biggest, economically most dynamic, and in terms of the EU's Common Agricultural policy (CAP) the most burdensome candidate in the first round of Eastern enlargement, but due to its revolutionary and early transformation to democracy and market economy was also one of the most interesting candidates for membership. Its political-geographic location between Germany and Russia, its history, and inner controversies concerning EU membership and its EU Foreign and Security Policy (CFSP) give Polish EU policies special significance.

With the accession to the European Union on 1 May 2004, Polish foreign policy achieved its main strategic objective since the beginning of the political transformation in 1989. The beginning and the successful conclusion of Polish EU membership was and is indisputably an event of historical dimension both for Poland and Europe, if one considers that for more than 20 years ago the perspective of a membership in the EU was for many Central and Eastern Europe Countries[1] (CEEC) not even a dream. But with the end of the East-West conflict and the transformation of Poland from a Socialist into a democratic political system the idea of becoming a member of the EU and NATO turned into reality. Although Poland's attempt to use the Visegrád cooperation for EU membership negotiations failed and thus improve the bargaining position, the Polish leadership nevertheless gained membership together with the Czech Republic and Hungary in the first round of Eastern enlargement. Furthermore Polish support to continue Eastern enlargement was equally successful in creating the second round of Eastern enlargement, to continue further Eastern enlargement negotiations, and to establish special relations between the EU and the Ukraine – and to sever, restrain, and limit EU relations with the new Russia. This enlargement, including the last accession of Romania and Bulgaria in 2007, constituted a major challenge not only for the European Union at the beginning of the 21st century, but for the 10 old respectively 12 new EU member countries as well.

---

1   The term of Central Eastern Europe (CEE) follows the definition of the Eurostat which considers the Central Eastern Europe to consist of the following countries: Albanien (AL), Bulgarien (BG), die Tschechische Republik (CZ), Estland (EE), die ehemalige jugoslawische Republik Mazedonien (FYROM), Ungarn (HU), Lettland (LV), Litauen (LT), Polen (PL), Rumaenien (RO), die Slowakei (SK) und Slowenien (SI).
The definition of Eastern Europe (EE) included formerly all states of the East Block, but currently refers to European states of the Commonwealth of Independent States (CIS).

The results of this accession and the common perspectives for the enlarged EU are currently the main issue of intensive discussion between the 27 member states with the main focus on the constitution and the related last treaty as well of on the future of CFSP/ESDP. The related so-called "debate about the future of the EU" or "finalité politique" of European integration not only includes key issues and problems of further institutional reforms, which are necessary for improving both decision-making efficiency and democratic legitimacy of the enlarged Union, but also regarding the political will and the political-economic-military ability to act as a global player in general and to take necessary political–military actions for peace-keeping, peace-building, and international crisis management in particular. These two issues are connected with the main question of the European Union as a whole – i.e. the amount and intensity of a future deepening of the integration process and the improvment of the existing institutional framework.

Poland is from the geographical point of view the sixth biggest and one of the most populous countries within the EU and, because of this, considers itself as one of the more powerful member states at the same time. After nearly four years of membership with several disputes between Polish government and the European Union, notably on CSFP in general and EU-Russian relations in particular, it is necessary to analyse the Polish policies as well as its long-term visions of the future development of the European Union or to deal with the question, of how Poland defines this and finally of ask what the EU expects from its new Eastern member states. This means to describe and analyse such policies including their objectives and dynamics in a step by step and multi-dimensional approach in order to better understand the current as well as the future Polish policies within and towards the EU. This means in particular to answer the following questions:

1) What have been the most important goals of the Polish policies and politics after the accession,
2) are the Polish interests and norms/values compatible with those of the other EU members, and if yes or no where and why,
3) how influential is Poland's policy towards institutional change within the European institutional structure and the EU integration process in general, and
4) how far is Poland willing to deepen and/or widen the EU's integration?

Evaluating the past and present of the Polish views on the EU and its future development leads then to the final question: How are the perception and what are the acceptance of the Polish view within the EU and what does this mean for the future position and role of Poland as a member of the EU?

The theoretical framework for the analysis of Polish policies towards and within the EU

Following the concept of Reimund Seidelmann on politics as a matter of norms, interests, and power[2] means not only to understand the important role of the historical factor in Polish policies but as well to analyse the Polish view on the consolidation and further development of the European Union after enlargement under three aspects:

1. First, in terms of norms and values, Poland considered the membership in the European Union not only as its legitimate historical place but as well a mean for outside-stimulated demand for democracy in support of the political transformation from a Socialist towards a Western democratic political system, i.e. giving the EU a role in the political transformation and West-orientation as a political demander, supporter, and stabiliser.
2. Second, in terms of interests, membership in the European Union had major economic, political and military advantages. Both for the transformation towards a market economy as well as for rapid growth and modernization of all sectors of the economy including the highly backward agriculture the EU membership was essential for trade, investment, and labour export. In security terms NATO-membership promised fullest security against any Soviet/Russian military-political threat as well as direct access to U.S. policies and EU-membership was considered as a political supplement or as a sort of political reassurance that European NATO-members would fully support Polish security needs and interests in general and towards Russia in particular.
3. Third, in terms of power, Poland understood that the political geography, situated between EU/Germany and Russia would not enable to exploit its re-established national sovereignty but that seeking EU- and NATO-membership would allow Poland to use EU's and NATO's power and influence to pursue its national interest better. In addition, Poland defined itself as the most important and influential Eastern country/central Eastern country both in the EU and NATO and as the born speaker of the Eastern European interests. And finally, NATO membership was perceived as the best way to establish direct access to U.S. foreign and security policy decision-making.

Due to this, Poland saw and then understood both the EU and NATO as being community of Western democratic values, of major economic and military benefits for Poland, and as an economic-political (EU) and a military-political (NATO) powerful actor, which could be instrumented for Polish interests and position and in which Poland could extend its absolute and relative influence in the new European power

---

2   See: Reimund Seidelmann 2007. "European Union and Eastern Europe". In: Mario Teló. European Union and new Regionalism. Regional Actors and Global Governance in a Post – Hegemonic Era. Brussels, p.235-253.

hierarchy – towards the West and towards the East – i.e. Russia, Belorussia, and Ukraine.

This rationale for Polish membership had and has the above-mentioned strong historical dimension. Poland understood itself traditionally as a European country – its political, economic, and cultural elites oriented themselves throughout its history always towards the West. Russia was traditionally regarded as a threat and not as an ally – a view, which was confirmed by Russia and the Soviet Union's policies towards Poland highlighted by the Ribbentrop-Molotov agreement before the outbreak of the Second World War, in which the Soviet Union not only took major territories from Poland's East but participated actively in the abolishment of the Polish state. Becoming part of or being forced into the Eastern bloc after 1945, Poland tried to reduce confrontation with the West through numerous initiatives[3] and understood détente policy as a means to re-establish relations with Europe in order to reduce Soviet influence, control, and military threat.[4] The special and influential role of the Catholic Church in Poland supplemented Poland's historical orientation towards the West, while Polish migration to the U.S. established additional links. Due to the importance of the historical factor in Poland's political and cultural identity, which goes far beyond the relevance of history for other Eastern European countries, EU-membership not only revitalized Polish traditional orientation towards West but was considered to be historically necessary and natural return to Poland's original place in Europe.

Because of the specific relevance of the historical factor for Polish policies as a whole, and for the EU-membership in particular, one has to go into further details to fully understand the specifics of Polish policies towards and within the EU. Looking at the West, Central- and Eastern Europe to search for compatibility in common values and interest and to understand the problems of the Europeans from a Polish perspective, one has to start with the fact that Poland although considered until 1989 in political point as a part of the Soviet Bloc, is rich in political and cultural European tradition and close relations to the West. Due to its geographical location between the two largest European powers Germany and Russia was created an ambivalent common history, in which cooperation changed into conflict and inversely during the last 1000 years of good and bad neighborhood with the Western and Southern (i.e. Austria) as well as the Eastern neighbours. Relations to Germany and the West included not only a very intensive cultural and scientific exchange, close cooperation and political

3   Recall the so called Rapacki Plan (1956) and the idea of an area free of nuclear weapons in Central Eastern Europe. See: „Memorandum des polnischen Außenministeriums zum Rapacki-Plan (Schaffung einer atomwaffenfreien Zone in Mitteleuropa), Warschau, 14./15. Februar 1958". In: Hans-Adolf Jacobsen/Mieczyslaw Tomala (Hrsg.)1992. *Bonn-Warschau 1945-1991. Die Deutsch-polnischen Beziehungen. Analyse und Dokumentation*. Köln, pp.89-92
4   Cf. Artur Hajnicz 2006. *Irrungen und Wirrungen der polnischen Außenpolitik 1939-1991*. Deutsches Historisches Institut. Warschau, pp. 105-132.

innovation[5], but at the same time several political and military conflicts, since Poland was often subject to foreign rule by the neighboring countries and object of their strategic-political interests. The Polish historical memory, which plays an important role in defining its foreign policies, was formed particularly through the three partitions of the Poland-Lithuania commonwealth in 1773, 1793, and 1795 between Prussia, Austria and Russia. It underlines the tragic chapters of the First and the Second World War and after that of over 40 years of Soviet domination. Both the specific Polish historical factor as such, as well as the general political history of the 20th century explain the special importance of regaining sovereignty and democracy in 1989 and Poland's wish for independence – not only from the Soviet Union/Russian Federation, but also from a reunified Germany – in terms of identity, position, and foreign orientation.

Thus, the creation of a Polish external and internal *raison d'être* [6] including the territorial integrity and political self-determination has highest priority in Polish foreign policy and the way to maintain it conducted various options for the political reorientation. The most important of those was the early participation in the political, economical, security and military structures of Western Europe. In 1990 – i.e. one year after independence and at the beginning of the political-economic transformation to the "New Poland", the Polish foreign minister had already signalized in a major statement the country's wish to seek full membership in the European Community[7]. With the political and economical transformation from an authoritarian regime to democracy Poland together with other CEEC, opened in 1989 a qualitatively new chapter of European history, in which Poland played a special active role. The disintegration of the Soviet empire, the Polish Round Table, and the fall of the Berlin Wall together with German unification then opened new perspectives and challenges for Poland's strategy to fully integrate into Western European political and security structures. And this included not only to reconfirm the Polish good-neighbourhood policy with the old Federal Republic of Germany towards the newly united Germany but as well to redefine Polish-Russian relations to be supported by the EU and NATO.

---

5   Consider the Polish National Education Commission of 1772-3 – the earliest European educational project, consider also the Constitution of 3 May 1791, first constitution in Europe, which established the Poland-Lithuanian commonwealth as a modern constitutional state. Cf. Norman Davis 1998. *Europe: a history*. New York, p. 608 and p. 699.

6   »raison d'être refers to the category of higher (…) national interest«, quoted by Krzysztof Skubiszewski, Minister for Foreign Affairs of the RP. In: Krzysztof Skubiszewski 1997. *Polityka zagraniczna i odzyskanie niepodległości. Przemówienia, oświadczenia, wywiady 1989-1993*. Warszawa, p.300.
     For a short insight into the classic perception of Stateness and Sovereignty see: Andreas Vasilache 2007. "Precarious Stateness and the Fleeting Boundaries of Sovereignty: Theoretical Considerations on Giorgio Agamben and the Indonesian Case". In: Bob S. Hadiwinata, Christoph Schuck (eds.). *Democracy in Indonesia. The Challenge of Consolidation. With a Foreword by former Indonesian President Abdurrahman Wahid*. Baden-Baden, pp.126-129.

7   See: Krzysztof Skubiszewski 1997. Polityka zagraniczna i odzyskanie niepodległości. Przemówienia, oświadczenia, wywiady 1989-1993. Warszawa, p.45.

Poland considered the willingness to enlarge the EC/EU and to accept the new candidates as full members not only as a rational and interest-based political-strategic motive, but also a historical and moral obligation. It was understandable that Poland then made at that time immediate use of this unique historical window of opportunity created by the end of the East-West conflict. The so called *Return to Europe* underlined the Polish attitude back to its historical basis, because "Poland was always in Europe. In the cultural and traditional point of view. Now, after the peaceful Revolution, it has joined it politically as well".[8]

Political dimension

Within the European enlargement process the question of the future political integration of the EU and its willingness and ability to act as a united body with one voice in the global perspective is currently of particular relevance both for the EU as such as well as for other regions, cooperating with the EU. But for Poland this is not only a question of the specifics of CFSP/ESDP but of the general institutional reform as well, which was an important element of the debate on the EU Charter. The starting point of the Polish view on the institutional reform is to provide and save the institutionalised equal distribution of power to all its member countries. With the partial or selected transfer of sovereignty towards the EU, Poland expected more political influence in the decision-making within the EU, more financial benefits, accelerated economic modernization, and better market competition conditions within the EU and abroad. But such expectations and the related pursuit of economic, political, and security interests have to be understood against the above mentioned historical background, for which four factors play an important role:

1. Poland's general experience with the problem of loss of sovereignty throughout its history and the experience of double dependence from the more powerful Germany and Russia,
2. Poland's specific experience with total dependency on the Soviet Union,
3. Poland's dilemma with EU membership, i.e. transferring newly reestablished and valuable sovereignty to the EU,
4. Poland's historical identity as a major European country and power.

In contrast to old members of the EU, this sort of political competition of national versus EU-identity is more intense because of Poland's history and specific national pride and self-esteem. Whereas compromises on concrete economic and military issues have been much easier to reach, political issues such as the formal distribution of power or shares in EU decision-making power have and will always revitalize the trauma of Polish national identity.

---

8   Lech Wałęsa, the President of the Republic of Poland at the Parliamentary Assembly of Council of Europe in Strassburg, on 4 February 1992. In: Lech Wałęsa 1995. Wszystko co robię, robię dla Polski. Przemówienia, posłania, listy 1990-1995. Kanzelaria Prezydenta RP.

Therefore, it is quite understandable that Poland pursues neither an integrationistic nor an intergovernmental approach towards present and future integration, but prefers a pragmatic combination of both to ensure concrete benefits of integrationalism and to preserve as much national identity as possible through intergovernmentalism expressed by a Polish Foreign Minister in the following way:

> "Foreign policy shows that the rigid dividing line between intergovernmentalism and the community method should be demystified. The practice of the intergovernmental method is often a prelude to community-based integration".[9]

This is not only a general but also a specific pattern of Polish views on CFSP as well. Poland is not a supporter of a fully integrated CSFP/ESDP and EU Crisis Intervention Force for two plausible reasons. Firstly, because of the above mentioned special sensitivity towards keeping its national sovereignty, particularly in the case of foreign relations. Secondly, because of its strong belief that integrating CFSP would contradict NATO, would damage U.S. interests in continuing as a European power, and therefore would reduce Polish access and leverage towards the U.S. Finally, understanding that CFSP is dominated by old EU members such as France, Germany, etc. and that Polish influence would always be marginal in a common approach, Poland traditionally does not support too much integration in this political field.

So far the co-existence of the vision "New United Union" and pragmatism has been considered as an unrelated and sometimes even contradictory parallelism.[10] But if one goes beyond the specific issue of CFSP/ESDP, the theme of the political integration in general and issues like the governance ability of the EU in particular revitalize this contradiction and has presented Poland with a difficult political choice. This places Poland in the camp of anti-integrationists and creates a major political difference between Poland and Germany as its most important neighbor, and as that EU member country which supported Polish membership in the EU from the very beginning.

The Polish understanding of European integration, which is rooted in Polish general views on the nation-state-EU relations, has been manifested very clearly within the last five years during the negotiations for the European Constitution Treaty (CT), officially known as *Treaty establishing a Constitution for Europe*, where Poland has developed into one of the strongest opponents of the Charter approach.[11] The set of fundamental institutional reforms of the EU was originally regarded by the "old" EU members as to significant as to be able to improve the preconditions for better and more effective governance towards the inside as well as the outside, and thereby further limit national sovereignty of member states through a more common effective governance.

---

9   See: Statement of Włodzimierz Cimoszewicz, Minister of Foreign Affairs of the Republic of Poland. In: "European Union the day after enlargement: the Polish perspective". London, 24 July 2002. (http://www.mfa.gov.pl/podstrona,3,1221.html)

10   Reimund Seidelmann 2008 (see article in this volume: EU's Enlargement to the East-Pattern, Causes, and Problems.)

11   See: Treaty establishing a Constitution for Europe, CONV850/03. (http://register.consilium.eu.int/pdf/en/03/cv00/cv00850en03.pdf)

In the Polish view this threatened to limit Poland's freedom in pursuing national, foreign and security policies, which might reduce Poland to a secondary European power. Although the Treaty of Nice (2001) was a difficult but acceptable compromise, the *Draft Treaty establishing a Constitution for Europe* in July 2003 constituted in the Polish view a less favorable basis for the institutional framework regarding the progress of integration including the modifications of the voting mechanisms in the EU, which were no longer based on weighted votes, but on the population criteria.[12] According to this proposal the debate about the future of decision-making and its legitimacy in the enlarged EU revitalized old dilemmas and contradictions in Poland's approach towards the EU. Therefore, Poland definitively disagreed with and contested the proposed regulations concerning this issue, in particular those of the forthcoming Treaty. Thus Poland pursued a consequent and continued hard line position in the course of negotiations, which reflected Poland's fears to lose its newly regained sovereignty on a supranational level, especially with reference to Germany. Therefore, Poland concentrated its efforts on defending the voting system in the Council, which constituted originally the component of the Accession Treaty and additionally defined the proportions between the member states in a way that met Poland's preferences.[13] The revision of this for Poland very substantial agreement caused a vehement reaction of the Polish side, which was underlined with the parole *Nice or Death*. As a result Poland, together with Spain, stopped the Draft for CT in 2003 but after the breakup of the Warsaw-Madrid coalition, Poland's left-wing government finally accepted the proposal and signed the final text of the new Constitutional Treaty on 29 October, 2004.

Following this the debate about the European Treaty achieved a new dynamic after the failure of the referendum in France and the Netherlands in 2005. In Poland the planned referendum was still on hold. The Polish conservative coalition, elected in 2005, considered the re-negotiation of the Constitutional Treaty as its top priority in its internal and foreign policy agenda and as a sort of defense of the Polish national interest. This 'radicalization' of the Polish attitude especially during the German Presidency in 2007 damaged Poland's reputation in the EU and let others – in particular the oldest six EU members including Germany – regard Poland as an anti-integrationist and non-progressive force in European integration. The central topic of the Polish government was the continually strict refusal to accept the voting proposal in order to maintain the political balance between Poland and Germany, in spite of all differences as formally equal. The fears of Poland to reduce its influence in decision-making power in favor of Germany and to establish a potential form of a hegemonial structure in Europe paralyzed any attempts for a political compromise. In addition, the exact opposite position of both of those countries regarding the questions of the voting system and the ratification of the CT, revitalized old historical and political polemics

---

12   Ibid. Art. 24: Qualified voting. In: CONV850/03, p.18.
13   See in more detail: Discussion about European Constitution – Arguments of the Minister of Foreign Affairs of the Republic of Poland, 2003;
     (http://www.msz.gov.pl/Discussion,about,European,Constitution,1602.html).

as well as disputes on a bilateral level.[14] While it was the major objective of the German Presidency in 2007 to come to terms with the EU Constitution Treaty project the Polish position vis-à-vis this priority issue finally turned into the blocking stone in negotiations. Concerning the central question of the decision-making system towards the *double majority* voting, Poland presented an alternative option based on square root[15], which would reduce the German power in the voting system. Although this proposal would have reduced Polish power as well, the main point seemed to reduce the German power by sheer weight of numbers. However, giving the preference to the pro-integration principle the European Council meeting on 21 June 2007 decided to act - if necessary - without Poland and in this way threatened Poland negotiators into a compromise concerning this key issue within the new EU Treaty and made Poland agree to convene an IGC to finalize a Reform Treaty[16] for the European Union. Thus, Polish pragmatism, power ambitions, and national identity problems lead not to an improvement but to a decline in political influence and position within the EU. Its continued pro-American policy in cases such as Iraq, its differences with EU members on issues like EU-NATO relations and the missile defence issue, and finally its reservations vis-à-vis EU-Russia relations caused for additional marginalization and loss of influence and relative power within the EU.

Security dimension

ESDP vs. NATO

As was mentioned above, the enhanced discussions about the further and future role and nature of the second pillar of the European Union reflect Poland's ambivalent position to the European Security and Defense Policy (ESDP). Since the early 90s, Poland's political and security grand strategy is clearly based on a combination as well as the division of labour between European and Atlantic orientation, i.e. between the EU and NATO.[17]

But although the Western European Union (WEU) at the time of the beginning of the Polish transformation process seemed both to eventually develop into the European security actor to be later fully absorbed in the post-Maastricht EU and to constitute an option for Polish membership, which the Soviet Union at that time would eventually tolerate, Poland gave priority to NATO membership despite heavy Soviet opposition

---

14 Consider the previous resentment by the diplomatic German and the Polish sides for example about the Second World War and the controversial Center of Remembrance in Berlin for so called Expelled Germans, which has to remember a painful common past.

15 Poland's proposal based the voting rights threshold not on the population, but on its square root; The so called »Penrose square root law« would give Warsaw more balance in reference to Germany.

16 Presidency conclusions-Brussels, 21/22 June, Draft IGC Mandate, 11177/07, ANNEX I

17 See: Statement of the 5th Congress on European Defense. "Poland as a reliable Partner for the Implementation of the European Security and Defense Policy", 2006-10-25; (http://www.mon.gov.pl/en/artykul/2349)

and despite the early lack of support for the widening of NATO within the U.S. In the Polish view,

- NATO had proven that it was the most effective military alliance to provide maximum security guarantees[18], particular against the USSR,
- NATO structures allowed a high degree of retaining national sovereignty in its political dimension,
- NATO would positively control the Polish military through military integration,
- NATO promised major military advantages for the Polish military in terms of the supply of modern weaponry[19],
- NATO membership would create positive spill-over effects for EU membership because of nearly-equal membership of major European nations in NATO[20] and the EU, and
- NATO membership would allow direct and unrestricted access to the U.S. foreign and security decision-making structures.

Upcoming Soviet opposition to the Polish membership in NATO was an additional factor, because forcing the Soviet Union into accepting Polish membership against its will, was considered as a major political victory, ready to be exploited for home consumption because of the long-standing anti-Soviet feelings in Poland.

Although the Polish foreign efforts to join the NATO had already begun in 1990 with the presidency of Lech Walesa, who was a very strong supporter of this Alliance and made a major first step in this issue hoping to get quick and full membership[21], NATO's final decision on Poland's membership needed much more time. First, NATO membership was a complicated issue and demanded certain changes in the organization of the Polish military. Second, while Germany in the very beginning supported the idea of Polish EU- and NATO membership, the political reluctance of other NATO members including the U.S. vis-à-vis full Polish membership with the consequent related burdens delayed Polish-NATO pre-negotiation talks. Third, at that time a number of NATO members and NATO itself hoped that in a gradual but lengthy political dialogue the USSR could be persuaded to accept Polish membership.

Therefore in case of Poland and as with all other Eastern European countries – NATO decided to offer membership in a new additional but non-binding-NATO supplement, i.e. the Partnership for Peace Programme (PfP) of NATO. Poland signed its first PfP agreement on 02 February 1994 and defined it as the beginning of entering

---

18 Cf. Christoph Humrich/August Pradetto 2001. "Poland". In: Hans J. Giessemann/Gustav E. Gustenau (eds.). *Security Handbook 2001. Security and Military in Central and Eastern Europe.* Baden-Baden, p. 336.
19 Ibid. p. 336.
20 Cf. Wojciech Multan 1998. "The Security Policy of Poland". In: Eric Remacle/Reimund Seidelmann (Eds.). *Pan – european Security Redefined.* Baden-Baden, p.196.
21 Recall the famous speech of Lech Wałęsa 1991 in Brussels about the eventually membership of Poland in NATO. See more in: *Prezydentura Lecha Wałesy 1990-1995.* Kancelaria Prezydenta RP. Biuro Obsługi Prezydenta, Warszawa 1995, p.96.

into European security cooperation. When finally German support for Polish full membership and a shifting U.S. attitude on the European security architecture which replaced soft guarantees of PfP through hard ones of full NATO membership, the political conditions changed and introduced the doctrine of widening of NATO towards the East, even in spite of Soviet/Russian opposition, official negotiations about Polish membership in NATO started because of the decisions of the NATO summit in Madrid in 1997. Two years later, on 12 March 1999, Poland's early goal to become a full member of the North Atlantic Alliance turned into reality.

It has to be underlined, that Poland's particular interest in a double strategy of seeking both NATO and EU membership was an essential part of the Polish political orientation since the early 1990s, which considered EU and NATO membership, despite the fact that the EU followed a Europeanistic model without the U.S. and NATO followed a transatlantic model under U.S. leadership, as basically not contradictory but as complementary. The Polish Prime Minister J. Buzek underlined this as following:

> "We do not perceive these two issues separately. (…) our Membership in the EU is a logical consequence of our NATO membership. Without participation in the EU our presence in the Alliance would make sense only partially".[22]

The reasons for the Polish double attitude – and later its contradictory - security and defense strategy were already formulated in the relatively early stages of the Polish foreign policy re-orientation process under the Wałęsa presidency and were motivated by both historical and political-military-geographical context. i.e. the geographical location between Germany and the USSR/Russian Federation. Leaving the Soviet controlled Warsaw Treaty Organisation (WTO), substituting East-orientation through an uncompromised West-orientation, and finally by replacing Soviet security guarantees through NATO ones on the one side, and still-existing Soviet military power and proximity of its best conventional forces near the Polish Eastern borders on the other side, created a new threat scenario of Soviet military blackmail or even intervention, which Poland alone could not adequately deter. The historical factor intensified and deepened this threat perception and made it survive even after the significant decline of Soviet/Russian conventional military power projection capability towards Poland. Thus, the Polish foreign minister contended already in 1991:

> "From the security point of view, Central Europe in particular cannot be turned into a kind of grey, buffer or neutral zone. An area so situated can, because of its location, easily become an object of rivalry among stronger states"[23].

The relation with the United States as the proven guarantor of political and military stability for Western Europe, its successful stand in the end of the East-Westconflict

---

22   Jerzy Buzek, Prime Minister of the Republic of Poland. "Poland's Future in a united Europe". In: *ZEI Discussion Papers*. 1998/C 6.
23   Krzysztof Skubiszewski, Foreign Minister of the Republic of Poland. In: Sejm Exposé by the Polish Foreign Minister Krzysztof Skubiszewski, Warsaw, 27 June 1991.

and as the traditionally most willing and able power to preserve peace, security, and stability in this region, won special attention in this context.[24] Understanding that the EU at that time did not have any adequate military dimension and the WEU was militarily by far to weak to counter even a minor Soviet threat or border conflict, NATO in general and U.S. conventional military presence in European NATO countries in particular played an enormous role during Poland's transformation period:

> "Poland should be – and is – interested in maintaining the presence of the United States in Europe and its role as a peculiar European power. For the presence of America in Europe introduces an unquestionable value added"[25].

And Poland as now the foremost central Eastern country of NATO and the fare most exposed country to near-abroad Soviet/Russian military threats subscribed to a strategy similar of that of the FRG during the East-West conflict: the closer the ties between Poland and the U.S., and the more U.S. troops, NATO infrastructure, and installations such as for missile defence the more would NATO and the U.S. live up to their security guarantees in the case of emergency – and the higher the political deterrence effect towards the USSR/Russia would be. This priority regarding NATO as the stability factor for the Polish security agenda has been maintained continually up to the present.

In the beginning of Polish EU membership policies as part of its double membership policy – i.e. the pre-Maastricht period – the former EC had neither political will nor military capability to project hard security guarantees for its members or towards its borders and WEU could not be considered as a major military actor, willing and able to serve security needs of the Europeans. Traditionally and conditioned by the East-West conflict military security services were left to NATO in general and to the U.S. as a traditional European power in particular. Thus, in this early period, Poland understood membership in the EC/EU as primarily in its political-economic interests and less in its concrete security needs. Given the overlapping membership between NATO and the EU, Poland calculated supplementary and indirect security-building effects of EC/EU membership. It understood that the EC/EU would not allow a direct military threat to one of its members and would press NATO to take necessary actions and that Germany in particular would do its utmost to prevent its new EC/EU and NATO-neighbour against any Soviet/Russian security threat.

With the end of the East-West conflict and in addition the new Maastricht-EU such considerations, in which NATO was the main and only military security agent and in which the EC played only a marginal and indirect role for such services, fundamentally changed and presented an unforeseen challenge to Poland's grand security strategy. With the creation of CSFP, ESDP, and later the European Crises Intervention Force as well as the debate about a future Common European Armament Market, the EU turned

---

24 Ibid.
25 Prof. Adam Daniel Rotfeld, Foreign Minister of the Republic of Poland - The session of the Sejm on 21 January 2005. In: Government information on the Polish foreign policy presented by the Minister of Foreign Affairs; (http://www.msz.gov.pl).

not only into a political-military actor, but into an indirect competitor to NATO in providing security, peace, and peace-keeping services. Given the early strong opposition of the U.S. towards a EU military dimension as a threat to NATO's role in Europe and beyond, this meant for Poland in concrete terms to choose between an orientation towards U.S.-led and militarily effective NATO and a militarily very weak and divided intergovernmental CSFP. In such a choice, Poland's political-military cost-risk-benefit calculations and its traditional reservations on transferring too many sensitive national sovereignties to Brussels and a common European decision, Poland continued its traditional support for U.S./NATO, while accepting CSFP/ESDP intergovernmentalism but not actively seek its political and military strengthening including introducing better and more effective common policies through the European Charter.

Torn between conflicting consequences of NATO and EU membership, Poland actively supports the development of a much deeper integration in the field of European security concept as far as the ESDP is not duplicating nor competing with NATO[26]. According to the official Polish Security Strategy of the Republic of Poland for 2007[27], Poland advocates the complementarity of the NATO and the European Security Strategies (Art. 25). In the global point of view Poland recognizes the key role of the US, which is the guarantor of the international security capable of stabilizing the political and military relations on the continent. In sum, Polish vital interests are that the NATO remains as the common and politically and militarily effective defense instrument of the member states (Art. 25). At the same time Poland accepts the crucial role of the European Defense Agency, but underlines the simultaneousness of the institutional cooperation concerning the security issues between the EU and the NATO (Art. 46). And as a potential danger for the external security of the Republic of Poland, Poland views the potential ambitions of EU's CSFP/ESDP not as an alternative but a complementary counterbalance (Art. 32). Thus, Poland regards itself as the supporter of U.S. objectives in keeping NATO as the main security agent for Europe and eventually limiting and restraining progress in CSFP/ESDP political will-building and military power-building.

Poland further regarded the September-11-case as the proofstone of the Transatlantic Alliance and a major possibility to demonstrate unrestricted political support to the U.S. But while in this case Poland's position was in full consensus with the other EU-members, the question of European involvement in the Iraq War divided not only the Europeans in general but marked a major political dissens between Poland and its Western neighbour Germany[28]. Polish clear and uncompromised support for the U.S.

---

26 See: Washington Summit Communiqué Issued by the Heads of State and Government participa-ting in the meeting of the North Atlantic Council in Washington, D.C. on 24 April 1999 (Art. 9c).

27 See: The National Security Strategy of the RP. Warsaw 2007. In: The Ministry of National De-fense the Republic of Poland; (http://www.mon.gov.pl/pliki/File/zalaczniki_do_stron/SBN_RP.pdf).

28 Refer to the contradictory positions of Germany, France and Belgium against the American ap-proach in Iraq on the one side, and the so called "Letter of Eight", a joint declaration of support

and its participation in the U.S. military activities in the post-war Iraq revitalized the debate about generally engagement and support of ESDP in view of the regional and global security challenges.[29] Poland's evoking of Art. 5 of the NATO treaty and its absolute solidarity with the U.S. during this period, as well as its participation in the Iraq military missions and the ISAF mission in Afghanistan, demonstrated and illustrated the Polish foreign and security concept for the near future. The Polish pro-American attitude, reflected recently in the Polish–American discussions about the MDI defense programme and the location of antimissile shields on Polish territory, provokes once again a controversial discussion within the EU states about the Polish involvement in "Europeanising" European security. The question of the implementation of this project as a joint NATO endeavor or as a separate Polish-U.S. bilateral cooperation, does not contribute constructively to the current discussion reflecting the EU's disappointment with Poland's political choice in this matter. But in spite of this, the newly elected Polish government will continue the strategic policy of its predecessors[30] and maintain Poland's strong relations with the U.S., but with some modification concerning the mode of its acting towards the EU:

> "If we decide jointly, in talks with our partners in the European Union and NATO partners, that this isn't an unambiguous project, then we are definitely going to think it over".[31]

Supporting the continuation of the policy of a conditional but constructive engagement towards the ECSP/ESDP could be a step towards solving the Polish strategic dilemma – i.e. between Europeanism and Atlanticism - because Poland on the one side pleads for more European integration, but on the other side it has shown until now only limited interest in considering the European project solely as a European one.

European Eastern dimension - the case of Ukraine

The enlargement of the EU built a new political-security-related imperative to establish a closer and deeper cooperation between the new EU and its neighboring countries in Eastern Europe, the Southern Mediterranean as well as the countries in the Southern

---

for the United States in its efforts to disarm Iraq (signed by Jose Maria Aznar, Spain/Jose Manuel Durao Barroso, Portugal/Silvio Berlusconi, Italy/Tony Blair, United Kingdom/Vaclav Havel, Czech Republic/Peter Medgyessy, Hungary/Leszek Miller, Poland/Anders Fogh Rasmussen, Denmark) on the other side.

29 See the Joint Declaration of the Heads of State and Government of Germany, France, Luxembourg and Belgium on European defense, Brussels 29.04.2003.

30 Governments of: L. Walesa/T. Mazowiecki /J. Bielecki /J. Olszewski /W. Pawlak /H. Suchocka/W. Pawlak; A. Kwasniewski/J. Oleksy/ W. Cimoszewicz /J. Buzek/L. Miller; L. Kaczynski/J. Kaczynski, D. Tusk.

31 Donald Tusk, Prime Minister of Republic of Poland. In: *Herald Tribune* "Poland's Tusk open to missile defense, reiterates plan to end military mission in Iraq", published: November 6, 2007.

Caucasus, whose accession to the EU is not anticipated. Despite the perspective of the external effects of a further widening to the East, the EU started to develop a new strategy towards its neighbors and to constitute the European Neighborhood Policy (ENP) at the beginning of 2000.[32] It is understandable that Poland supports strongly such a policy and the idea of sub-regional cooperation towards the East. From the Polish point of view, one of the main EU security goals of the enlarged Union have to be the 'Eastern Dimension', in particular towards the so called *Western Newly Independent States* (WNIS) like Ukraine, Belarus and Moldavia. Apart from the relative success in adaptation and implementation of the ENP towards the cooperation with the new partners[33], Poland is attempting to create additional new tasks and arrangements within the framework of the Action Plan (AP)[34]. Reflecting the individual interests of the EU countries, Poland's objectives to guide and to strengthen the EU attention towards the Eastern part of Europe are related on one hand to the Polish bilateral, geopolitical, strategic and historical basis, and on the other hand are associated with the new conditions for common political activities within the EU framework. In terms of security strategy, such a good neighbourhood policy together with creating economic-political dependencies resembles Germany's policies towards its Eastern neighbours during détente and after: turning neighbours – particularly those between Poland and Russia - into cooperative but dependent friends enhance economic-political advantages and extends security towards the East.

The creation of good and friendly relations with the new Eastern neighbors after the turning point of 1989 constituted one of the highest priorities on the Polish foreign policy agenda. Considering the vacant political and security situation in Central and Eastern Europe in the early 90s, Poland's attitude towards the East was more reserved and guided by a double foreign strategy.[35] These relationships developed a new dynamic with the start of Polish EU accession negotiations and gained a new quality and intensity with Poland's membership in the EU in 2004. Poland signaled its support for the Eastern Countries and declared its willingness "to be a good advocate of their integration with Europe"[36] – again counting those policies would enhance Poland's role within the EU as well as towards the further East. After the last two rounds of enlargement in 2004 and 2007 the political and geographical reach of EU influence has been widened

---

32 Please see the files: http://ec.europa.eu/world/enp/documents_en.htm,
   (http://ec.europa.eu/world/enp/pdf/com03_104_en.pdf)
33 See: Communication from the commission. A Strong European Neighborhood Policy, Brussels 05.12.2007, (http://ec.europa.eu/world/enp/pdf/com07_774_en.pdf)
34 See: http://ec.europa.eu/world/enp/pdf/action_plans/ukraine_enp_ap_jls-rev_en.pdf
35 »Good-neighborly relations will link us with both the USSR and the republics, especially those on our borders - the Russian Federation, Ukraine and Belarus. We will cultivate relations in these two directions - the Union as a whole and the Republics - without interfering in the internal transformations on our eastern border«. In: Sejm Exposé by the Polish Prime Minister Jan Krzysztof Bielecki, Warsaw, 5 January 1991.
36 Włodzimierz Cimoszewicz, Polish Minister of Foreign Affairs. In: "EU Eastern Policy - the Polish perspective". Lecture by Włodzimierz Cimoszewicz, Polish Minister of Foreign Affairs. Prague, 21 February 2003.

towards Eastern and Southern Europe. Due to the fact that the Polish Eastern border equals - with the exception of Lithuania - the EU and NATO border as well, Poland advocates rightly that more attention is demanded on stability and economic interests in this region per se.[37] Taking into account that the situation of Eastern Europe has been changing significantly in the last few years to the very positive[38], the Polish government emphasizes the fundamental necessity of more assistance and a more active policy of the EU in the Eastern part of Europe, especially in Ukraine.

Although Ukraine has already been declaring its willingness for integration into the EU for a long time, the visible results of progress have been relatively limited in the last years.[39] Therefore, Poland is actively supporting the transformation process and the democratic reforms, even with the option of an EU membership within the near future, although this objective is not on the EU agenda at the moment. Instead the EU neighbourhood concept is offering a *third option* between partnership and integration, but without any perspective of the accession. For the Ukraine, the absence of the membership option and the equal positioning with the countries in the Mediterranean area is unacceptable - from a political and historical perspective.[40] To gain more efficiency in developing and strengthening the Eastern Policy, Poland is again cooperating with its partners from the Visegrád Group concerning the definition of common positions with the new Eastern neighbors, as well as in regard to the effective realization of joint projects.

Although Polish policies vis-à-vis the European Charter and CSFP/ESDP have damaged Polish influence and role in European decision-making bodies as well as the Polish image in major pro-integration-oriented EU member states. Nevertheless, in the case of further Eastern enlargement, neighbourhood, and cooperation policies, Poland acts not only in Polish but in EU long-term interests as well. Acting bilaterally and regionally, the new members of the EU can and want share their accumulative experiences in consolidation of the common values of the democratic transformation and thereby help to accelerate the Ukrainians aspirations towards the EU. And its logical, that in addition Poland believes that the successful future development of this country is dependent on its timely integration in the Euro-Atlantic structures and therefore Poland promotes not only EU but NATO enlargement as well.

---

37 With the full membership in the Schengen-agreement (21.12.2007) Poland have gotten much more obligations and responsibility to safe the east border of the EU.

38 Remember the "orange Revolution" in the Ukraine and the political changes as well as the return to oppressive policy in Belarus after the reelection of president Lukaszenko in 2006.

39 Cf. Volodimir Vergun/Oleksy Kuznestov 2002. "EU, NATO und Ukraine: Nation building and Democratization between East and West". In: Reimund Seidelmann (ed.) *EU NATO and the Relationship between Transformation and external Behavior in Post-Socialist Eastern Europe. The cases of the Slovak Republic, Bulgaria, Romania and Ukraine*. Baden-Baden, p.301.

40 Cf. Christos Skevas 2006. Die Osterweiterung der EU. Der Fall der Ukraine. Marburg, p. 68.

Poland, Russia and the European Union

As it has been mentioned several times above, Polish-Soviet/Russian relations are conditioned by both objective historical and geographic factors and subjective perceptions of political and geographical history. In addition, Polish national identity as European and Russian identity as Russian, add a further dimension to the Polish-Russian relations.

Looking at recent EU – Russian relations one can begin with the political, security and economical interests, which are very different for the member of the EU, especially after the Eastern Enlargement in 2004 and 2007. The strong national interests as well as the resulting bilateral approaches towards Russia of certain member states of the EU such as Germany's traditional bilateral policy of constructive engagement illustrate the limitations for a common EU strategy and policy towards Russia. The basis of the EU relations with Russia is *The Partnership and Cooperation Agreement* (PCA) of 1997 which has intensified its institutional form in the last 10 years and consists currently of several levels of political dialogs including »promotion of international peace and security, support for democratic norms as well as for political and economic freedoms. It creates a spirit of equality and partnership aimed at strengthening political, commercial, economic and cultural ties, and envisages the eventual establishment of an EU-Russia free trade area«[41]. In addition, Russia as the most important partner in the ENP constitutes the other power counterweight in Europe resulting from its role in energy and resources supplier. This underlines the special status of Russia within the ENP and explicitly the EU-Russian relations, visible in several agreements between both actors. Finally, the EU and Russia adopted the so called "road maps"[42] at the Moscow Summit in May 2005 as their common agenda for removing the common spaces and improving the implementation of the different aspects with an ongoing cooperation. However, until now, the links between objectives and the results in some of the issued mentioned, in particular those concerning democratic values, are very vague.[43] In addition to that, this relatively close network illustrates that the established concept of the EU-Russia co-operation has become more or less important depending on the constellation between the participating actors, but is not adequate as a standard co-operation platform for each member of the EU. The internal incoherence of the EU regarding this issue can affect further efficiency of the EU on the international level, because on one side the current framework model allows the extension of the co-operation in certain sectors at the regional level but on the other side disregards support for a dialog between Russia and the, in this aspect, disadvantaged EU member states.

Poland is a prominent example. Because of the political dictate, the historical ties between Poland and Russia were very close in the past and caused a heritage of fear

---

41 See link: http://ec.europa.eu/external_relations/russia/intro/index.htm (downloaded 28.12. 2007)

42 See link: http://ec.europa.eu/external_relations/russia/russia_docs/road_map_ces.pdf

43 For more details see: Kirsten Westphal 2007. *European Union and Russia. Face to face*. Tomsk, pp. 34-67.

and distrust as well as, especially in the 90s, problems in matters of political dialogs between these countries.[44] To understand Polish perceptions of Russia further, one can refer to the view that the introduction of military dictatorship in Poland in the early 80s was forced by the threat of a Soviet military intervention to repress early political reforms. The collapse of the Soviet Empire, Poland's West-oriented political course, its membership in EU and in particularly in NATO, and its further ambitions towards the *Westernisation* of Eastern Europe has enhanced hackles in neighboring Russia motivated by unresolved historical grievances and current political-security challenges from the regional and global point of view. The Polish foreign and security policy with its strong support of NATO and the U.S. plus its ongoing support for the further enlargement of the EU and eventually NATO provide further conflict potential with Russia. By fully supporting the Ukrainian's efforts concerning political, security and economical transformation, Poland and Lithuania adopted a course in open contrast to Russian interests and policies vis-à-vis those countries.[45] Poland's support for Viktor Yuschenko during his election and the attempts towards a Western orientation and democratization in Ukraine in 2004 as well as the official critical line towards Russia worsened the relationship and created a major issue of dispute in bilateral relations. However, such conflicts in Polish-Russian relation became overshadowed by EU policies, which adopted a position equal to that of Poland and critical towards Russian attempts to influence the political developments in Ukraine and thus shielded the bilateral relations of Poland and Lithuania with Russia from further worsening.

A further main conflict between Poland and Russia is the energy policy which caused a serious security problem in Poland within the last two years. Considering Poland's high dependency on energy imports from Russia – and related Russian pricing policies -[46] and the increasing Russian tendency to exploit the energy policy for its political purposes at the same time, Poland raised this aspect to the primary issue of its foreign and security policy and will encourage the EU in strengthening its competence in energy matters as well as promoting a multilateral solution in this issue.[47] Despite several advances in selected areas of the EU-Russia relation, there have not been major improvements yet – neither quantitative nor qualitative[48] – and this reconfirms Polish political reservations, when it comes to EU-Russian cooperation. Poland's problem, however, is that up to the present energy

---

44 See in more detail: Elżbieta Stadmüller 2003. Pożegnanie z nieufnością? Rozszerzenie NATO i UE a stosunki polsko-rosyjskie w kontekście bezpieczeństwa europejskiego. Wrocław.
45 Cf. Kirsten Westphal 2007. European Union and Russia. Face to face. Tomsk, pp.46-47.
46 Poland depended for example in 2005 on 97,5% of the Russian oil supply and on 65,4% of Russian gas supply. For more details see: Kai-Olaf Lang 2007. "Polens Energiepolitik. Interessen und Konfliktpotentiale in der EU und im Verhältnis zu Deutschland". *SWP Studie*, Berlin, p. 13.
47 See: EU Foreign Policy 2006-2010. Key points of the speech by the Polish Foreign Minister Anna Fotyga, at the conference of the European Union Institute for Security Studies and European Center Natolin: European as a Global Power, Warsaw-Natolin 19-May 2006, p. 3.
48 For more details see: Kirsten Westphal (ed.) 2005. *A Focus on EU-Russian Relation*. Frankfurt am Main, Berlin, Bern, Bruxelles, New York, Oxford, Wien.

policies in the EU are not integrated neither intergovernmental but still national. This means, that in the case of energy imports from Russia, Poland depends mainly on itself and on its bilateral relations with Russia.

As a result, it is one of Poland's vital interests to develop new instruments for the realization of a common strategy in regard to energy policy including the active support of the entire EU for Polish energy needs. But the problem for Polish efforts towards a stronger common strategy is that the Polish interests in the energy sector are not always in conformity with the objectives of other EU members[49] and thus this issue has not gained a very high degree of effective enforcement so far. Poland regards as main objectives to reduce the dependency on Russian gas and to search for new alternatives as well as to promote the idea of a strong integration of the EU regarding the energy sector. Furthermore the Polish prime minister proposes an "Energy-NATO"[50], committing the EU and NATO to join forces if their energy supplies are threatened. However, the political test for EU-Russian-Polish relations was the clash between Poland and Russia during the Summit of Helsinki on 24 November 2006, originally planned to focus on the EU's energy partnership with Russia[51]. Retalliating to the Russian embargo for Polish meat exports of 2005 and the increasing problem of energy supplies from Russia, Poland decided to use its EU membership position to veto against a re-negotiation of the Agreement for Partnership and Cooperation (PCA)[52] between the EU and Russia, since Russia would not fully incorporate the *Energy Charta Treaty* and its Transit protocol, which grants mutual access to energy markets according to these regulations.[53]

In summary, the Polish veto demonstrated not only Polish will to pursue national interests within and through the EU but at the same time EU's lack of willingness and ability to develop a common stand in energy policy issues, which was in Polish eyes a significant demonstration of a lack of EU solidarity for its Polish member. At the same time, Poland's opposition created a major acceptance problem for the EU policy of the Polish government in opening and focussing the political discussion on the instruments, which a single member of the EU has to pursue its national aims and how far this affects the common EU position on the international level.

To finally understand the Polish position towards EU-Russian relations, one have to put this into the broader framework of Polish-Russian/Soviet/Russian relations as well as Polish hopes that both NATO and EU would do its utmost to support Poland against dependency from Russia in general and secure Poland against any political-economic-military threat from Russia. If it comes to EU-Russian relations, Poland

---

49 Consider the German-Russian Baltic pipeline project, which underline, in Polish point of view, the principle of inderpendence between Poland, the Baltic States and Russia.

50 Cf. Polen-Analysen. Das polnisch-russische Verhältnis und EU-Ostpolitik. Nr. 5, 16.01.2007.

51 For more details see: "EU-Russia Energy Dialog". *Seventh Progress Report*; (http://ec.europa.eu/energy/russia/joint_progress/doc/progress7_en.pdf)

52 For more details see: http://trade.ec.europa.eu/doclib/docs/2003/november/tradoc_114138.pdf

53 See: The EU Council supported Polish proposals for principals of energy policy; (http://www.premier.gov.pl/archiwum/english/402_8150.htm).

tried and will try to convince the EU that the most effective way to prevent Russian dominance, to control and limit Russian influence in the Eastern neighbourhood of the EU, and to introduce positive change to Russia including not only its foreign and security but its energy policies as well is primarily both to take Polish reservations towards Russia adequately into account and to *act* in consensus.

Conclusion

The open-end character of the integration process has enabled all member states of the EU with its different national policies towards integration not only to share its experiences within the European bodies but also to express their interests and ideas, and to seek for its contribution to the European integration project in the future. In particular after Eastern enlargement of the EU there are many different political coalitions with different projects and different modes and political instruments to realize it. Evaluating Poland's past and present ways of acting within the EU and its efforts in regard to the future of the EU, this analysis has shown that Poland's objectives concerning the future integration process of the EU are divided and could be with four imperatives:

1. forwarding intergovernmentalism in substantial questions like the reform of the Union's constitutional architecture and legal system especially the mode of decision-making in the EU,
2. limited and sometimes ambivalent support of pro-integrationism in key questions of the foreign and security policy of the EU – particularly how far Poland is willing to deepen the EU integration -,
3. continued support for an uncompromised widening to the East – particular vis-a-vis the Ukraine and Moldavia – as a major responsibility for both Poland and the EU in the coming years, and
4. to accept role, influence, and interests of Poland as a major European power.

Given Polish self-perception as an EU member, which legitimately co-defines, delays, and if necessary blocs the further integration process was of minor political relevance as long as Polish interests, sensitives, and historical missions were accepted by the European Union in general and by Germany as a major power in EU policies and politics in particular. Poland's final acceptance of the treaty, which substitutes the European Charter, has demonstrated despite all problems that Poland is willing and able to pursue common and effective political will-building within the EU.

In sum, the membership in the European Union was a crucial historical success for Poland's identity, its economic and military interests, and its power. Transferring sovereignty towards the EU was regarded as a small price, limited by Poland's subscription towards intergovernmentalism and compensated by many advantages - in concrete benefits as well as in rehabilitating and legitimizing Poland as a major power in a Central Eastern Europe, which had become part of the greater Europe and the EU.

Divergences in the Euro Area and Stability of the EEMU: In Prospect of the Eastern Enlargement of the EMU

Soko Tanaka

Introduction

A euro-participating country loses its sovereign power in the monetary policy areas in exchange for gaining advantages of the euro as a common currency. The lost of the Sovereign power is related with always choosing its optimal policy interest rates, since the ECB sets common interest rates based on the average economic and monetary conditions in the euro area as a whole. The other lost of it is concerned with changing its foreign exchange rate. Though a country with relatively high inflation rates loses gradually competitiveness in the euro area, the country cannot devalue its currency any more. These two constraints stem from true nature of a common currency.

The EEMU (European Economic and Monetary Union) consists of the developed and developing (cohesion) economies. This structural divide can lead to instability of the EEMU. Because of the inflation gap between the two groups of countries, real interest rates in the developing countries tend to be lower than that of the developed countries, which can lead to another gap of economic growth rates between the two groups. It may be hopeful that the economic growth rates of the developing countries is stimulated by the lower real interest rates, but high economic growth rates may stimulate higher inflation. The high real interest rates in the developed countries may dampen low inflation further, or even lead to deflation. Let us call the divergent development of inflations between the groups the "divergence 1". An interesting example of the divergence 1 took place between Spain, which has kept long-lasting prosperity, and Germany whose economy stagnated in the first several years of the 21st century.

The inflation gap also leads to a divide in the real foreign exchange rates. The real forex rates get down in the low inflation developed countries and they tend to become more and more competitive over time. The economic growth of the countries is stimulated gradually by the growing net exports. In contrast, the real exchange rates of the developing countries rise and they tend to become less and less competitive, if other conditions are equal. The economic growth of the high inflation countries is depressed by the decreasing net exports. Let us call the divergent development of this type the "divergence 2". An interesting example of the divergence 2 also existed between Spain and Germany in the beginning of the 21st century.

The divergence 1 stimulates domestic demands in high inflation countries and depresses them in the low inflation countries. The divergence 2 facilitates gradually exports in the low inflation countries and depresses gradually exports in high inflation countries. What are the composite results of these two divergences in the early years in the euro area? Did the two kinds of the divergences lead a country or even the

115

TABLE 1. REAL GDP GROWTH (Annual avg. 1999-2005)		
	CONTRIBUTIONS FROM:	
Real GDP	Domestic Demand	Net Exports
Ireland	6.3	4.4	1.9
Greece	4.1	4.5	-0.4
Spain	3.6	4.6	-1.0
Finland	2.7	1.9	0.8
France	2.2	2.6	-0.4
Belgium	2.0	1.7	0.3
Austria	2.0	1.4	0.6
Netherlands	1.6	1.2	0.4
Portugal	1.5	1.8	-0.3
Italy	1.3	1.5	-0.2
Germany	1.2	0.4	0.8
Euro Area	1.9	1.8	0.1

Source: Eurostat

EEMU to instability or economic crises? Are there any other elements to be considered in the debates on the divergences? A case study about Spain and Germany will be presented in this article to investigate the above questions.

At the last part, we will sum up our investigations in the case study about the divergences and consider policy implications of the enlargement of the euro area to the Eastern European EU members from viewpoints of the divergences and the SGP constraints.

1. Economic Divergences in the Euro Area

1.1. Economic Performances in the Euro Area

A remarkable feature of the first seven years of the EEMU (European Economic and Monetary Union) was divergences in economic growth, inflation and export performances among the participating countries.

Table 1 documents the differences in real GDP growth rates across the euro area between 1999 and 2005. Growth in Ireland, Greece and Spain outpaced the average

116

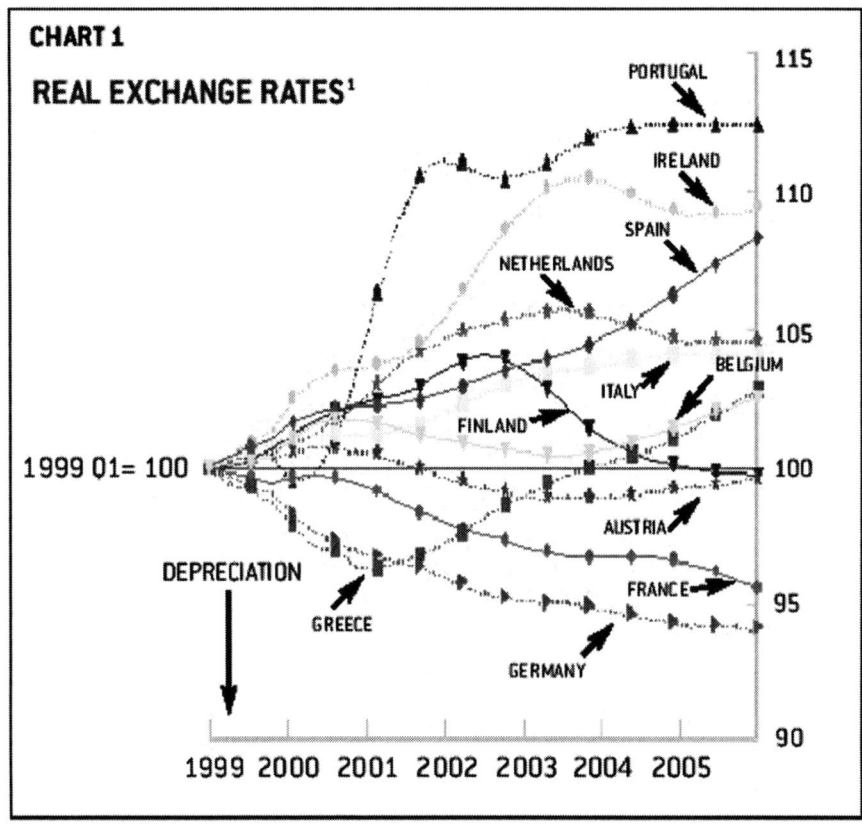

CHART 1

REAL EXCHANGE RATES[1]

PORTUGAL
IRELAND
SPAIN
NETHERLANDS
BELGIUM
ITALY
FINLAND
1999 Q1= 100
AUSTRIA
DEPRECIATION
FRANCE
GREECE
GERMANY

115

110

105

100

95

90

1999 2000 2001 2002 2003 2004 2005

Source: OECD

euro area growth rates, while Germany, Italy and Portugal underperformed. Between these two groups, there were five countries which showed the average performances.

The strong growth in Spain and Greece was driven by robust domestic demand, whereas their net export performances were mediocre. Weak net exports also depressed growth in France, Italy and Portugal. In contrast, the German growth came entirely from net exports, and the German domestic demand barely grew during the seven years. In the four small developed countries (Finland, Belgium, Austria and the Netherlands), the economic growth depended on both domestic demands and net exports.

The growth differentials in the euro area were persistent during the seven years. As business cycles became strongly synchronised in the euro area, the growth differentials were not due to different stages of the business cycles. Such growth differentials had been caused by several factors, to which we will refer in detail later.

Chart 1 shows the development of real foreign exchange rates of the twelve countries in the euro area (intra-euro area trade-weighted exchange rates) from 1999 to 2005. We can categorise them into three groups. Germany and France belong to the 'group 1' in which the real foreign exchange rates got down and reached around 95 at the end of 2005. In contrast, the real forex rates rose in Portugal, Ireland and Spain and came over 105 at the end of the time span ('group 2'). In the remaining five small developed countries, the real exchange rates existed at the end of 2005 between 100 and 105 ('group 3').

Since the real exchange rates are based on consumer price indices, the divergences in Chart 1 reflect differences in inflation rates among the countries. Comparing Table 1 with Chart 1, we can recognise that the strongest growth in domestic demand came hand in hand with the highest level of inflation in the eruo area. Portugal is the only notable exception.

1.2. Two Divergences Arising from Inflation Gap and Their Effects on Economic Growth

A monetary union which consists of developed and developing countries may have performance differentials of structural nature stemming from differences of the economic development level. The inflation rates of the developing countries tend to be higher than those of the developed countries, since the developing countries have normally economies of the demand-pull type. Under the common nominal interest rates set by the ECB, the real interest rates of the developing countries are normally lower than those in the developed countries. However, we can divide the developed countries in two groups: the group 1 (the big developed countries: Germany and France) and the group 2 (the small developed countries) during the above-mentioned time span.

As the ECB sets the common nominal interest rates based on the average monetary and economic conditions in the euro area as a whole, the rates tend to be oriented towards the average inflation countries, namely the small developed countries in the above case. The real interest rates tend to be too low for the high inflation countries and too high for the low inflation countries. In the former, economic growth tends to be stimulated and the inflation tends to be accelerated. In the latter, the economic growth tends to be depressed and the inflation rates tend to be further depressed. Let us call such contrasting developments as "divergence 1".

Table 2 "Divergence 1" in the Euro Area

Country group	Inflation(t_1)	Rit & Growth	Inflation(t_2)
1. developing c's	high	Low Rit→high growth	Higher
2. Small developed c's.	average	Average Rit→average	Average
3. Big developed c's	low	High Rit→low growth	Lower

[Note] Rit: real interest rate, c's: countries.

In parallel with the "divergence 1", the second divergence appears in the movement of the real foreign exchange rates. The real exchange rates go up in the high inflation countries and vice versa. The high inflation countries lose competitiveness step by step and vice versa. We call these divergent developments between the two groups of countries in the monetary union the "divergence 2". Its main features are shown in Table 3. As the countries with low inflation get more and more competitive in the euro area, the foreign demands contribute to their economic growth. In the high inflation countries, the real rates keep rising and the country becomes less and less competitive.

Table 3 "Divergence 2" in the Euro Area

Country group	Inflation	Real foreign exchange rates	Competitive-ness
1. Developing c's	high	rising	Deteriorating
2. Small developed c's.	average	unchanged	Average
3. Big developed c's	low	coming down	Rising

The changes in competitiveness resulting from the movements in real exchange rates have affects on the current account balances. Portugal and Spain registered large deficits, while Germany and several other small developed countries ran large surpluses as Table 1 shows.

Among these countries, we will pick up three countries, Spain, Portugal and Germany, and propose a brief case study.

2. Case Study (1) - High Inflation Countries -

At first, let us pay attention to the two high inflation countries: Spain and Portugal. Spain was a typical country which moved along the upper channel in the divergence 1 and divergence 2. Spain enjoyed prosperity in the low real interest period, but its current accounts deteriorated. Portugal was exceptional. Though its real interest rates were very low or negative like the Spanish case, Portugal recorded very low domestic demand growth in contrast with Spain. What are the reasons of the differences?

2.1 Portugal and Its Policy Mistakes

Portugal succeeded in catching up with other EU countries after the membership in 1986. Per capita GDP rose from 55 (in PPS) of the EU-average in 1986 to 76 in 1999. But, the gap widened after 2000. The real economic growth rate was negative in 2003 and near 1 % after 2004. The unemployment rates soared from 4% in 2002 to 7.6% in 2005. Why did Portugal fall into the low growth trap?

In order to be one of the first members of the EEMU, the people and the government exerted efforts to pull down inflation and cut down the budget deficits in the 1990's.

Portugal got its inflation rate down from 9.5% in 1992 to 2.3% in 1999. real The interest rates declined by more than 6 percentage points in the 1990s. Portugal enjoyed a spurt in growth in domestic demands under the construction sector boom thanks to the lowering real interest rates.

However, the good time was short. After Portugal was nominated as one of the euro-participating countries in May 1998, the government changed its sound budget principle and took a series of lavish spending policies: grade-up of social welfare system, raising salaries of civil service workers and cutting down the VAT etc. Inflation rate went up suddenly in 2000 and 2001. In 2001, the budget deficits amounted to 4% of GDP. The European Commission proposed a recommendation to cut the budget deficits, based on the Stability and Growth Pact.

Portuguese government took correction measures: privatisation, integration of old-age pensions and raising VAT from 17% to 19%. The timing was very bad, because European economy went on the road to the bottom of the recession. After the tax rise, Portuguese economy fell into negative growth and the low growth continued. In 2005, the budget deficits rose to 6% of GDP because of decreased receipts of the state and increased government expenditure to the unemployed etc. The socialist government led by Mr. Socrates took further austerity measures with which the deficits would be cut under 3% until 2008. Raising tax and structural reforms of the budgets aggravated the economic situation and the low economic growth may continue further.

The high inflation in 2000 and the next year led to a marked deterioration in competitiveness, which depressed exports in the upper channel of the "divergence 2". Before the participation in the euro area, Portugal used to take competitive devaluations to recover its competitiveness. This measure could not be applied in the euro area. The trade deficits in Portugal were as high as 10% of GDP during 2001-2006. The share of the Portuguese exports in the world fell by 15 percent during 1995 and 2005.

The third reason of the low economic growth in Portugal was the geopolitical change in Europe. Portugal had become a part of the production bases with cheap labour in the European Community in the 1980s and developed with the growth of West European production network. The FDI inflow from core EC countries supported the economic growth and the catching-up towards the EC average. The core of the manufacturing industry was changed to the automobile and semi-conductor industry from the traditional textile, clothing and footwear industry or winery industry. But, the collapse of the cold war reversed the Portuguese economic life.

The Central and Eastern European Countries (CEECs) became a strong production base in Europe. The FDI (foreign direct investments) inflow which came into Portugal in the 1980's was converted to the CEECs. After the mid-1990s, the FDI inflow to the Central Eastern European countries increased dramatically. The FDI inflow to Portugal fell and several foreign companies got out of the country.

Portugal's inflation and budget deficits may be corrected until 2010. But its competitiveness problem will remain much longer. The country will have to struggle with very difficult problems in order to find new ways to prosperity.

2.2 Spain in Long-Lasting Prosperity and the Divergences

Spain has enjoyed a long-lasting economic prosperity since 1996 and celebrated its twentieth anniversary of the EU membership in 2006. The Spanish success was basically based on the euro.

The reasons of prosperity look similar to those of Portugal. In order to become an original member of the euro area, Spanish people and the government decided to pull down inflation and cut its budget deficits in the middle of 1990s. The last devaluation of the Spanish Peseta took place in 1995. The long-term interest rates went down from 6.8% in 1995 to 2.2% in 1999. The lowering real interest rates stimulated private consumption and residence construction supported also by the continuous inflow of immigrants. The contribution of private consumption and construction to economic growth rates had been as high as three to four percentage points. The contribution of the government consumption has been around 1% point. These three factors cancelled the negative contribution of the foreign demands of one percentage point and Spain succeeded in accomplishing economic growth rate of 3% to 5% every year since 1996.

With the above-average inflation, the two divergences began to develop. But, there was a decisive difference between Portugal and Spain: economic policy stance. Spanish government succeeded in checking the "divergence 1" to develop to the vicious circle by a series of economic reforms like improvements of the government system (for example, abolishment of subsidies), liberalisation of the economy, privatisation and the tripartite cooperation (employers, trade unions and the government) to depress inflation. Economic reforms promoted competition to dampen price rise and the tripartite cooperation mitigated wage rise.

The government also succeeded in cutting the budget deficits gradually even after the introduction of the euro. The high economic growth helped the Spanish government bring its budget deficits into balance in 2003. The budget changed finally into surplus in 2005.

Ahearne/Pisani-Ferry (2006, p.5) pointed out about Spain and Greece as follows: "Greece and Spain showed poor exports performances. …Our concern is that when the temporary boost from the EMU-induced drop in real interest rates and rising property prices eventually fades, they may well be facing similar problems to those Portugal is facing today".

Concerning Spain, this criticism does not hit a mark. First of all, Spain's prosperity is not a "temporary boost from the EMU-induced drop." The high economic growth is lasting over ten years, based on not only the low real interest rates but also wise government policies and a rapid increase in population due to a lot of immigrants. It may be called a demand-based growth model. Spain's per capita GDP (in PPS) reached 90% of the EU15 average in 2006. The country is approaching to a developed country.

The Spanish government made the most of the regional policy funds given from the EU budget (the structural funds and the Cohesion fund) in order to construct traffic infrastructures all over the land. From Madrid radial traffic ways extended to all of the peripheral regions. The underdeveloped regions were connected with developed regions with AVE (high-speed train), highways and airways. Such traffic ways backed up balanced development of the regions, though there remain a lot of gaps between the south and the other regions.

There are more than 1000 Spanish firms which went to foreign countries. Spanish multinational firms and big banks have advantages in Latin America because of linguistic and cultural reasons. They could invest big sums of funds raised in the euro financial markets.

Until today, Spain has succeeded in making use of the advantages of the euro in full. But, the "divergence 2" seems to have led to a marked deterioration in Spain's competitiveness. Trade deficits rose to 7.5% of GDP in 2005. In spite of flourishing tourism industry, Spanish current account deficits are bigger than the trade deficits because of the money transfers by a lot of immigrants to their home countries. The current account deficits in 2008 may become about 10% of GDP. The long-lasting house price rise will stop in the near future. The residence construction boom will come to an end. Household indebtedness and external imbalances could finally put a brake to economic activity and a slowdown in GDP growth might happen. Then, Spain will be faced with the adjustment problem. The adjustment will include factors underlying low productivity growth, the external imbalances and a possible downsizing of the housing sector. The nature of adjustment will be different from that of Portugal. Spanish government will have to realise a soft landing.

3.   Case Study (2) - Germany and the EMU -

3.1. Germany as a "Problem Country"

Ahearne/Pisani-Ferry (2006, p.6) criticised Germany as follows:

1. "Germany kept inflation below the euro area average, based on weak domestic demand and persistent excess capacity. The above-average real interest rate in Germany depressed further domestic demand and inflation. Germany's very low inflation pulled down average euro area inflation. In response, the ECB would have run a more expansionary monetary policy than would otherwise be the case. The resulting looser monetary conditions would have pushed up inflation in other EMU member countries, leading to greater divergence".
2. "The euro area should avoid putting itself in a situation where its members pursue inconsistent goals. In this respect, further depreciation of Germany's real exchange rate vis-à-vis the rest of the euro area would be inconsistent with the need to restore price competitiveness in several other countries."

The first criticism is concerned with the "divergence 1" and its spillover effect [1]. The second criticism is concerned with the "divergence 2". A problem of the criticism is that the authors did not even ask why Germany's inflation was so low in the first five years in the 21st century. Without answering this question, nobody can have a right prospect on the German behaviour in the EEMU at that time. What kind of policy recommendations will come out from the second criticism? The critics may have in mind an idea that Germany has a dogmatic inclination to low inflation without paying attention to the economic situation in the other euro area countries. Such criticism cannot be justified as we will see in the next section.

3.2. The German Depression at the Beginning of the 21st Century

The German economy fell into the severe recession (depression) from 2001 to 2003. The growth rate was 0.0% in 2002 (0.9% in the euro area) and minus 0.2% in 2003 (0.7% in the euro area). The economy recovered slightly to 1.2% in 2004, but got down again to 0.9% in 2005. Was the main reason of the mid-term stagnation of the German economy form 2001 to 2005 the "divergence 1", namely the high real interest rate? The real interest rate must have been a factor, but perhaps not a major one. Germany had several serious problems of structural nature at the beginning of the 21st century.

There were several factors which made the German depression so serious. The most important was the burst of the stock price bubble in 2000 following the burst of the American NASDAQ bubble. In the second half of the 1990s, German business world was so eager to follow the American model of economic prosperity: ICT-sation, orientation of the big German banks to the American-style investment bank, listing of the big German enterprises at the New York Stock Exchange and the large-scale M&A. When the American ICT bubble broke in 2000, the European stock price fell dramatically in parallel with the NYSE stock price fall. But, the fall of the EUROSTOXX index was mach larger than that of Dow Jones index. Based on 1994 price, the American Stock price fell from 300 to 180 while the index of the euro area fell from 330 to 130. The price fall in Germany was much bigger. Based on the value of January 1994, the EUROSTOXX index fell from 100 to 58 while the German DAX index fell to 47. This stock exchange shock hit the euro area economies, very hard especially German economy, as was symbolically shown in the close of the venture-business-oriented Neuer Markt in 2002.

---

1   Experts of the Bank of Japan indicated at the end of 2003 that the high real interest rate due to its low inflation rate and the common policy rate of the ECB hampered its economic upturn and the ECB should have lowered its policy interest rate from 2% to 1.5% or 1%. They criticised the common currency, but Ahearne/ Pisani-Ferry (2006) criticised German low inflation rates. Belke/ Gross (2006) criticised the ECB because the monetary policy during the recession was too soft that the problem of bubbly real estate price rise happened. Ahearne/ Pisani-Ferry (2006) did not criticise the ECB, but criticise the spillover effect emanating from Germany.

The big business in the euro area suffered from the big fall of stock prices. In the 1990s, Japanese economy passed through the "lost decade" as a consequence of the long-lasting price fall of stocks and real estates. Some economist defined the long-lasting Japanese recession as the "balance sheet recession". The asset side of the balance sheet of the big business shrank by the price fall of their assets. In order to rebalance the balance sheet, companies concentrated on settlements of their debts. Companies cut down or stop their investments to repay their debts to the banks. With lowering propensity to invest, the economy was depressed for a long time. Banks were faced with a lot of non-performing loans and were reluctant to lend. This also depressed the economy. I guess that the German economy fell into a similar balance sheet depression for the first five years of the 21st century, though the depression was much shorter and lighter than the Japanese one since Germany had no serious price fall of the real estates.

The European Commission (2005, pp.26-27) pointed out as follows: "Investment activity in the euro area has been sluggish for several years amid a gradual decline in the net financial position of non-financial corporations to less than 0.5% of GDP in 2004. The decline in net lending reflects weak demand and can be explained as a reaction to the accumulation of substantial corporate debt in the period 1999-2001. More specifically, companies have made use of low interest rates to re-finance their expenditure on physical investment. As a result, the level of accumulated corporate debt has stabilised about 62% of GDP since 2002. As a result of lower interest rates and balance-sheet restructuring, companies have reduced their debt-serving costs, with net interest payments to the banking sector declining to slightly over 1.5% of GDP in the second quarter of this year".

As the Commission referred, the euro area enterprises fell into a balance sheet depression. In proportion to the biggest stock price fall in Germany, the damage to big German companies was quite severe.

The second factor that influenced the German depression was structural stagnation in the construction sector, which continued from 1996 to 2005. The sector employed 1530 thousand workers in 1995. It decreased to 720 thousand in 2005.

The third factor was outflow of FDI from Germany to other EU countries, America, the CEECs and other emerging market economies like China. The outflow of FDI amounted to 80 billion euro in 1999 and to 100 billion euro at its peak in 2000. German big business and banks held off domestic physical investments and constructed subsidiaries and affiliates overseas. The FDI outflow was a factor which influenced weak German growth. But, the construction of global production networks by German business world looks to be completed in 2002, since the outflow of FDI came down to nearly zero in 2003 and 2004.

3.3 Prospects on the "German Problem"

The balance sheet depression finished in 2005 and German companies at last restarted physical domestic investment. In 2006, German economy recorded 2.7% real economic growth and unemployment rate came down to 7.3% in 2007 from 9.5% in 2004. Consumer price inflation rate has been rising. The gap of inflation rates (harmonised index of consumer price inflation) between euro area and Germany was 0.9% points in 2002 and 1.1% points in 2003. But, it became only 0.3% points in 2004 and 2005 and minus 0.1% points in 2006. It will be zero in 2007 according to the European Commission's forecast (2007).

The second criticism to Germany by Ahearne/ Pisani-Ferry (2006) expressed at the head of this sector was clearly wrong. As they disregarded the specific feature of the German depression, they misunderstood the abnormal economic situation as normal. From 2006 on, the "spillover effect from low inflation Germany" does not happen. The "German problem" will not reappear in the future.

4. Prospects on Stability of the EEMU

4.1. From Three Groups to Two Groups

There were three groups of countries in the logic of the divergences: developing, small developed and big developed countries. As German economy recovered and inflation rates in France and Germany are coming close to the average in the euro area, the last two groups in developed countries are going to become one. Since the economic weight of developed countries is overwhelmingly large in euro area, the divergence 1 and 2 will happen in developing countries vis-à-vis the base inflation rate of the developed country level. The convergence of inflation rates in the developed countries will facilitate stability management in euro area. If the governments of developing countries can evade policy mistakes, low real interest rates can contribute to the high rate of economic growth for a long time as the example of Spain showed.

There remain problems between France, Italy on the one hand and Germany on the other hand, though inflation rates are converging. A gap in industrial production between Germany and the other two countries has been widening. In the middle of 2007, industrial production in Germany rose to 118 while 104 in France and 99 in Italy. German big business constructed global production networks. Germany gained the most from the Eastern enlargement of the EU. German companies organised regional production networks in Europe. It is by far superior to the French and Italian networks. Net exports of Germany exceeded 100 billion euro in 2005 and has been rising. Germany conquered the long-lasting damages of the German reunification when the country passed through the balance sheet depression. The strong Germany seems to be reappeared. The industrial production gap may be a symptom of the resurgence of Germany. If industrially strong France and Italy will come true in the near future, we may see another type of divergence in euro area.

4.2. *Eastern Enlargement and Stability of the EEMU*

Today, convergence issues are paid much attention in the enlarged EU. The new members from central and eastern European (CEE) countries are candidates of the EEMU. Slovenia took part in the euro area at the beginning of 2007 and Malta and Cyprus will be members in 2008. But, current situations in the remaining nine CEE countries show divergences vis-à-vis the euro area countries. It is sure that the CEE countries have shown strong and sustainable catching up with the euro area since the middle of 1990s. But, per capita income gap between the euro area and the CEE countries is still very large and the countries belong to developing countries in our picture of the divergences.

The nine CEE countries expect Slovenia, Malta and Cyprus are the euro candidates. These countries are divided into two groups based on their underlying monetary and exchange rate regimes. The 'group 1' countries (currency board system) are Bulgaria and the Baltic Three (Estonia, Latvia and Lithuania), which adopt hard pegs with the euro. These countries experience rather similar macroeconomic and financial patterns. In recent years, these patterns have appeared to differ significantly from the second group of countries with more flexible exchange rates, namely the Czech Republic, Hungary, Poland, Romania and Slovakia.

The countries with hard peg regimes have recently experienced a very rapid catching-up process, with real GDP growth standing average at 9% per annum in the past two years, which is almost twice as fast as the growth rates observed in the countries with flexible regimes. Likewise, inflation in the hard peg countries was almost one and a half times higher than that in the countries with flexible regimes.

The hard peg countries show also signs of overheating economy in the form of labour shortage and strong upward pressures on wages. The very strong credit growth in 2006 was well above 40% under negative real interest rates. The house prices in the Baltic countries have doubled on average since 2004. The countries with hard pegs face substantial external imbalances: current account deficits increased over past two years to more than 15% of GDP.

As these countries have fixed their foreign exchange rates towards the euro, we can recognise that these countries have followed the upper channel in the two divergences. As these countries have given up monetary policy independence because of the hard pegs, it will be very difficult to bring inflation under control. Before participation in the euro area, these countries will have to recover sustainable development paths by monetary policy and foreign exchange rate policy. For the sake of recovering the healthy paths, the countries should regain their monetary independence to quickly deal with the too strong imbalances. They should give up the currency board arrangements and take fixed exchange rate system with the wide fluctuation band (plus minus 15% around the central rates) in the ERM2 (for the Baltic countries) or take part in the ERM2 (Bulgaria). Otherwise, they would suffer from the burst of the housing price bubble or the further acceleration of inflation which can lead to an economic debacle.

For countries with flexible exchange rate regimes, inflationary pressures continue to be more muted, but fiscal policy has been very loose, with fiscal deficits standing on average at above 4% (excessive deficit situation). Comparing the economic situations in the hard peg countries, the flexible rate countries have much better position for the participation in the euro area. But, inflation is likely to increase once catching-up process will gain momentum. A fully sustainable level of convergences should be achieved before the participation.

The Maastricht criteria based on inflation, long-term interest rates, exchange rate stability and public finance do not seem to be suitable for the CEE countries outside the euro area. Article 121 of the EC Treaty explicitly mentions "high degree of sustainable convergence" of the each criterion. This should be taken as a basis of the participation in the euro area.

Concluding Remarks

The two divergences had effects on inflation and economic growth in the euro area countries. High inflation countries can enjoy low real interest rates and relatively high economic growth with growing current account deficits. Low inflation countries must endure high real interest rates and low domestic growth, but net exports contribute to the economic growth.

What are the composite results of these two divergences in the early years in the euro area? From the case study on Spain, Portugal and Germany, we could say that to draw a single and simple conclusion is quite difficult. Spain and Portugal, even with the low real exchange rates, experienced quite opposite economic results. Policy mistakes can cancel all of the advantages of the introduction of the euro like the Portugal example. To keep sound economic policies is quite important to get fruitful results from the introduction of the euro.

The logic of the two divergences can propose basic recognition to analyse the economic situation in the EEMU. But, it is not the only criterion to judge a country's behaviour. I referred to Ahearne/ Pisani-Ferry (2006) and the suggestions of the article were very important. But, the article was too straightforward to apply the logic of the divergences and disregards other factors which have much effect on economic behaviours of the euro area countries. The case of Germany has shown that the balance sheet depression and other structural factors may have been more influential on the economic performance of the country than the effects of the two divergences. It would be an exceptional case, but we should be cautious to apply the logic of the divergences to the real world.

The two divergences take place mainly between developed and developing countries. As the CEE countries are developing countries, they will develop on the upper channel of the two divergences. Today, the countries with hard peg show economic overheat phenomena. The countries do not seem to recognise the importance of the "EMU mentality". These countries should recover their policy independence in the monetary and foreign exchange rate policy before the participation of the euro.

References:

Ahearne/ Pisani-Ferry (2006), The Euro: Only for the Agile, bruegel policy brief, February.

Belke, Ansgar and Daniel Gross (2006), Instability of the Eurozone? On Monetary Policy, House Prices and Structural Reforms (mimeo).

Bini-Smaghi, Lorenzo (2007), Real convergence in Central, Eastern and South-Eastern Europe, Speech at the ECB Conference, 1 October.

European Commission (2005), Economic forecast Autumn 2005.

European Commission (2007), Economic forecast Spring 2007.

Stark, Juergen (2007), Fast, but sustainable? Challenges and policy options for the catching-up process of central and eastern European countries, Speech on October 1.

Tanaka, Soko (2007), The Enlarging Euro Zone, Nikkei Publishing Company (in Japanese language).

Impact of the Eastern Enlargements on the EU's Legitimacy:

From the perspective of Intergovernmentalism or Supranationalism?

Jian Junbo

After having been discussed for about 30 years,[1] now the issue of legitimacy deficit of the European Union (EU) is becoming more and more outstanding in theory as well as in practice, especially after the two latest widenings of the Union respectively happened in 2004 and 2007. Nonetheless, the comprehensive relations between enlargement and legitimacy are not analyzed explicitly through systematic method.

This article will discuss how the EU legitimacy deficit becomes a serious problem in the stage of recent enlargements and what the relation between enlargement and legitimacy is. In common sense, modern legitimacy in theory has two dimensions, i.e., normative legitimacy and empirical one, in which the first one is based on democratic bureaucracy, identity or public consensus on political system, and traditional values, while empirical legitimacy consists of effectiveness of institutions and sufficient public goods provided by political system.[2]

Methodology

In this article, the classification method will be utilized by which the EU legitimacy after enlargements will be analyzed in different dimensions step by step and the whole picture of the EU legitimacy can be depicted clearly.

This paper will be based upon the clear concept of legitimacy. Historically, the idea of legitimacy can be traced back at least to the period of ancient Rome when the people recognized *legitimus* as "lawful, according to law". In the Middle Age, it was transmuted into "what conforms to ancient custom and to customary procedure".[3] Only in modern time, the idea of legitimacy had a chance to evolve into an academic concept and the first definition of it was given by a famous sociological philosopher Max Weber, who was also the first man studying legitimacy systematically and

---

1 In 1979, a British Labor Party academic, David Marquand in his book *Parliament for Europe*, used democratic deficit to describe the weakness of democratic legitimacy of the European Community institutions. Quoted in Meny Yves, on the democracy of Europe: old concept and new challenges, *Journal of Common Market Studies*, 2002, Vol. 412, No.1, pp.1-13.

2 Some scholars prefer this classification of legitimacy, for example, Janet Mather, see his article The Citizenry: Legitimacy and Democracy, in Neill Nugent (edited), *European Union Enlargement*, Palgrave Macmillan, 2004.

3 See Ian Clark, *Legitimacy in International Society*, Oxford University Press, 2005, p.17.

intellectually.[4] After his research, more and more scholars and specialists focused on legitimacy issue because of its importance for the continuity of power and the protection of public interests.

Unfortunately, legitimacy is always a confusing concept used in all disciplines in different ways and for different aims. In a common sense, it is related to legality, legitimization of institution and public support for power. In a short term, legitimacy means the appropriate utilization of power under the rule of law, regulated by shared social-political values and supported by publics. Namely, power with justified legitimation, public approval and effectiveness is legitimate.

In this paper, it tends to classify legitimacy into two dimensions: normative one and empirical one, both of which cannot be divided at the same time when the integrated legitimacy of power (or political system) is considered. Janet Mather argues that "normative legitimacy is almost entirely dependent upon popular *input*, yet empirical version has no prerequisites, and theorists suggest ... governance might win the support and approval of its citizens by means of its *performs*".[5] Nevertheless, his definition is too constricted to be used in a more complicated context in which power (political system) and its ruled interact at many different levels. The paradigm of "input-performance" cannot shed light on some cases in a far more complicated society. For instance, some authoritative regimes are supported by publics in that regimes have good performs though the 'input' (transformation of public opinions into governments) is restricted; in other cases, citizens won't support their political leaders who cannot keep their promises declared toward the public in presidential or governor's campaigns. So the "input-performance" or "input-output" paradigm is too simple to analyze a complicated society.

In this article, normative legitimacy is a "should-be" legitimacy focusing on legitimation of power which is realized by embedding societal shared values into power and by approval of the mass. A legitimate power in terms of normative version indicates it should comply with the constitution and other positive laws, respect for dominant social shared values and of course, be approved by most residents within its jurisdiction. Commonly, normative legitimacy is generally grounded in political democracy, basic social values and public identity of citizenship.

Conversely, empirical legitimacy is mainly in relation to performance of power, including effectiveness of institutions and public goods as outcome of policies. Summarily, the integrated legitimacy depends on democracy or other basic social values, identity, effectiveness and public goods.

---

4   Even he is "one of the founders of twentieth-century social science and probably its great prac-
    tioner". In legitimacy study, he reviews legality is the most important factor for bureaucracy's
    legitimacy. See Max Weber, Legitimacy, Politics and the State, in William Connolly (edited),
    Legitimacy and the State, Basil Blackwell Publisher Ltd, 1984, pp.33-61.
5   Janet Mather, The Citizenry: Legitimacy and Democracy, in Neill Nugent (edited), *European
    Union Enlargement*, Palgrave Macmillan, 2004, p.104.

Why legitimacy matters is that legitimacy is of importance for any kind of power (political system) to work smoothly. As a supranational organization to some extents and an international actor, the EU can simply exist if it's approved by European public and functions depending upon universal values and positive laws at the level of the EU. Power's continuity, stability and capability all rely on legitimacy, which indicates those principles such as democracy, equality of member states and rule of law ought to be worked together in the Commission, the Council, the Parliament and other institutions, further more, to narrow the gap of trust between the elite and the mass in Europe. Namely, the EU can become stronger with legitimacy but weaker without it; on the other hand, as to the public, their interests and preferences can only be protected and kept through a legitimized EU since the public are ruled to some extents by the EU. Ironically, in some cases, the demands for legitimacy of the EU is a pragmatic means for public to against national governments in which the EU is a victim of domestic affairs of member states.[6] However, not only those institutions of the EU but also European citizens need a legitimized EU to keep their own interests.

Legitimacy deficit in the enlarging EU?

Legitimation

Legitimation in the sense of modernity is in relation to liberal democracy, equality, justice, rule of law, human rights and so like, which are resulted from secularization after the end of the Middle Age. As regards to the EU, such as democratic institution (for instance, the Council of Ministers), equal and just allocation of votes power, spirit of coordination and cooperation are basic characters of the EU's legitimation.

1. Democratic deficit?

Democracy of the EU should be analyzed in two levels—member states and Europe. In 1993, leaders of 15 member states declared the fixed principle of accession, i.e., Copenhagen Accession Criteria, which says that any candidate country can be accepted to be a member of the EU only after meeting several criteria, such as domestic democratic politics, respect for human rights, social freedom, free market economy and so forth. Obviously, the EU cannot be legitimized until each member state is democratic politically and keeps those beliefs in liberalism and free market economy, etc.

---

6   For example, in 2005, the case of Constitution Treaty draft refused by French and Dutch's publics to some degree resulted from dissatisfaction in their domestic governments for weak capability to cope with domestic affairs such as unemployment, social security or educational equality, and so on.

In 2004, the eastern enlargement enclosing ten pre-communist countries in which the degree of political democracy and free market economy was clearly lower than that of the EU-15. Most eastern members had a very short experience of democratization and immature capitalist markets. Thus after the eastern expansion, the average degree of the Union's democracy and market economy declined relatively, although all candidate states on the whole met Copenhagen Criteria, only a basic principle for accession.

Another factor undermining the EU's democracy is the defect of institutions' structure. Commonly, scholars have an agreement to an idea that among EU institutions, the Parliament is most democratic than any other institutions. It's true to an extent since the Parliament is elected by citizens directly. Nevertheless, two problems should be considered -- the "representativeness deficit" arises and the would-be "direct election" is not a truth. In view of the first problem, in accordance with the Treaty of Nice, the representatives number in the Parliament will switch from 626 of EU-15 to 732 of EU-27, which indicates, for example, in 2002, a member of the Parliament (MEP) represents 600,944 citizens on average, however, in 2007 after two enlargements, the number of ratio of one MEP is 622,267[7]. Accordingly, the degree of representativeness in the Parliament reduces. As to the second problem, the election of MEPs is also a domestic political issue but not happens in the level of the EU since representatives are elected from members of national parliaments and meanwhile, this election is full of domestical political discussions and political parties' competition. So the so-called direct election of the Parliament is perhaps recognized as a domestic affair since European citizens cannot vote for any candidate member of the Parliament from any member state. Unfortunately, this didn't change after the eastern expansion in 2004 and in 2007.

2. Equality and the allocation of votes power in the EU

In a community, the equality of actors (member state) is another basic value to construct legitimacy of the institute having ability to control or manage this community. The distribution of votes power is just a very important parameter to evaluate the legitimacy degree of a political system. In the Treaty of Nice, a complicated voting system was designed in order to approve a proposal introduced by the Council of Ministers, and this system was completely available till some slight amendments were made in the Treaty of the European Constitution (EC), but those amendments were not carried out since the EC treaty was refused by France and the Netherlands in 2005. In Nice Treaty, so-called Qualified Majority Voting (QMV) was re-affirmed and re-explained so as to be fit for the aftermath of the enlargement. In details, apart from keeping the continuity of QMV principle in the Council of Ministers, two extra criteria

---

7   Janet Mather, see his article The Citizenry: Legitimacy and Democracy, in Neill Nugent (edited), *European Union Enlargement*, Palgrave Macmillan, 2004, p.107.

were added when concerning the rising number of the countries. So there are three principles in voting system of the Council as follows:

– The decision receives at least a specified number of votes, namely the qualified majority as the most important criteria and a threshold,
– The decision is approved by a majority of member states and,
– The qualified majority represents at least 62% of the total population of the European Union.[8]

Specifically, for instance, in 2005 the vote threshold set in Nice Treaty was 72.27 percent (232 of 321 votes) and a proposal should be supported by 13 member states and appropriate number of delegates of the Council who represented 281.822426 million people of EU-25. Then after the accession of Bulgaria and Romania, the number of QMV changes due to the increase of member states, yet the QMV as a principle doesn't shift at all.

Table 1: Allocation of vote power in the Council of Ministers (EU-25)

Member State	old votes power	Share of old votes power	New votes power	Share of new votes power	Popu- lation x 1000	Share of total P.
Austria	4	4.5977	10	3.2725	8067.3	1.775
Belgium	5	5.7471	12	3.9103	10355.8	2.278
Cyprus			4	1.3292	715.1	0.157
Czech Republic			12	3.9103	10407.5	2.290
Denmark	3	3.4483	7	2.3102	5379.2	1.183
Estonia			4	1.3292	1356.0	0.298
Finland	3	3.4483	7	2.3102	5206.3	1.145
France	10	11.494	29	8.5606	59328.9	13.052
Germany	10	11.494	29	8.5606	82536.7	18.158
Greece	5	5.7471	12	3.9103	11018.4	2.424
Hungary			12	3.9103	10203.3	2.245
Ireland	3	3.4483	7	2.3102	3963.6	0.872
Italy	10	11.494	29	8.5606	57321.0	12.610
Latvia			4	1.3292	2331.5	0.513

---

8   Commission of the European Communities, Secretary-General, Brussels, January 18, 2001, Memorandum to the Member of the Commission. Summary of the Treaty of Nice. From *the Draft Treaty amending the Treaty on European Union and the Treaty establishing the European Community* (which was passed at the Intergovernmental Conference, Heads of State or of Government, meeting in Lisbon on 18 October 2007.), a new regulation about the voting system was introduced without changing the QMV, which proclaims that "As from 1 November 2014, a qualified majority shall be defined as at least 55% of the members of the Council, comprising at least fifteen of them and representing Member States comprising at least 65% of the population of the Union". See *Draft Treaty amending the Treaty on European Union and the Treaty establishing the European Community*, p. 13.

Member State	old votes power	Share of old votes power	New votes power	Share of new votes power	Population x 1000	Share of total P.
Lithuania			7	2.3102	3462.6	0.762
Luxembourg	2	2.2989	4	1.3292	448.3	0.099
Malta			3	0.9933	397.3	0.087
Poland			27	8.1221	38218.5	8.408
Portugal	5	5.7471	12	3.9103	10142.4	2.231
Slovakia			7	2.3102	5383.5	1.184
Slovenia			4	1.3292	1995.0	0.439
Spain	8	9.1954	27	8.1221	41550.6	9.141
Sweden	4	4.5977	10	3.2725	8940.8	1.967
The Netherlands	5	5.7471	13	4.2284	16192.6	3.562
United Kingdom	10	11.494	29	8.5606	59630.1	13.118
Total	87		321	100	454552.3	100
Qualified majority			232			

Sources: Voting power in the European Union, Federico Perea Justo, Puerto_MaMaEuSch, Management Mathematics for European Schools

According to table 1, the number of vote power of EU-15 increased after enlargement in 2004, but the weightings of vote power of all biggest member countries including Germany, France, UK and Italy decreased in comparison with the weightings of their votes power before the Treaty of Nice. For example of Germany, before 2005 when Nice Treaty was put into practice, the share of votes power was 11.494 percentage, nonetheless, after enlargement of 2004, it reduced to 8.5606%, since its share of population was 18.158 percentage compared to the total population in the EU-25. In practice, all the biggest members' vote power decreased and totally the EU-15 vote rights slightly or sharply changed in terms of the Treaty of Nice. And the eastern members acquired much more shares of vote rights compared to their shares of population in the EU. Correspondingly, the quarrel about allocation of vote power among member states continues. Those used to set the allocation of weighting of vote power should be considered carefully and completely, such as equality of state, national GPD, demography, distribution of national power, etc. Nevertheless, there will be no full legitimation before the discussion or quarrel regarding shares of vote power among member states disappears.

European citizenship, collective identity and nationalism

Public identity of belonging to an existing political system or community is a basic precondition of the legitimacy of the power controlling or ruling the system or community. Correspondingly, citizenship providing people with a sense of belonging to a community is a quite important factor to shape identity. Whilst the word 'citizenship' to some degree is a confused concept that cannot be used to explain someone's identification or his status in a giving society exactly.

1. European citizenship and its limitation towards new member states

John Crowley argues that at least there exist three main understandings of citizenship as follows: (1) citizenship is often used as a more or less close synonym of nationality in the legal sense; (2) citizenship is a political philosophical concept used to refer to true membership of a genuinely democratic state; (3) citizenship may be a sociological concept used to designate true membership of a truly egalitarian society (or at least, at a normative level, of a society truly governed by a generally recognized norm of equality).[9]

In a common sense, some authors believe the main feature of citizenship is linked to nation-state. For instance, David Miller claims that "nationality and citizenship complement one another. Without a common national identity, there is nothing to hold citizens together."[10] Thus Dimitry Kochenov writes "It is, of course, possible to argue that European citizenship is not real; the European Union is not a state; there is no European people; and, political representation at the European level is only a myth. At the same time, the notion of European citizenship, which is sometimes seen as accidental and arbitrary in national policy debates, has considerable potential as the basis for the guarantee of important rights and for the future of European integration."[11]

In 1993, the clear concept of European citizenship was introduced by the EU. In view of its history, the Treaty of Rome had established an area without frontiers and to abolish checks on persons at internal frontiers, irrespective of nationality, and then this regular was re-affirmed in the Single European Act (1986). In 1993, the Treaty of Maastricht declared the European citizenship and then was re-affirmed and amended to a minor extent in the treaty of Amsterdam (1997) and in the Treaty of Nice (2002). In the treaty of Amsterdam it reads that "Citizenship of the Union is hereby established. Every person holding the nationality of a Member State shall be a citizen of the Union. Citizenship of the Union shall complement and not replace national citizenship." From the angle of law, European citizenship is regulated under a range of secondary legislations which defend the following rights such as "to move and reside freely within the Union, to vote and stand in municipal and European Parliamentary elections, to petition the European Parliament, to complain to the European Ombudsman, to receive diplomatic and consular protection, to communicate with the Institutions in

---

9   John Crowley, Some Thoughts on Theorizing European Citizenship, *Innovation,* Vol. 12, No. 4, 1999, p.474.

10 David Miller, *Citizenship and National Identity*, MA:Polity, 2000, pp.31-32.

11 Dimitry Kochenov, The European Citizenship Concept and Enlargement of the Union, *Romanian Journal of Political Science*, Volume 3, Number 2, Winter 2003, p.71.

your own language and lastly, the right to have access to documents of the European Parliament, the Council and the Commission".[12]

However, facing the eastern enlargement, the Act of Accession (2003) imposed a limitation of citizenship on those new member states of Eastern Europe. It implicitly rejected the *'citoyen pur'* concept and created a body of "second class" citizens of Europe. Namely, the EU citizenship of the new member states is not sufficient.

The restriction of citizenship will lead to the limited freedom of individual movements in the "transitional stage" when new member states chase after the western countries and finally reach the same level of social and economic development as that of the old ones. However, the free movement of labors is a key symbol of citizenship. In theory, the EU has set out a road map to reduce the restriction of European citizenship by so-called "2+3+2" years scenario, which implies the transitional stage will be 7 years at least and end by 2011 since the accession of new members in 2004.

2. European identity and nationalism

The meaning of European identity can be understood as a collective identity. In terms of Pollak, collective identity has two dimensions, ideational one and political one. Ideational identity means the common values, traditions and expectations for the future, and political identity is the externalization of the ideational identity in acts.[13] In accordance with his classification, citizenship can be regarded as the outcome of the externalization of the ideational identity. Clearly, in consideration of those related culture and values which are intrinsic factors of ideational identity, European identity can be traced back to a long time ago, albeit European identity, in the sense of feelings of "Europeanness", has existed for a very long time (even since the Renaissance), although such feelings are not the same as those which undermine national identity.

But without question, reviewing European history and its culture is really a very boring work. In order to simplify the research in this paper, it's better to investigate the public attitudes to the EU, especially, the enlarged Union, albeit the public attitudes to the EU reflect their feelings and sense towards this typical international organization. Just as mentioned, European identity can be defined as a general feeling of "Europeanness" and loyalty to Europe, in a cultural sense, which does not conflict with national identities of member states. The following section will examine the degree of European citizens' knowledge about the eastern enlargement, their satisfaction with the EU institutions, the collective identification in the EU level, and their common values, and so forth.

As to information of enlargement that public received, regardless of detailed contents, in accordance with Eurobarometer, it showed the common citizens knew well because at the European level, for instance, 80% of citizens in the European

---

12 See Article 8 of the EC treaty.
13 See Pollak and Mokre 1999, p.320, quoted in Monika Mokre, Collective Identities in the enlarged European Union (IWE- Working paper series, No.32, September 2002, p.3.

Union claimed they had already heard about the Enlargement, according to the results of a survey carried out from November 2002 to March 2003 within EU-15. However, At the European level, only a minority of respondents (39%) believed the European Union was prepared for the Enlargement when questionnaire was carried out in 2003 before the sixth expansion. In other hand, the public claimed with a relatively positive view of enlargement that the European Union would have a stronger voice on the international scene, and the average percentage of this view was 79.67 in the surveys of September, November 2002 and March 2003.[14] From September 2000 to September 2007, the image of the European Union in the minds of the EU's public was more positive with more 45% ratio than negative with less 20% ration. And around the time of accession of new candidate countries (2003-2005), the image was not changed much at all.[15] It showed enlargement had not depressed public confidence in the EU's future. The same or similar results of surveys about other topics in 2003 were made. According to Eurobarometer 2007, a very large majority of citizens in the Union believe the Enlargement that will open up new markets to companies (86%), will be highly beneficial from a cultural point of view (82%) and will benefit the environment (65%). There are also 63% who 'rather agree' with the fact that the Enlargement will allow the agricultural sector to expand to new markets.[16]

Additionally, in terms of investigations from 2002 to 2007, EU citizens' supports for membership of the European Union, their recognition of benefits from being a member of the EU and their trust in European Union's institutions are all also stronger in comparison with those negative attitudes. At the same time, there was also no sharp change around the enlarging year 2004.

Apart from the public attitudes to the EU and its enlargement, the high level of sharing of values among the mass of accession states shows a clear presence of European identity since self-identification of common values is a main factor of identity shaping. From Eurobarometer, it shows in 2004 when being asked about their top three terminal values among citizens of accession countries (ACs) and candidate countries (CCs), the majority of them considered the most important value was family (82%), then health and work are respectively the second (63%) and third (35%) important ones among the most issues. In 2004, citizens from new 10 ACs considered the first value representing the EU is human rights,[17] which indicates the public of ACs shared common values about the EU, which is helpful for them to consolidate to be a community with the same collective identity.

---

14 Report of Eurobarometer 2003, http://ec.europa.eu/public_opinion/archives/eb/eb60/eb60_en.pdf
15 Report of Eurobarometer 2007, http://ec.europa.eu/public_opinion/archives/eb/eb68/eb68_first_en.pdf
16 Ibid.
17 Report of Eurobarometer 2004, http://ec.europa.eu/public_opinion/archives/eb/eb62/eb_62_en.pdf

Maybe the upper analysis gives a too much positive picture about public attitudes to and feelings of the EU around the stage of enlarging. Nevertheless, the identity is also mixed with some negative attitudes and feelings.

For example, although most part of citizens was informed of enlargement and others, they didn't know about them in details because the information was not insufficient. Almost two-thirds of respondents share the view that the EU-related information provided by the national media is too little (62%). Only about a quarter of European citizens think that the information they receive is just about the right volume.

Table 2: number change of complaints from EU-15 (2003-2006)

Table 3: number change of complaints from EU-10 (2004-2006)

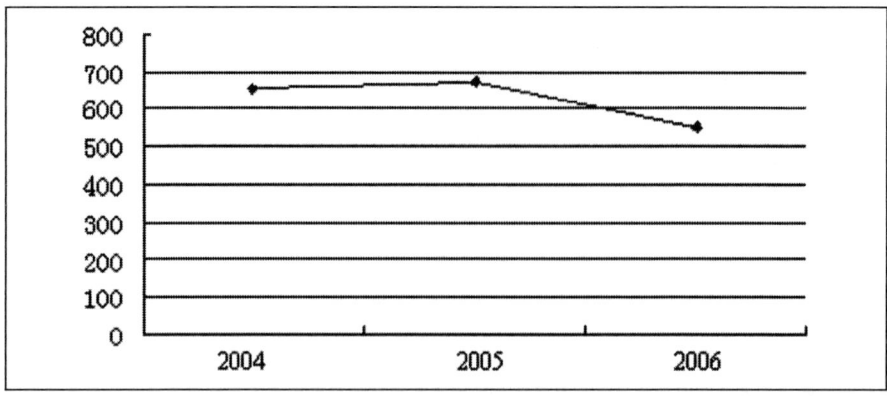

Exception for insufficient information provided to the public, complaints from citizens to the EU are should be taken into consideration as well. In accordance with the European Ombudsman, complaints increased around 300% from 1996 to 2006 where most part of complaints were sent by individuals. But it's interesting that from 2004 to 2006, the number of complaints to the EU increased in EU-15 but conversely, decreased in EU-10. It can be explained through the enlargement which led to many issues the old members had to face, for instance, they would burden more budget to help the eastern members and absorb more labors from the east.

Another very serious problem is nationalism which is partially stimulated by immigrants when the EU is expanding to the eastern region where many workers travel borders to seek better chances of jobs and lives in the west, which is considered by some politicians and citizens of old member states as a terrible wave of occupying their own chances. Partially for this background, fledging nationalism arises in some western countries like France. For example, an extreme-nationalist party led by Jean-Marie Le Pen won the rights for the second round of presidential campaign.

Clearly, in theory the strong nationalism will undermine the base of collective identity, thus if western countries' nationalism becomes too strong, the EU's legitimacy will become weak. Though many authors always carefully reconcile European identity with national identity which has a close relation to nationalism, but no one argues that strong nationalism can exist together with regional identity. So after enlargement of 2004 or 2007, if nationalism stimulated partially by immigrants or labor movements from the eastern member states is backed by some publics of EU-15, the European identity and citizenship will be hard to shape.

Effectiveness of bureaucracy and public goods stemmed from common policies

Effectiveness and public goods are pretty important sources of power's empirical legitimacy which is a base of public belief in legitimation of power. Effectiveness means a good performance of bureaucracy in decision-making and policy-implementing, meanwhile, rich public goods indicate common people can benefit from those policies bureaucracy makes and implements. If the EU can provide citizens with abundant public goods by good performance of policy process even after enlargement, it will be legitimate in the empirical sense undoubtedly.

1. Limited coordination among institutions

In practice, some reasons that can account for the low degree of the EU's empirical legitimacy are clear because the EU cannot perform effectively and provide rich public goods that citizens need. Namely, in the level of EU, there are some negative factors undermining EU empirical legitimacy, such as limited coordination among institutions of the EU, relative weak power of decision-making, and shortage of influential common policies.

Originally, the Treaty of Nice was prepared for the forthcoming enlargement of May 2004 and further widening in future, and amended some regulations of previous treaties in order to make the EU fit for the reality – more member states, huger population and more complicated settings than before. But this emendation doesn't generate a harmony within the EU whilst it wants to deal with those debated problem, because in accordance with the Treaty of Nice, unanimousness principle should be taken seriously and obeyed restrictively when decision-makings are done in those sensitive fields such as foreign affairs, defense, customs and social affairs, and so forth. However, after enlargement, the unanimousness principle will be more difficult to be implemented for more debates, quarrels, bargaining, competences and conflicts within more member states.

For making up this defect of Nice Treaty, leaders of the EU decided to make a Constitution partially due to the openness article for emendation of the Nice Treaty. Some major reformation articles were written in Constitution which was in relation to reformation and formation of institutions and their functions. For example, it officially considered the European Council as an institution of the EU but deprived its some power of legislation, on the contrary, strengthened the Parliament's legislative power, and reduced the number of the Commission to strengthen its effectiveness, and so on. Yet this reform in Constitution Treaty is criticized by some scholars because the utilization of the principle of "community institutional balance" somehow makes the distribution of power among institutions be more indistinct. For instance, the Constitution Treaty reclaims the balance of legislative power between the Council and the Parliament by the co-decision procedure (Article 251), which was introduced by the Treaty of Maastricht firstly. It means the Constitution Treaty allows the European Parliament to share legislative power with the Council yet through an unclear division of power.

Accordingly, on the one hand, these principles such as Balance and Co-decision procedure cannot be carried out successfully for its unclear boder of power among these institutions; on the other, the Constitution Treaty is beyond the possibility of being passed and signed because of being refused by French and The Dutch in 2005. So encountering enlargement, the EU hasn't prepared well to ease conflicts between inefficient institutions and more complicated conditions within an enlarged EU.

2. Public goods deficit

Sufficient public goods shared freely by common people should be provided by powerful government at the national level, which implies a weak political system doesn't have strong ability to meet public demands. At the EU level, those policies can benefit citizens isn't easy to generate for two causes-- unclear allocation of power among different institutions and weakness of institutions' power in comparison with national governments.

For the first reason, just mentioned above, although the institutions reform was set out in the Treaty of Nice followed by the EC draft, the distribution of power was not explicit, typically among the Council of Ministers, the Commission and the Parliament. In accordance with Nice Treaty and the EC treaty, the Council has reduced but not abandoned the power of legislation, so it should cooperate with the Parliament. Additionally, the Council in the recession of legislative power will compete with the Commission in the field of decision-implementation. For example, according to article of the EC treaty and the Lisbon Treaty, the president of the Council will be on behalf of the EU and become the special delegate toward the external world, yet what's the exact position of the president of the Commission or the Foreign Affairs representative of the EU? Further more, how can these two big men work together in harmony?

This fuzzification of power distribution in the EU after enlargement either in practice or in theory will undermine its effectiveness of the EU, which leads to weak policies and less public goods. So the second reason is linked with the first one. Namely, inefficiency of bureaucracy leads to public goods deficit.

The weakness of the EU institutions is also related to their vulnerable positions compared to national governments which have much stronger capabilities to implement domestic policies which can be translated into public goods. Thus the weak ability of the EU is resulted from both its unclearness of power allocation within EU and its vulnerable position in comparison with member states in the field of decision-making and policy-implementing.

Correspondingly, public goods deficit become inescapable, typically in some areas such as home and international affairs. Within the building of the EU policies, there are three pillars-- community policy, home and justice policy and common foreign and security policy where only the community policy is a true "common" one which is decided mostly in the EU level; however, not only home and justice affairs but also diplomatic ones cannot be determined by the EU alone. In these two fields, the EU can simply share the power of decision-making with member states, especially influenced by the willing of those powerful states, like France, Germany or Britain. Subsequently, a lot of public goods European citizens enjoy are not provided by the EU but by national governments. This phenomenon will continue, if not more serious, when expanding policy is continuous.

Intergovernmentalism or supranationalism?

To some degree, legitimacy is an idea, in view of this, the EU's legitimacy is also an idea rather than a reality, according to which reviewing the legitimacy of EU is not only an empirical analysis but also an selection of one special perspective at first, which means the evaluation of EU legitimacy depends upon the author's philosophy, morality, feelings or even his social status, and so on.

Notwithstanding, if to simplify the perspective to be in search of the EU's legitimacy regardless of personality or subjectivity of the individual researcher, it's necessary to introduce two common perspectives: intergovernmentalism and supranationalism. So it indicates when selecting one of these two perspectives, the EU's legitimacy will be very different from that if selecting another.

Intergovernmental perspective and the enlarged EU legitimacy

Theoretically, intergovernmentality is in relation to bargaining between or among member states and adherence to sovereignty to preserve state's independence and freedom in international society. Cooperation, multilateralism or deliberative democracy may be adopted by member states; nonetheless, these should be recognized as some good methods of reaching national interests more than fixed criteria or aims. In light of intergovernmental perspective, legitimacy is mainly based on equilibrium between national interests and regional stability.

So from this perspective, the normative legitimacy is grounded in indirect democracy and a mixture of European identity and national identity; correspondingly, the empirical legitimacy still consists of effectiveness of institutions and good policies, but the meaning of effectiveness and good policy is different from that if based on supranational angle.

In details to say, firstly, the operation of the EU doesn't need using the principle of mass participation and comprehensive discussion between elites and publics, whilst which is considered seriously in the theory of direct democracy. Legitimacy of the EU institutions relies on degree of success in cooperation among member states in the EU. Consequently, the conflict between equality of member states in principle and inequality of member states in practice becomes a core issue regarding the EU's legitimacy.

Secondly, intergovernmentality argues European identity is not the unique base of legitimacy as regards of identity, and the national identity should not be neglected. It presents national citizenship should be equal with the European citizenship, if not overwhelming at least, and an ideal identity is a mixture or entangled interdependence of national identity and European identity. Just mentioned in the Treaty of Amsterdam, European identity should not replace national identity, which exactly is a manifesto of intergovernmentality.[18]

Thirdly, the legitimacy of the EU does not only rely on effectiveness and public goods of the EU institutions, but also on those of national governments of member states, especially on the efficiency of implementing of common policies approved through co-decision among member states within the EU. Namely, national government's ability to carry out common policy is more important than power-strengthening of the EU institutions.

---

18 This mixture of identity is also expressed clearly in the Amended on European Union and the Treaty Establishing the European Community in which it declares that "The Union shall respect the equality of Member States before the Treaties as well as their national identities, inherent in their fundamental structures, political and constitutional, inclusive of regional and local self-government". See the draft of Amended Treaty passed on 18 October 2007 by IC, p.5.

However, supranational legitimacy is different from that of intergovernmental one. The former adheres to direct democracy, more importance of European citizenship and European identity than national citizenship and national identity, powerful institutions and more influential common policies.

Thus from the supranational perspective, bargaining or functionalist cooperation among member states on national interests is an old and obsolete approach which should be replaced by Universalist cooperation beyond national interests. Anyway, the first approach to pave a road toward the family of community is direct democracy, i.e., direct election of delegates to the EU in the level of the EU. Simultaneously, direct democracy also means those delegates to the EU from a non-democratic member state will undermine the base of the EU's normative legitimacy. In other words, when those institutions formed by delegates or representatives from democratic member states, the EU will be legitimate.

In addition, a weakness of European identity is a shortage of the EU's legitimacy in the process of its integration and expansion toward the East. Although a single European identity without national or sub-national identity is a dream, in reality it can be pushed by strengthening European citizenship and prevented from attack of nationalism, an enemy of community identity.

Of course, the empirical legitimacy has direct linkages with the strong power of institutions and common influential policies made by the EU's institutions. Effectiveness means the EU is more powerful to make policies enclosing common interests of all EU citizens and has full capability to carry out them without resistance. The authority of the EU over member states is much of importance to shape empirical legitimacy by providing better and more public goods to European citizens. An effective, authoritative, unified and powerful EU will be full legitimate in the sense of empirical legitimacy undoubtedly.

Table 4: The comparison of intergovernmental legitimacy and supranational legitimacy

	Normative legitimacy		Empirical legitimacy		Theory
	Legitimation	Identity	Effectiveness	Public goods	
Intergovern-mental per-spective	Indirect democracy & equality	A mixture of national citizenship and European citizenship	Cooperation and bargaining	Intergovern-mental policy	Realism
Supranational perspective	Direct de-mocracy & consolidation	European citizenship	Strengthening the EU's power	Supranational policy	Universal-ism

Conclusion

That more and more discussions about the EU's legitimacy arise is mainly due to the increasing complexity within the EU after enlargement or while enlarging. To an extent, the EU motto "United in diversity" is a dream more than a reality, and the ongoing enlargement will make legitimacy issue be a core problem in political and academic fields. Anyway, according to upper analysis it can be concluded as follows:

Firstly, the problem of the EU's legitimacy is an idea rather than a reality. Although enlargement leads to a more complicated problem of legitimacy at European level from supranational perspective; however, from intergovernmental angle, this problem is not as serious as that supranationalists imagine. In other words, different perspectives result to different cognitions on the legitimacy issue of the EU, allowing for this, legitimacy deficit somehow is a myth which is a problem regarding idea rather than a reality.

Secondly, the EU's legitimacy problem results from the shortage of consensus on the EU's status and its future. Exactly, those adhering to supranational perspective will recognize the EU as a supranational political entity whose destiny will be the United states of Europe or the European Federation; while the EU regarded by intergovernmentalists is only a typical international organization consisting of sovereign states just like the UN or ASEAN, or somehow a kind of multi-level governance system where national governments are key actors. Theoretically, supranational perspective is based upon universalism which argues a united community with strong-shared values, identity and interests; notwithstanding, intergovernmental perspective is dependent on realism adhering to relative rights and bargaining and competence which are utilized as main approaches to realize national interests. Unfortunately, in consideration of the EU, those features belonging to universalism and realism both exist simultaneously. That is, the EU's nature is a mixture of supranational political system and intergovernmental international organization, which is the mainly genuine reason that legitimacy issue will be debated continuously. So before a clear nature and future of the EU, those quarrelling or discussion about the EU's legitimacy problem will not disappear.

Part III:

External Implications

The Enlargement of EU:
Some Lessons for East Asian Regionalism[1]

Cae-One Kim

This article will focus on the lessons learned especially during the accession process of Central and Eastern European Countries (CEECs) to the European Union, and how they can apply to East Asian regionalism, as market integration receives greater attention in this region.

Of course, it is needless to say that the European integration model as such cannot be trans-implanted in East Asia. There are significant historical and cultural differences, in addition to variations in the geo-political and geo-economic conditions of both regions. Nevertheless, by closely examining the historical development process of the EU, we can easily find many principles commonly applicable to East Asia as well. The only caveat is that it will take the wisdom and the will to materialize these principles so that they can be modified to fit the particular conditions in East Asia.

1. Rationale for a future-oriented pragmatic approach

The European Union is often considered to be largely a product of history, one that developed with the confluence of changing events and conditions both on and off the continent. That is not to say that the EU is inherently passive; the Union has been able to flexibly adapt and successfully change directions in its basic purposes as a response to the drastically changing times.

The EU Treaty is based on the premise that all European countries will eventually be admitted. While the Copenhagen criteria adopted in 1993 made the conditions for adherence more specific, this has not changed the overall principle. Rather, the Union has taken care to enlarge only when conditions are opportune. Membership enlargement has taken place gradually in six different stages, instead of in a simultaneous fashion. In the process, the EU has been consistent and circumspect in making sure that potential member countries fulfill the necessary conditions.

The inclusion of the CEECs which corresponds to the 5th and the 6th enlargement of the EU typically reflects, I believe, the existing traditional Community spirit that has become the trademark of the EU with its long historic background. It is worth noting that the multilateral efforts to improve economic relations between Eastern and Western Europe had already begun in the post World War II and Cold War eras.

---

1   This article originally is a keynote speech at the 4th EU-NESCA Workshop, Shanghai, October 2007. There is a slight amendment in comparison of the speech—by editor.

Soon after the end of the Cold War in the early 1990s, the EU was imparted with the opportunity to pursue one of its long-cherished dreams of strengthening economic cooperation with the CEECs. Multilateral support measures were implemented immediately, including the establishment of the European Bank for Reconstruction and Development (EBRD), and concrete preparatory measures for CEECs admission into the EU; for example, various agreements between the EU and individual Central and Eastern European countries began to be initiated.

Turning to East Asia, it is unfortunate to see that no step has been taken towards multilateral market integration in the region, nor have any agreements concerning how such a measure should take place been initiated. While it is true that the international trend of FTA proliferation has elicited the proposal of the East Asian Free Trade Area (EAFTA) at the 2004 ASEAN+3 Summit Meeting; the Meeting also agreed to pursue in the long-run the creation of an East Asian Community (EAC). But the majority of the concerned nations have offered a tepid attitude toward the EAFTA agreement and have given little official consideration to the agreement within their governments.

In order for market integration to take place in East Asia, first and foremost, the countries involved must reach a consensus on its necessity. In Europe, the idea of 'European integration' as a means to establish long-lasting peace and stability in Europe has a long history, with the creation of the EU being the first step in the realization of this concept. In East Asia, however, the first priority of market integration, inter alia, should be on what economic advantages can be gained through the process. The region is already progressing toward a natural economic area considering the high intra-regional trade dependency and deepening division of labor. The rationale for an FTA is that the institutionalization of such trends would help create the advantage of a larger, more stable market.

One of the lessons learned from the EU experience is that the pursuit of economic integration is a effective means to materialize two objectives at the same time: higher economic gains and greater peace and stability. By forming an EAFTA, if the countries of East Asia are able to collectively pursue mutually beneficial goals, traditional barriers to intra-region cooperation, such as nationalism, legacies of historical disputes and hegemonic competition between major countries in the region will progressively lose their significance. As can be seen from the EU experience, market integration provides an institutional framework for countries to discuss the issues of common concern.

Following this conclusion, it would behoove East Asia to pursue common prosperity through the introduction of an EAFTA with an economy-first, market-led and pragmatic approach.

As the 6-stage EU enlargement process shows, a gathering of 'like-minded nations' will be a prerequisite condition for the launching of East Asian market integration. It is desirable, then, that ASEAN+3, first of all, agree upon the 'necessity' of market integration by formulating an action plan. East Asian regionalism should extend from ASEAN+3 to include other countries in the region which share the common endeavors of the EAFTA.

East Asian market integration should therefore begin with the steps that are feasible to attain and, drawing on the experiences of the EU, to 'deepen' and 'widen' market integration through gradual enlargement to those countries which are ready to join.

2. The necessity for an institutional approach

Many studies regarding East Asian market integration, and monetary and financial cooperation rely on comparisons between East Asia and Europe on their respective degree of trade dependence, factor mobility, economic openness and convergence of macro-economic variables. Primarily based on the theory of optimum currency area and convergence criteria of EMU (Economic and Monetary Union), these researches in comparing mainly the changes in macro-economic variables, derive a favorable conclusion for promoting East Asian economic cooperation.

But the results of such studies show only one of the necessary conditions in realizing East Asian market integration. The lack of meaningful progress towards this integration is evidence of this myopia.

More importantly, the EU experience with the CEECs manifests the need to determine the basic conditions required for market integration with an approach focused on policy coordination. From the early 1990s, the EU pursued two different approaches in negotiations with the CEECs. The first was to implement gradual transformation of those countries, which had different economic systems, into the market economy, while the other was to carry out continuous assistance for development.

Adhering to the Copenhagen criteria, the focus of cooperation was on implementation of diverse policies and institutions to promote market economy in the CEECs. The reason for this was that the CEECs would not have to be able to adopt the EU's 'acquis communautaires,' including 'internal market' and common policies, immediately after their accession. While the CEECs were undertaking system reform, they needed to accept more stringent discipline as required by a market economy in order to become EU members.

However, questions have arisen of whether or not such a rigorous policy approach as adopted in the EU is necessary when considering the mode of integration in East Asia, which is as a mere free trade zone.

The answer is nuanced in several aspects. A free trade area is an early form of market integration, and has the advantages of minimizing constraints in the economic sovereignty of participating countries. Therefore, in the case of East Asia, there is no need for membership conditions as strict as those in the EU. Nevertheless, what is undeniable is that irrespective of the mode of market integration, it should be in principle based on market economy.

While the establishment of a free trade area may be a rudimentary form of market integration, it is imperative that the minimum requirements for this essential step towards integration be met. The removal of trade barriers between countries will vitalize competition in the region, which will in turn increase the static and dynamic efficiency of resource allocation. Countries that have not established a market economy system on a domestic level can hardly be expected to benefit from an enlarged market following the removal of trade barriers. Also, if distortions resulting from market intervention, which we often observe in developing countries, are significant, the removal of trade barriers alone will not generate free movement of goods in the region according comparative advantages.

Now there have been many regional trading arrangements established in East Asia and throughout the world. But the successful instances of market integration have been very limited, especially in developing nations. The main reason is that these arrangements failed to fulfill the basic premises of market integration.

Most East Asian countries have pursued outward-looking growth strategies, ostensibly in the fashion of market economies. Of course, there is no standard model for a market economy, and its practical mode will differ depending on the period and locus. It is not surprising that in East Asia, with its wide variety of cultures and institutions, one can find many different forms of market economy including the diverse role of governments' role according countries.

One thing is clear that the higher a country's degree of economic freedom, the easier it can achieve market integration with other countries. At the institutional level, there is a need for increased economic freedom in the region, on the one hand, and intra-regional convergence in the degree of economic freedom among the countries concerned in order to facilitate the liberalization of intra-regional trade on the other. In this regard, East Asian countries show a lower level of economic freedom and a larger institutional gap among countries in the region compared to other regions, such as the EU and NAFTA.

Considering the extant conditions, it would be desirable to establish 'a multilateral economic cooperation organization' in East Asia to systematically and effectively pursue trade liberalization. The purpose of such an organization would not only be to provide mutual trust in economic policies and performance between East Asian countries, but also to allow market economy to take root in the region through intensive multilateral cooperation and assistance. It would also provide a forum for debate and cooperation on numerous issues, such as mutual consultation on economic policies, elimination of trade barriers, government market intervention and deregulation, the coordination of economic policy and achievement of common goals.

Without question, East Asian market integration can succeed only if it is implemented based on the foundation of systematic cooperation. This would require member countries to sufficiently respect mutual economic sovereignty and multilateral cooperation must focus on realizing common benefits.

3. Systematic implementation of multilateral cooperation - Community spirit

Recalling that from the Rome Treaty (EEC) through to the Maastricht Treaty and the Nice Treaty, the EU has consistently emphasized the fundamental objectives of 'balanced growth' within the region, 'economic and social cohesion' among member nations and the strengthening of solidarity. We could be especially impressed by the extensive preparation undertaken during the fifth and sixth enlargements, which welcomed the accession of the CEECs.

As mentioned earlier, the EU provided the CEECs, large-scale financial and technical assistance and expertise in order to support their gradual transition into market economies. Having lived under a radically different system for such an extended period, the CEECs needed massive amounts of support in adopting a market economy. The most well-known instances include the EBRD, setting up of various structural adjustment funds and the implementation of common regional policies for the CEECs.

In East Asia, the promotion of an East Asian Free Trade Area (EAFTA) creates an opportunity for the convergence of economic systems and the intensification of multilateral economic cooperation among member countries. These two goals are closely interconnected. There are large disparities in the social and economic levels between East Asian countries, as well as within the countries themselves. Without a conscious effort to lessen such differences, market integration will not bear successful results.

The purpose of an EAFTA aims to increase mutual benefits for its members through trade liberalization. But such an increase in total gains resulting from intra-region trade itself would be meaningless if liberalization is implemented under unequal conditions or the benefits are concentrated in a specific country due to socio-economic disparities in the region. Consequently, strengthening measures at the government level for multilateral economic cooperation is a sine qua non in order for the gains to be efficiently allocated according to market mechanisms.

If East Asian countries succeed in the reinforcement of economic and technological cooperation and the multilateralization of ongoing bilateral relations, two considerable merits will be recognized.

Firstly, the 'will' of the participating countries in the region to overcome the economic difficulties of certain countries will contribute to the development of a 'Community spirit'. Economic cooperation will benefit not only the recipient countries but in the long-run also bring about benefits to the donor countries as intra-regional economic transactions increase. Moreover, if the countries in the region prepare and establish a common development plan for certain regions through an exchange of views and open discussions, these efforts will contribute to enhancing the transparency in each country, as well as increasing mutual trust for its management.

Secondly, a multilateral cooperative system will help member countries to systematically establish and implement development plans. In particular, on-going bilateral economic cooperation initiatives can be reviewed and readjusted in an efficient way. The establishment of a common, comprehensive development program for certain regions in difficulty would avoid redundancies in bilateral assistance plans. It would also allow an efficient allocation of resources to concentrate to the regions which need them the most according to the priority plan. With this objective in mind, it is desirable to establish and execute a medium and log-term multilateral development plan after adjustments, if necessary, with the agreement of member countries.

As we can see in the example of the EU regarding its cooperation with the CEECs, the introduction of assistance organizations such as a common development bank and restructuring funds in the region can be appropriate alternative measures.

The EU/China Relationship and the Impact of the Recent EU Enlargements on It[1]

Ali M El-Agraa

I. Introduction

China is in the limelight and rightly so. By this, the reference is not to the country's recent international leadership activities, including enticing the Democratic People's Republic of Korea (DPRK) back into the 6-nation talks[2]; holding/hosting the Summit of the Forum on China-Africa Cooperation (FOCAC) in November 2006 with 48 of the 50 African nations, a feat never achieved by the Africans in their own fora; and the eight-nation 12-day tour of Africa by Chinese President Hu Jintao in January/February 2007[3]. One could even admire these initiatives, because despite the self-interest, i.e. securing China against an influx of escapees from DPRK if that country were

1   This paper was published in the *Asia Europe Journal*, vol. 5, no. 2, 2007. It is reproduced here with updates, amendments and additions with AEJ's kind permission.
    I wish to express my gratitude for comments and helpful suggestions from Professor Philip Arestis, Director of Research, Cambridge Centre for Economic and Public Policy, the University of Cambridge, UK, Professor Marius Brülhart of HEC, Université de Lausanne, Switzerland, Jean Monnet Professor Alan Matthews of Trinity College, Dublin, Ireland, Brian Ardy, Head of the European Institute, London South Bank University, UK, and Dr Albrecht Rothacher, Editor-in-Chief of the *Asia Europe Journal*. I am especially indebted to Professor Matthews for provoking me into pursuing directions that I had not envisaged. Nevertheless, I must absolve all of them of any responsibility for any of my errors.— by Ali M El-Agraa
2   The six nations are China, Japan, the two Koreas, Russia and the US.
3   The tour is his third during the past two years, with the second taking place during April 2006. The latest tour began on 30 January 2007 and included stops in Liberia, Sudan, Zambia, Namibia, South Africa, Mozambique and Seychelles. It marked his first visit to Africa after holding/hosting the FOCAC in November 2006, when he pledged $5 billion in loans and credits to Africa during 2006-2009 and declared the formation of a $5 billion China-Africa 'development fund' aimed at encouraging Chinese enterprises to invest in African countries as well as provide them with support; for details, see Worldpress.org (2007) 'China to double aid to Africa': http://www.worldpress.org/print_article.cfm?article_id=2674&dont=yes The Chinese have claimed that the visit was remarkably successful in enhancing friendship and cooperation between China and African nations (see *China View*, 'Chinese President Hu Jintao wraps up successful African trip', published in 2007 and can be accessed from their website at: http://news.xinhuanet.com/english/2007-02/11/content_5724926.htm) and the Africans are pleased with the mentioned cheaper credit it has promised to extend to them. Note that: in the first ten months of 2005, Chinese companies invested $175 million in African countries, mainly on oil exploration projects and infrastructure; at the end of October 2005, China's trade with Africa amounted to $32.17 billion, making it Africa's third most-important trading partner, behind the US and France and ahead of the UK; and China's foreign direct investment (FDI) in Africa reached $900 million in 2005 out of a total of $15 billion (i.e. 6%). Detailed information can be found in Pan (2007) 'China, Africa and oil' under the Council on Foreign Relations, to be accessed at: http://www.cfr.org/publication/9557.

completely isolated from the international community, not to mention securing a nuclear-free Korean peninsular, and attracting much needed energy and mineral resources from Africa, these are moves which are bound to impact positively not only on the Asian but also global security.

China is in the limelight because it has been one of the fastest growing economies in the world, averaging about 10% Gross National Income (GNI) growth over the past decade or so. Indeed, by 2004 the Chinese economy surpassed that of France to become the world's fifth largest, after the US, Japan, Germany and the UK. This trend is confirmed by the latest figures, released in the press in early 2006, which place China ahead of the UK; not surprising given that in 2003 the UK's GNI amounted to $2.01 trillion while China's was $1.94 trillion, a difference of a mere 3.5%. Yet these figures are based on market exchange rates; in terms of purchasing power parities (PPP), which are what any responsible economists would use, China has been the number two economy after the US for some years now. What is even more striking is that China is now an increasingly substantial player in global trade. In 1980, its total trade was $38 billion, accounting for 1% of total global trade. By 2003, however, this has increased to $851 billion, raising the share to 5.6% to elevate China to the rank of fourth largest world trader, following the US, Germany and Japan. Indeed, this trend seems to have been maintained since the latest data[4] shows that in 2005 China replaced Japan as the third largest world trader with $1.42 trillion of trade, of which $762 billion were exports (up 28% from 2004) and $660 billion were imports (up 18%). Furthermore, and much to the surprise of many countries headed by Japan, 2006 OECD projections reveal that China would be second to the US in the league of R&D expenditure, measured in terms of 'Purchasing Power Parity' (PPP), for the first time relegating Japan to third place[5].

Over the same period, the pattern and composition of China's trade have also experienced dramatic changes. Instead of having its exports continuing to be concentrated on primary products, a characteristic of very poor nations, they have become dominated by industrial products, especially those of the capital-intensive type, which is a feature of advanced nations. Such a speedy transformation under China's circumstances is most unexpected, i.e. could not be predicted by any trade model, given that China is still a

---

4   Released on 11 January 2006 and published in all the major news media, including the *Financial Times*, on 12 January 2006.

5   According to the OECD's *Science, Technology and Industry Outlook 2006*, published in 2007, China's R&D expenditure in 2006, as measured in PPP terms, is expected to be $136 billion while that by the US, Japan and EU-15 would be $330, $130 and $230 billion respectively. The OECD arrives at the figures for 2005 and 2006 by projecting on the assumption of a continuation of growth in R&D spending in these years 'at the same average rate as was observed over the period 2000-2004'; a fairly standard projection practice. Japan's shock is due to its obsession with nominal exchange rate valuation which reduces China's R&D to only $33 billion or 1.3% of its GDP; under the same terms, Japan's would be 3.17% of its GDP; see OECD (2007), which can be accessed at: http://www.oecd.org/sti/outlook. However, no economist would or should settle for comparative data that is not based on PPP valuation.

very poor nation, ranking 108 in 2004 in terms of per capita PPP GNI, with $5,890.[6] This raises several questions. What has been happening to the Chinese economy that enabled such a transformation? Have the policies being adopted by China been the main instigators of this? What is the precise nature of the export commodity composition brought about by this change? How has the change in the composition of exports impacted on China's direction of trade? What has been the consequence of this transformation on the nature and composition of China's imports?

These questions are however not the subject of this paper, not only because they have been addressed elsewhere,[7] but also because my concern here is with the extent to which the European Union (EU) has been preparing itself to deal with China's transformation and how to capitalize on China's huge economic potential for trade and investment. Hence, the paper commences by describing the efforts exerted by the EU in this respect which it formalised in 1995 in its EU-China relationship policy document. The paper then proceeds to consider China's responses which culminated in 2003 when China produced its own first ever China-EU policy paper. The reasons for this long gap between action and reaction are then explored. It is obvious from this that the EU has been driving this relationship so the rationale for this is then explored. The nature of China's reciprocation is then examined before this main part of the paper is concluded. The main finding is that the relationship means more to the EU because China perceives the EU as only having a limited role within its overall global aspirations, of becoming a world power in economic terms, resulting from its impressive rate of economic growth, increasing R&D expenditure and continually enhancing sophistication of its technology, and politically with its developing links and military prowess. Finally, a short section looks into how the recent EU enlargements have impacted on the relationship; short, because my other paper covers practically all aspects of this issue.

II. Initiating the relationship

In its Communication (COM) of 1995 concerning a strategy for the establishment of a long-term policy for relations between the EU and China[8], the European Commission expressed its realisation of the uniqueness of China's ascendance since the end of the Second World War. Unique because while Japan acquired economic prowess and Russia continued to survive on the basis of military strength, China was 'increasingly strong in both the military-political and the economic spheres'. On the economic front, the Commission relied on, inter alia, IMF and World Bank extrapolations, based on then prevailing PPP GDP and its growth rates, to forecast that China would become the world's largest economy in a generation's time. The EU obviously had an interest

---

6   At nominal exchange rates, it ranks 128 and its per capita GNI is only $1,740.

7   El-Agraa and Wei (2006a,b).

8   Commission of the European Communities (1995). This was the culmination of efforts on the part of the EC to promote bilateral political dialogue with China that started in June 1994.

in developing its economic relations with a future superpower but its interest went beyond the economic. With population increasing, despite the one-child policy, by 15 million annually and China already second only to the US in terms of energy consumption, it would impact greatly on energy demand; hence on the physical environment. The Commission concluded that the consequences for the environment of a huge China reaching western consumption, and pollution, levels in the future would be impossible to ignore. It was therefore vital that China should play a full part in the wider policy exchange on such key issues as the environment, population and health. Moreover, with China still poor[9], a substantial number of Chinese would seek emigration, which would increasingly become subject to illegal trafficking due to limited licit access to EC and other nations. It was therefore essential to tackle the 'very real resultant problems' in close cooperation with China.

As to the military-political, the Commission emphasised that China's size (in terms of both area and population, then 1.2 billion), nuclear power status and permanent membership of the UNSC clearly indicated that it would become impossible to tackle international issues without factoring in China's impact on their development and management, especially since the country was 'one of the world's biggest arms producers and exporters'. Hence China's 'role across the whole *security* spectrum is central to global, as well as regional security'.

The Commission pointed out that while China was domestically undergoing sustained and dramatic economic and social change, it was simultaneously increasing its involvement in the world security and economic systems. On the domestic side, China's hugeness was reflected 'in the multiplicity of players...who can influence Chinese policy and practice': central government agencies, both in Beijing and elsewhere, provincial and municipal authorities; emerging economic actors; and the like. This, together with the rapid devolution in economic power was delegating policy responsibility and implementation for economic and trade matters to the provincial level. The Commission concluded that it would thus be vital to have firm commitments on the enforcement of China's international obligations at the sub-national level, for example, during the World Trade Organization (WTO) negotiations. It reiterated that this 'makes it crucial to expand our bilateral trade and cooperation discussions to include provincial and local authorities which, de jure or de facto, are in charge of economic and trade policy in many fields'.

All this was happening at a time of 'globalization'[10] with problems such as the protection of the environment and nuclear non-proliferation requiring coordinated action by all countries. We were reminded that in its endeavours to become part of this

---

9   In 1995, China had a per capita GNP of $2,920 in PPP terms ($620 in nominal exchange rate terms), ranking 42 from the bottom in the World Bank's list of 'low-income economies' (see the World Bank's *World Development Report 1977*).

10 A fashionable and over-played term since those specialised in International Economics have always referred to 'international interdependence' and its increasing occurrence. See, inter-alia, Bhagwati (2002), Fischer (2003) and El-Agraa (2004).

global dynamic, China joined the IMF and the World Bank in the early 1980s; became a member of the APEC forum[11] (in 1991); was actively negotiating membership of the WTO; contributed significantly to the outcome of the World Conference on Human Rights in Vienna in June 1993; and would be hosting a major UN conference on women later in 1995.

The Commission pointed out that two decades had passed since the EC and China engaged in diplomatic relations in 1975[12] and a decade since the signing of the Trade and Cooperation Agreement[13] between them in 1985; the agreement was: both broader in scope relative to that of 1975, providing a framework for cooperation in industry, mining, energy, transport, communications and technology; and more flexible with regard to trade and economic cooperation.[14] Although bilateral relations were severed in 1989[15] in the aftermath of the Tiananmen Square brutal crack down on Chinese dissidents[16], their normalisation, especially during the early 1990s, had led to enhanced

---

11 Not that such membership has any significance when the mere mention of possible discussions on the creation of a free trade area for the 21 member nations of APEC is met by complete silence by all as happened during their meetings in November 2006, held in Hanoi, Viet Nam. See, inter alia, El-Agraa (1999; 2007b).

12 Diplomatic relations were established in May 1975, following the visit to China by Commissioner Sir Christopher Soames. The resumption of diplomatic relations was supposed to quickly pave the way for trade and economic relations, but the chaos that beset China in the aftermath of the passing away of Mao Zei Dong in 1976 put on hold all contacts between the Commission and China (Kapur 1981, p. 201). However, in 1980 China was admitted into the group of developing nations granted special treatment under the EC's Generalised System of Preferences (GSP). Griese (2006) claims that EC-China *trade relations* after that progressed so rapidly and positively that the 1978 agreement had to be considered inadequate for its purposes and hence a new agreement was in order.

13 Commission of the European Communities (1985).

14 Examples of this cooperation are the *Science and Technology Agreement* of 1999, which was renewed in 2004, and the *Maritime Agreement* of 2002, which aimed 'to improve conditions for the maritime transport of EU and Chinese companies moving from the EU, China and third-party destinations' (see Griese 2006, p. 546).

15 After EC Commissioner Sir Christopher Soames' visit to China in 1975, there followed in 1979 the first ever visit by a president of the European Parliament (EP), Mr Emilio Colombo, and a month later the first such visit by a president of the Commission, Mr Roy Jenkins, who met personally with the Chinese leader Deng Xiaoping. These visits would seem (as claimed by Griese 2006) to have paved the way for a meeting in Strasbourg in June 1980 between delegations from the EP and the Chinese National People's Congress, but there is no concrete evidence to support this conjecture. They also led to: the launching in 1983 of the first *EC-China Scientific Cooperation Programme*; and the setting up in 1988 of the EC Delegation offices in Beijing. However, no high-ranking official visit to the EC by a Chinese took place until Prime Minister Zhu Rong-ji visited the Commission in Brussels in June 2000.

16 Two days after 4 June 1989, the EC condemned the 'incident' and during the 26-7 June 1989 Madrid European Council meetings, the EC imposed several sanctions on China, eliminating high-level EC-China meetings and leading to the suspension of new cooperation projects and the curtailment of programmes then in action. However, in 1990 the EC relaxed its embargos on contacts and cooperation, when it was realized that no change in Chinese leadership was going to ensue from the incident; the only exceptions being the ban on arms sales and cooperation in the military field (see Griese 206, p. 547).

trade and investment[17] and culminated in the 1994 arrangement for 'political dialogue'.

With that background in mind, the Commission thus urged that it was high time to 'redefine' the EU relationship with China, within the context of the new Asia Strategy endorsed by the Essen European Council[18]. It emphasised that the EC 'must develop *a long-term relationship with China* that reflects China's worldwide, as well as regional, economic and political influence'. That was because 'relations with China are bound to be a cornerstone in Europe's external relations, both with Asia and globally'. It added that the EC 'needs an action-oriented, not a merely declaratory policy, to strengthen that relationship'.

The rest of the Communication examined the specific concerns of the EC, especially how to enable EC enterprises compete successfully in the expanding Chinese market, and developed a detailed picture of all these considerations as well as articulated policy recommendations and actions on each. These details will become apparent in the following section when I turn to China's response, but here it can be briefly stated that the conclusions drawn by the Council on the basis of the Communication set the aims of the EC-China relationship to be:

1. To engage China further, through upgraded political dialogue, in the international community;
2. To support China's transition to an open society based upon the rule of law and the respect of human rights;
3. To integrate China further in the world economy by bringing it more fully into the world trading system and by supporting the process of economic and social reform underway in the country, including in the context of sustainable development;
4. To make better use of existing EC resources; and
5. To raising the EC's profile in China.

All the essential elements in the Communication were formally adopted by the Commission on 25 March 1998 in its 'Building a comprehensive relationship with China'[19] and endorsed by the Council on 29 June 1998. Hence this 1998 document establishes the reference point for the EC's policy for the relationship.

---

17 Indeed, Algieri (2002, p. 64) argues that the Tiananmen incident caused no ' major disturbance [in] EU-China economic relations.'

18 This relates to the endorsement by the Council, held on 9/10 December 1994, of the Commission's 'Towards a New Asia strategy' (COM(94) 314). The Council concluded that it 'emphasizes the economic and political significance of the countries of the Asia-Pacific region and reaffirms that the European Union and its Member States wish to strengthen cooperation and dialogue at all levels with the countries and regional organizations in the Asia-Pacific region, in particular ASEAN'. It urged the Council (of Ministers) and Commission to report to it as soon as possible on the practical measures taken in that respect. See *Bulletin of the European Union*, 1994, No. 12, p. 14.

19 Commission of the European Communities (1998).

III. China's reciprocation

For a long time, no *equivalent* response was forthcoming from China. That however would/should not have surprised the EC since its policy paper was not only an act of 'unilateral declaration' and hence the EC had to follow it by endeavouring to sell it to China by negotiating its various aspects, item by item, especially if China did not see the need for a policy. But also, and vitally, the EC policy sent a double-edged message: wanting to benefit from the vast economic potential of China yet simultaneously dictating conditions which countered China's socio-political stance. Beggars cannot be choosers, although much needed sanctioning of China's bid for WTO membership provided a counterweight – see below. Indeed, the very fact that the EC deemed it necessary to publish a Report on progress with the policy on 8 September 2000[20] under the circumstances is a clear manifestation of an EC having been engaged in a 'selling exercise'. The Report stated that since the adoption of the 1998 Communication, the EU-China relationship had greatly intensified, with the annual EU-China summits in 1998 and 1999 laying the foundations for a broader political dialogue. Also, simultaneously, an increasing succession of meetings and dialogues at all levels, and in numerous areas of concern to both sides, 'improved communication and promoted mutual understanding'. Moreover, the agenda were extended to regional security, economic/trade concerns as well as to human rights and the EC expressed its wish for the inclusion of other global issues such as illegal immigration and 'eventually drug-trafficking, money laundering and organised crime'. Furthermore, the two signed a Bilateral Agreement on 19 May 2000, needed for China's accession to the WTO, and in this regard, it was stressed that once a member, 'a key challenge for the EU will be to develop mutually acceptable methods to monitor and assist with China's compliance with its WTO commitments'. The EU would also carry on pressing China to tackle remaining barriers to its markets. Finally, the EU-China Cooperation Programme had expanded steadily, focusing on 'sustainable development to assist China's overall reform process' and its priorities and contents would be re-examined in the light of 'the pace of constant change, as well as to improve the impact and visibility of EU assistance to China'. Nevertheless, none of the mentioned items suggests that China saw its role in them as anything but one of being engaged in a 'buying exercise': participation in the China-EU summits should be seen in the wider context of the Asia-Europe meetings (ASEM)[21] instigated by Singapore; including new items to the agenda was an EU, not a mutual, wish; and so on and so forth.

It could of course be argued that pursuing the relationship, especially on facilitating WTO membership in 2001, must have impacted the EU favourably on China[22]. This

---

20 Commission of the European Communities (2000).
21 The first ASEM meeting was held on 2-3 March 1996 in Bangkok and the second in April 1998 in London. For a detailed discussion, see El-Agraa (2001).
22 Indeed, the EU was a positive, almost vehement, advocate of China's bid for WTO membership and acted as a vital mediator between the US and China in their negotiations on the membership

is because on 13 October 2003, China published its formal document on the subject: China's EU Policy Paper[23]. Since about two years had lapsed by then, obviously the Paper did not immediately follow the Report, but that could be due to the factors just mentioned and/or the time-consuming Chinese political decision-making process. Other reasons could be the need for further consideration of some issues by China and/ or that some points needed further clarification from the EC; I shall return to this point later. An alternative scenario for China's response however would be the one mentioned above; that China had to bend somewhat to the EC since without EC endorsement a safe passage to WTO membership would have been out of the question, when that aim was uppermost in China's priorities at the time. Be that as it may, it is pertinent to look into what the Paper had to say.

The Paper commenced in a grandiose, EU-detached, fashion:

> The international situation has been undergoing profound changes since the advent of the new century. The trend towards world multipolarity and economic globalisation is developing amid twists and turns. Peace and development remain the themes of the era. The world is hardly a tranquil place and mankind still confronted with many serious challenges. However, preserving world peace, promoting development and strengthening cooperation, which is vital to the well-being of all nations, represents the common aspiration of all peoples and is an irreversible trend of history.

> China is committed to turning herself into a well-off society in an all-round way and aspires for a favourable international climate. China will continue to pursue its independent foreign policy of peace and work closely with other countries for the establishment of a new international political and economic order that is fair and equitable, and based on the Five Principles of Peaceful Co-existence. China will, *as always, respect diversity in the world and promote democracy in international relations in the interest of world peace and common development* (italics added).

It was only after this grand gesture, emphasising China's awareness of its place in the world, what it stood/aspired for and how it saw the entire globe within that context, vitally omitting any hint to the 'promotion of democracy' applying 'domestically', that it turned to the relationship:

> The…EU…is a major force in the world. *The Chinese Government appreciates the importance the EU and its members attach to developing relations with China.* The present EU Policy Paper of the Chinese Government is the first of its kind and aims to highlight the objectives of China's EU policy, and outline the areas and plans of cooperation and related measures in the next five years so as to enhance China-EU all-round cooperation and promote a long-term and stable development of China-EU relations (italics added).

It is interesting that the Paper should mention the importance the EU and its member states attach to the relationship, without a reciprocation of the sentiment by China; a

---

status for China: the US was adamant that China should be treated as an 'industrialised nation' while China was all for being deemed a 'developing nation' with all the privileges such a status would entail, e.g. GSP treatment; see footnote 8. This point is fully set out in Eglin (1997).

23   Ministry of Foreign Affairs of the People's Republic of China (2003).

vindication of the double-edged nature of the EC policy, one edge of which China wants off the agenda. It could of course be argued that that could have been merely a manifestation of the fact that China was acting in reciprocation to being approached by the EC, or that it was a question of style, may be even of semantics, or that the devil was in the detail, and so on and so forth. I shall return to dispute this alternative later, so keeping it in mind for the time being, let me turn to the details.

The main body of the Paper consisted of three parts. The first comprised three short paragraphs, ten full lines in total, about the EU itself. The last paragraph confidently stated that '[d]espite its difficulties and challenges ahead, the European integration process is irreversible and the EU will play an increasingly important role in both regional and international affairs'.

Part two was less brief and set out the general tone of China's EU policy. Its gist was that the establishment of diplomatic relations between China and the EC in 1975 bestowed benefits on both. That, irrespective of 'twists and turns', the relationship as a whole was 'growing stronger and more mature' and was 'on the track of a comprehensive and sound development', citing as evidence some of the items mentioned above in the EC Report. What is significant was the statement that the relationship was 'now better than at any time in history'.

After adding that there were no fundamental differences between the two and that neither posed a threat to the other, the tone however changed somewhat dramatically: 'given differences in historical background, cultural heritage, political system and economic development level, *it is natural that the two sides have different views or even disagree on some issues*' (italics added). And was quick to reiterate that China-EU relations, based on mutual trust and mutual benefit 'cannot and will not be affected *if the two sides address their disagreements in a spirit of equality and mutual respect*' (italics added).

The tone then became more positive and less self-assertive:

> The common ground between China and the EU far outweighs their disagreements. Both...*stand for democracy in international relations* and an enhanced role for the UN. Both are committed to combating international terrorism and promoting sustainable development through poverty elimination and environmental protection endeavours. China and the EU are highly complementary economically thanks to their respective advantages. The EU has a developed economy, advanced technologies and strong financial resources while China boasts steady economic growth, a huge market and abundant labour force. There is a broad prospect for bilateral trade and economic and technological cooperation. Both China and the EU member states have a long history and splendid culture each and stand for more cultural exchanges and mutual emulation. The political, economic and cultural common understanding and interaction between China and the EU offer a solid foundation for the continued growth of China-EU relations (italics added).

Again, there was no mention of democracy being extended to 'domestic relations'.

Before the details got set out, it was indicated that the strengthening and enhancement of the relationship was 'an important component of China's foreign policy' and that

'China is committed to a long-term, stable and full partnership with the EU'. The objectives were then stated to be:

1. To 'promote a sound and steady development of China-EU political relations *under the principles of mutual respect, mutual trust and seeking common ground while reserving differences*, and contribute to world peace and stability'.
2. To 'deepen China-EU economic cooperation and trade *under the principles of mutual benefit, reciprocity and consultation on an equal basis*, and promote common development'.
3. To 'expand China-EU cultural and people-to-people exchanges *under the principle of mutual emulation, common prosperity and complementarity*, and promote cultural harmony and progress between the East and the West'. (Italics added.)

Part three came in five major sections, covering the policy for the various facets of the relationship. One section dealt with the political elements, stressing various aspects. There was a call for the strengthening of the exchange of high-level visits and political dialogue. Abiding by the 'one-China principle' was stressed, clearly telling the EU to not engage with Taiwan or help it endeavour for independence. The encouragement of the cooperation of Hong Kong and Macao with the EU was agreed, but within the context of the 'one country, two systems'. The promotion of the understanding of EU 'personages of various circles' of Tibet was mentioned, with the important proviso that the EU should not have any contact with the 'Tibetan government in exile' or 'provide facilities to the separatist activities of the Dalai clique'[24]. The continuation of the dialogue on human rights was acknowledged on the understanding that 'both consensus and disagreements' exist between China and the EU in this regard. The strengthening of international cooperation, including on UN matters, advancing Asia-Europe cooperation by working together as equals to 'make ASEM a role model for inter-continental cooperation' and 'a channel for exchange between the oriental and occidental civilisations and a driving force behind the establishment of a new international political and economic order', joint combating of terrorism and promoting arms control all find a place. So did the enhancement of mutual understanding between Chinese and EU legislative bodies, including with the European Parliament. A final aspect was the increase of the exchanges between the Chinese Communist Party and EU parties at all levels *'on the basis of independence, complete equality, mutual respect and non-interference in each other's affairs'* (italics added).

---

24 Thus, when German Chancellor Angela Merkel met the Dalai Lama in the German Chancellery on 23 September 2007, although she was by then no longer the president of the EU Council, she clearly indicated that Germany had no intention of abiding by this Chinese demand. China was so upset that it cancelled a scheduled high-level meeting between its officials and their German counterpat, including German Justice Minister Brigitte Zypries, on patent rights protection that was meant to take place on the following day, 24 September, but on the pretext of 'technical reasons'; earlier in the month China summoned Germany's ambassador in Beijing to protest in the streongest of terms.

The second section covered various the economic matters. One of these was China's commitment 'to developing dynamic, long-term and stable economic cooperation and trade with the EU' with the expectation that the EU would become China's largest trading and investment partner. Another related to financial cooperation, including between central banks and deepening cooperation 'in preventing and managing financial crises and combating the financing of terrorism and money laundering'. Agricultural cooperation, including the intensification of exchanges in production, processing technology and sustainable development was mentioned. Environmental cooperation, calling for the creation of a mechanism for dialogue between ministers of the environment got a place. Another was IT cooperation, with China expecting EU 'participation in China's IT promotion'. Energy cooperation, with efforts to be exerted to ensure a successful China-EU Energy Conference was also stated. A final aspect was transport cooperation, including within the framework of the China-EU Agreement on Maritime Transport, cooperation in highway technology and management and the deepening of exchanges in civil aviation.

The third section was reserved for education, science, technology, culture, health and press and personnel exchanges. With regard to cooperation in science and technology, there was mention of the protection of intellectual property rights, the encouragement of Chinese institutions to participate in the EU Framework Programme for Research and Technological Development, and China's partaking in the EU Galileo Programme. The enhancement of cooperation in international 'big science' projects; the elevation of the role of the Scientific and Technologic Cooperation Steering Committee; insuring the success of the China-Europe Science & Technology and Innovation Policy Forum and the like were the remaining aspects.

As to the other mentioned areas, China would seek 'a multi-level and all-dimensional' framework for cultural exchanges, establish Chinese cultural centres in both EU capital cities and at the EU headquarters in Brussels and encouraged the EU to do likewise. Educational exchanges would be enhanced at all levels, a China-EU education cooperation mechanism established and cooperation strengthened in such fields as mutual recognition of academic qualifications, student exchanges, language teaching, exchange of scholarships and teacher training. Vitally, efforts would be exerted to ensure a successful China-Europe International Business School in Beijing by employing top professionals. The teaching of each other's languages was to be encouraged and supported. Health area cooperation should be reinforced especially regarding the prevention and control of SARS, HIV/AIDS and serious diseases, and efforts made to create a mechanism for mutual information and providing technical assistance in the advent of public health hazards. Exchanges and cooperation between the press and those concerned with the media would be enhanced. And exchanges at the personal level and between non-governmental organisations would be encouraged such that visa problems would be promptly handled, illegal immigration combated and so on.

The fourth section addressed social, judicial and administrative concerns. It called for strengthened cooperation on the employment of legal immigrants and the protection of their work rights, and for the two to strive for a bilateral social security agreement, implement their joint social security programme and broaden exchanges in social insurance of various types. It asked for the continuation of legal and judicial cooperation, a broadening of related areas and the like and specifically for exploring cooperation in judicial administration in the combating of cross border crime and the possibility for the creation of a mechanism of annual meetings between high-level judicial officials. China would strengthen exchanges with relevant EU police agencies and with Europol, broaden substantial cooperation with EU member state law enforcement agents and increase coordination in case handling and information sharing, and China and the EU should support and actively participate in UN peacekeeping and other activities.

The fifth section related to the military. High-level exchanges between the militaries of China and the EU would be maintained and the two gradually develop and improve a strategic security consultation mechanism, exchange more missions of military experts and expand exchanges concerning the training of military officers and defence studies. The EU was asked to lift its ban on arms sales to China at an early date 'so as to remove barriers to greater bilateral cooperation on defence industries and technologies'; yet another point consistent with China's asking the EC to keep off its socio-political domain.

IV. Comparing the EU/China policies

One can construct a table listing the details, item by item, with the EU policy on the left column and China's policy responses on the right. That is however not necessary, not only because it should not be a daunting task to recall the details from the description given above, but also because space limitations dictate otherwise. However, every item in the China Paper is more or less a direct response to one mentioned in the EU's. Also, and vitally, that the dominant concern in both policy papers is with issues relating to trade and investment, and particularly for China, investment embodying technology transfer. The essential differences are political in nature: China's reiteration of its being an equal, its integrity respected, its domestic 'democratic' practices not questioned and that the EU should keep out of matters Taiwanese/Tibetan and other 'internal' human rights' considerations. To put it differently, China's response clearly indicates that it will not move an inch on matters concerning its socio-political stance[25];

---

25 It could be claimed that item 9 of the latest EU-China Summit, held in Helsinki on 9 September 2006, contradicts this assertion, but all that it stated was that the 'two sides underlined their commitment to the protection and promotion of human rights and continued to place a high value on the EU-China human rights dialogue. They underlined the importance of concrete steps in the field of human rights and reaffirmed their commitment to further enhance co-operation and exchanges in the field on the basis of equality and mutual respect, while making every effort to achieving more meaningful and positive results on the ground. The EU welcomed China's commitment to ratifying the International Covenant on Civil and Political Rights…as soon as possib-

hence confirming the double-edged nature of the message in the EC policy and its rejection of the second edge.

V. Following up the relationship

The Commission followed up its own policy by offering regular assessments on progress. The first was issued on 15 May 2001[26], the second on 10 September 2003[27] and the latest on 24 October 2006.[28] The first assessment concluded that the global and long-term aims set in 1998 remained largely valid, but there was scope for making EU policy more effective by 'broadening dialogue and co-operation and fine-tuning existing instruments', after taking into consideration developments that took place since then. The emphasis was mainly on 'defining concrete and practical short and medium term action points' that led to the final objectives.

Major changes not only in the EU and China, but also worldwide took place before the second assessment in 2003. In the EU, the € became a reality, enlargement to include ten new members from central and Eastern Europe was imminent and responsibility for justice and home affairs (JHA) introduced[29]. China acceded to the WTO in 2001 and had new leadership installed. Globally, terrorism, in the aftermath of 9/11, weapons proliferation, major threats such as SARS (Severe Acute Respiratory Syndrome) and protectionism dominated. Hence, the assessment not only considered the progress to date but also reiterated the goals set in 1998 and endorsed and concretized in 2001 as well as added these new dimensions. The assessment was endorsed by the European Council on 13 October 2003.

The third assessment began by noting China's enhanced world prowess: emergence as a major power over the previous decade; becoming the fourth largest economy and third largest exporter; and, increasing political dominance. It claimed that impressive economic performance steered China towards a 'significantly more active and sophisticated' foreign policy and aspirations for '*a place in the world commensurate with its economic and political power*' (italics added). With phenomenal growth and

---

le. Both sides confirmed their commitment to co-operate with UN human rights mechanisms and their respect for international human rights standards provided for in relevant international human rights instruments including the rights of minorities'. Affirmations do not add up to a changed Chinese stance, especially when they are 'international', rather than domestic. See press.office@ cnsilium.europa.eu and http://www.consilium.europa.eu/Newsroom. It is because all the summit joint statements are in this fashion, no space has been devoted to them in this paper.

26 Commission of the European Communities (2001).
27 Commission of the European Communities, 'A maturing partnership – shared interests and challenges in EU-China relations', Communication from the Commission to the Council and European Parliament, COM(2003) 533 final, Brussels.
28 Commission of the European Communities (2006b,c). The strategy set up in this document was preceded by that in Commission of the European Communities (2006a), and an overview of the relationship can be found in Commission of the European Communities (2006e).
29 Details of these and other EU developments can be found in El-Agraa (2007a).

huge size, these changes therefore 'have a profound impact on global politics and trade'. As to its own counterpart, it reiterated that apart from being the largest world market, the EU became the home to a global reserve currency; was playing a pivotal role in seeking sustainable solutions to today's challenges, on the environment, energy and globalization; had shown its ability to exert progressive influence internationally; and became the top provider of development assistance. It called on the EU 'to respond effectively to China's renewed strength', because dealing with the main issues the EU was facing such as climate change, employment, migration and security, 'we need to leverage the potential of a dynamic relationship with China based on our values' as well as taking interest in endorsing the Chinese reform process. It concluded that this implied 'factoring the China dimension into the full range of EU policies' at all levels whether domestic or international and 'close co-ordination inside the EU to ensure an overall and coherent approach'. Given these developments and that the 2003 EU-China agreement on a strategic partnership reflected the significance of the relationship between the two, the overall evaluation was that some differences remained, but were being 'managed effectively, and relations are increasingly mature and realistic'. Also, that together with the EU, China was 'closely bound to the globalization process and becoming more integrated into the international system'.

Yet this was a glossy picture since the assessment immediately went on to state that although the fundamental stance must continue to be one of engagement and partnership, with closer partnership, 'mutual responsibilities *increase*' (italics added). Since a partnership must address the interests of both participants, the assessment stressed that 'the EU and China need to work together as they assume more active and responsible international roles, supporting and contributing to a strong and effective mutual system', the aim being that 'China and the EU can bring their respective strength to bear to offer joint solutions to global problems'. In other words, not all was rosy:

> Both the EU and China stand to gain from our trade and economic partnership. If we are to recognise its full potential, closing Europe's doors to Chinese competition is not the answer. But to build and maintain political support for openness towards China, the benefits of engagement must be fully realised in Europe. China should open its own markets and ensure conditions of fair competition. Adjusting to the competitive challenge and driving a fair bargain with China will be the central challenge of EU trade policy in the decade to come. This key bilateral challenge provides a litmus test for our partnership, and is set in more detail in a trade policy paper...[30]

The bottom line was that the EU and China together '*can do more to promote their own interests than they will ever achieve apart*' (italics added).

In sum, since 1995, the Commission's Communication established the fundamentals of the EU's long-term relationship with China, covering political dialogue, including specifically human rights; economics and trade; and the EU-China Cooperation Programme. To these three items, a fourth has recently been added relating to sectoral

---

30 Commission of the European Communities (2006d).

166

dialogues and agreements in more than 20 various fields, encompassing the protection of the environment, science and technology, industrial policy, education, culture and the like. The way China sees its role in the relationship is as depicted in 2003 in the China's EU Policy Paper which largely highlights the trade and investment aspects, but down plays, if not altogether categorically discarding, those relating to the socio-political arena. China's insistence on its 'domestic' socio-political stance is too obvious to warrant discussion, but its delay in the economic response needs explanation and the following section tries to do so.

VI. Explaining China's late reciprocation

As argued above, the trade and investment considerations have been the driving force behind the EU initiation of the relationship. It is therefore pertinent to have the relevant data on them not only for their own sake but also to see if they help explain the late reciprocation by China and its relative coolness to the relationship.

Seen from the EU's own perspective, Table 1 and Figure 1 show the evolution of EU commodity trade with China for two distinct periods: 1985-94, with values in ECUs, the period immediately preceding the initiation of policy; and 1998-2002, in €s, the period of the follow up of the relationship. The data is shown in one chart not just for mere convenience but also because there is no problem with the use of different units of value since the € simply replaced the ECU at par.

Table 1 EU commodity trade with China (ECU/€ billion)

Year	Exports	Imports	Balance
1985	7.181	3.936	3.245
1986	6.533	3.223	2.316
1987	5.533	5.239	2.946
1988	5.801	7.539	Δ1.204
1989	6.372	9.148	Δ2.276
1990	5.271	10.587	Δ5.316
1991	5.605	14.972	Δ9.367
1992	6.852	16.783	Δ9.931
1993	11.302	19.538	Δ8.236
1994	12.447	22.706	Δ10.259
1998	17.411	41.974	Δ24.563
1999	19.351	49.655	Δ30.304
2000	25.498	70.275	Δ44.777
2001	30.087	75.915	Δ45.828
2002	33.981	81.289	Δ47.308

Note: Δ means minus.
Source: collected from Commission of the European Communities (1995), COM(1995) 279 final and (2006) from http://ec.europa.eu/comm/external_relations/china/intro/

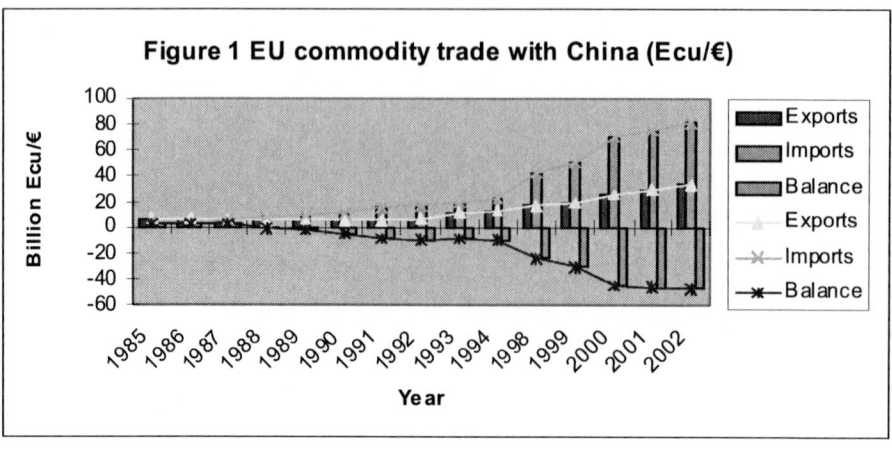

Figure 1 EU commodity trade with China (Ecu/€)

The picture is strikingly clear. After running trade surpluses with China during 1985-87, the EC went into deficits which, apart from a slight decrease in 1993, increased consistently during 1988-94. What is crucial here is that the deficit was not due to declining exports since they were increasing fast during 1991-3, after declining during 1986-90; it was due mainly to the faster growth in imports. In other words, not only was the EC benefiting from China's economic growth, through increasing FDI[31] and national income there stimulating higher imports from the EC, but so too were EC consumers through cheaper imports from China. On the other hand, cheaper imports from China were a manifestation of the reality that EC producers were suffering from lack of competitiveness vis-à-vis Chinese exports, if not from worldwide exports. The combination of looming larger trade deficits with and deteriorating competitiveness relative to the fast-growing China, at a time when competitiveness was uppermost in the EC agenda, must therefore have been instrumental in prompting the EC to pursue the relationship with China. It could of course be argued that the concern with EC competitiveness was not endorsed until 1999 and not formally adopted until 2000[32] in Lisbon as the commitment to galvanize the EC in the following decade into 'the most competitive and dynamic knowledge-based economy in the world, capable of sustainable economic growth with more and better jobs and greater social cohesion'. In other words, the relationship policy preceded them by 4 years. Such an argument would however display complete ignorance of the average time taken by the EC to evolve a 'common position' on a new policy initiative, let alone formally adopt it; indeed competitiveness was what my 1997 paper[33] was all about and journals have very long gestation publications periods.

This disturbing realisation was reinforced by the extent of the flow of EC foreign

---

31 See El-Agraa and Wei (2006b) for the major role played by FDI in increasing Chinese imports.
32 European Council (2000).
33 El-Agraa (1997).

168

direct investment (FDI) going to China. As the data in Table 2 for 1979-93 clearly shows, the EC lagged behind both the US and Japan in all respects, i.e. the EC was suffering from its enterprises not gaining a proportionate share in the fast growing Chinese economy.

Table 2 FDI flows to China, 1979-93

	Project	Contracted capital ($ million)	Used capital ($ million)
EU(12)	2,741	6,952	2,442
EU(15)	3,070	7,319	2,549
US	12,019	14,659	5,237
Japan	7,182	8,935	5,203

Source : Commisson of the European Communities (1995), COM(1995) 279 final

Turning to the Chinese perspective, Tables 3 and 4 provide the global distribution of China's exports and imports during 1980-2003. They show that just over half of the exports and almost two-thirds of China's imports were conducted with Asia, with Europe not only lagging far behind (20.1% and 16.9% respectively), but also less important than North America in terms of exports but slightly more important in terms of imports. Naturally, the picture was even more depressing for the EU relative to the whole of Europe as Figures 2 and 3 reveal[34]. Since the centre of gravity for China's trade was Asia, it was therefore natural for China to be more concerned with that Continent and that goes a long way towards explaining China's cool response to the China-CU relationship. This is reinforced by the investment side of the relationship. As can be gathered from Table 5, the FDI coming to China from the EU, represented by Germany and the UK combined, was minuscule, amounting to 4.04% of actually utilised FDI (3.88% of contracted FDI). This compared with 68.53% (67.32%) from the five Asian nations, of which Japan contributed 7.28% (7.43%), and 8.79% (9.17%) from the US.

---

34   The tables for these figures can be found in El-Agraa and Wei (2006a) or obtained from the author.

Table 3 China's exports by continent and major Area, 1981-2003

year	Asia		Europe		North Amercia		Latin Amercia		Australasia		Africa	
	$ billion	%	$ billion	%	$ billion	%	$ billion	%	$ billion	%	$ billion	%
1981	14.4	66.6	3.6	16.7	1.7	7.9	0.6	2.9	0.3	1.3	1.0	4.6
1982	14.6	66.9	3.2	14.7	1.9	8.8	0.6	3.0	0.3	1.2	1.2	5.4
1983	15.0	67.6	3.7	16.7	1.9	8.7	0.5	2.4	0.2	1.0	0.8	3.5
1984	17.8	68.2	3.9	15.1	2.7	10.3	0.6	2.2	0.3	1.1	0.8	3.1
1985	18.8	68.9	4.5	16.5	2.6	9.4	0.6	2.3	0.2	0.9	0.6	2.0
1986	19.6	63.4	6.9	22.4	2.9	9.5	0.5	1.5	0.3	0.8	0.8	2.4
1987	26.4	67.0	7.3	18.4	3.4	8.7	0.5	1.2	0.4	0.9	1.4	3.7
1988	32.6	68.6	8.4	17.6	3.8	7.9	0.4	0.8	0.4	0.9	1.9	4.0
1989	37.2	70.8	8.8	16.7	4.8	9.2	0.6	1.0	0.5	0.9	0.7	1.4
1990	44.6	71.8	9.3	15.0	5.6	9.0	0.8	1.3	0.5	0.9	1.3	2.1
1991	53.3	74.2	9.4	13.1	6.7	9.3	0.8	1.1	0.6	0.9	1.0	1.4
1992	61.1	71.9	11.4	13.4	9.2	10.9	1.1	1.3	0.8	0.9	1.3	1.5
1993	52.6	57.4	16.4	17.9	18.2	19.8	1.8	1.9	1.2	1.3	1.5	1.7
1994	73.4	60.7	18.8	15.5	22.9	18.9	2.5	2.0	1.7	1.4	1.7	1.4
1995	92.0	61.8	23.0	15.5	26.2	17.6	3.1	2.1	1.9	1.3	2.5	1.7
1996	91.2	60.4	23.9	15.8	28.3	18.7	3.1	2.1	2.0	1.3	2.6	1.7
1997	109.0	59.6	29.0	15.9	34.6	18.9	4.6	2.5	2.4	1.3	3.2	1.8
1998	98.2	53.5	33.4	18.2	40.1	21.8	5.3	2.9	2.7	1.5	4.1	2.2
1999	102.6	52.6	35.5	18.2	44.4	22.8	5.3	2.7	3.1	1.6	4.1	2.1
2000	132.3	53.1	45.5	18.3	55.3	22.2	7.2	2.9	3.9	1.6	5.0	2.0
2001	141.0	53.0	49.2	18.5	57.6	21.7	8.2	3.1	4.1	1.5	6.0	2.3
2002	170.4	52.3	59.2	18.2	74.3	22.8	9.5	2.9	5.3	1.6	7.0	2.1
2003	222.6	50.8	88.3	20.1	98.1	22.4	11.9	2.7	7.3	1.7	10.2	2.3

Source: El-Agraa and Wei (2006a), p. 39.

Table 4 China's imports by continent and major areas, 1981-2003

year	Asia		Europe		North Amercia		Latin Amercia		Australasia		Africa	
	$ billion	%	$ billion	%	$ billion	%	$ billion	%	$ billion	%	$ billion	%
1981	8.9	41.3	4.2	19.4	5.8	27.0	0.9	4.2	0.9	4.2	0.4	1.6
1982	7.0	36.8	3.8	20.1	5.5	29.3	0.9	4.6	1.1	5.7	0.4	1.9
1983	8.7	40.7	5.4	25.1	4.4	20.4	1.5	7.0	0.8	3.8	0.4	1.9
1984	13.4	48.8	6.0	21.9	5.2	18.8	1.1	3.9	1.1	4.1	0.4	1.5
1985	22.6	53.4	9.8	23.1	6.2	14.8	1.0	2.5	1.3	3.1	0.3	0.8
1986	21.0	49.0	12.5	29.2	5.7	13.3	1.6	3.8	1.7	3.8	0.3	0.6
1987	21.6	49.9	11.8	27.3	6.2	14.4	1.2	2.9	1.6	3.7	0.2	0.4
1988	27.7	50.0	13.5	24.4	8.5	15.4	2.2	4.0	1.5	2.8	0.3	0.5
1989	30.7	51.9	14.7	24.9	8.9	15.1	2.4	4.1	1.8	3.0	0.4	0.7
1990	29.0	54.4	12.8	24.1	8.1	15.1	1.5	2.8	1.5	2.8	0.4	0.7
1991	37.6	58.9	12.7	19.9	9.7	15.1	1.6	2.5	1.7	2.7	0.4	0.7
1992	49.0	60.8	16.1	20.0	10.8	13.4	1.9	2.4	2.1	2.6	0.5	0.6
1993	62.6	60.2	24.0	23.1	12.1	11.6	1.9	1.9	2.4	2.3	1.0	1.0
1994	68.8	59.5	25.0	21.6	15.7	13.6	2.2	1.9	2.9	2.5	0.9	0.8
1995	78.1	59.1	27.8	21.1	18.8	14.2	3.0	2.2	3.0	2.3	1.4	1.1
1996	83.4	60.1	27.7	19.9	18.7	13.5	3.6	2.6	3.9	2.8	1.5	1.1
1997	88.4	62.1	25.8	18.1	18.3	12.9	3.8	2.6	3.7	2.6	2.5	1.7
1998	87.2	62.2	26.3	18.8	19.1	13.6	3.0	2.1	3.1	2.2	1.5	1.1
1999	101.7	61.4	32.7	19.7	21.8	13.2	3.0	1.8	4.2	2.5	2.4	1.4
2000	141.3	62.8	40.8	18.1	26.1	11.6	5.4	2.4	5.9	2.6	5.6	2.5
2001	147.2	60.4	48.4	19.9	30.2	12.4	6.7	2.8	6.3	2.6	4.8	2.0
2002	190.3	64.5	53.4	18.1	30.9	10.5	8.3	2.8	6.8	2.3	5.4	1.8
2003	272.9	66.1	69.7	16.9	38.3	9.3	14.9	3.6	8.6	2.1	8.4	2.0

Source: El-Agraa and Wei (2006a), p. 41.

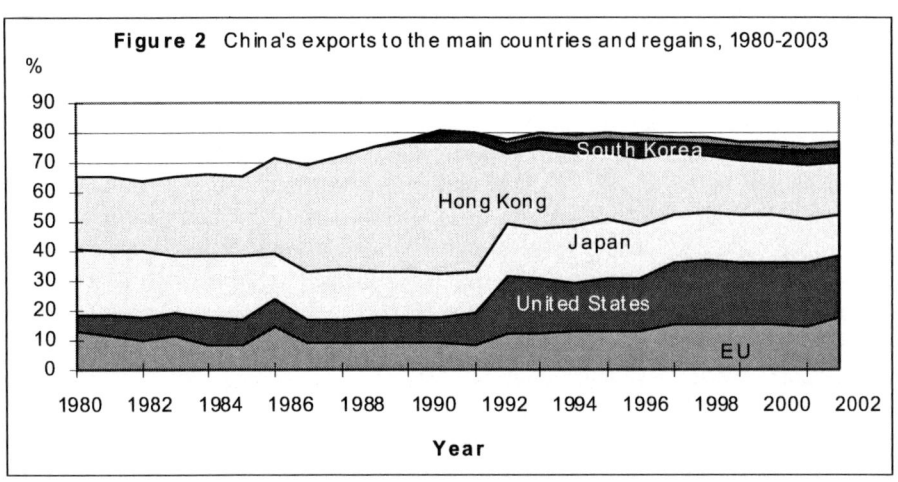

Figure 2 China's exports to the main countries and regains, 1980-2003

Figure 3 China's imports from main countries and regions, 1980-2003

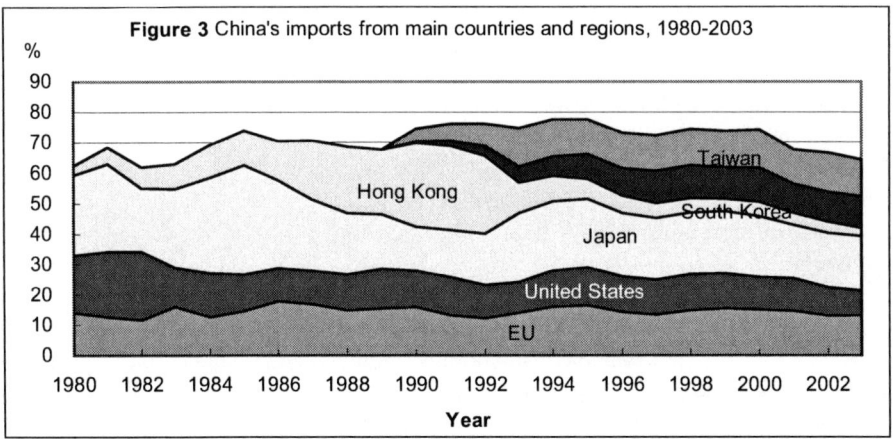

Table 5 The inflows of FDI into China by origin country or region, 1979-2003

Country /Region	Number of Projects	%	Contracted FDI ($ billion)	%	Actually Utilized FDI ($ billion)	%
Hong Kong	224,509	48.25	414.51	43.95	222.58	44.38
United States	41,340	8.89	86.44	9.17	44.09	8.79
Japan	28,401	6.10	57.49	6.10	41.39	8.25
Taiwan	60,186	12.94	70.03	7.43	36.49	7.28
Virgin Islands	8,877	1.91	62.01	6.58	30.17	6.02
Singapore	11,871	2.55	43.57	4.62	23.53	4.69
South Korea	27,128	5.83	36.65	3.89	19.69	3.93
United Kingdom	3,856	0.83	20.84	2.21	11.44	2.28
Germany	3,504	0.75	15.71	1.67	8.85	1.76
Others	55,605	11.95	135.90	14.38	72.27	12.62
Total	465,277	100.00	943.15	100.00	501.50	100.00

Source: El-Agraa and Wei (2006b), p. 10.

Figures 2 and 3 also show that during 1998-2002, the period before the China's EU Policy Paper was issued, the EU's shares of China's imports and exports were, *on the whole*, not changing much; China's exports actually increased in 2002, but that reinforces lack of concern on the part of China[35]. There was therefore no reason for China to have been having concerns about trade relations with the EU. When this is combined with the miserable FDI coming to China from the EU, this conclusion is reinforced. Given no worries and that Asia was the centre of trade and investment gravity for China, one cannot escape the conclusion that it was the bargaining inherent in the WTO negotiations process that persuaded China to indulge in the relationship offered by the EU. Of course, one could counter by asking why the response came after China formally joined WTO in 2001. Again, however, the answer would be that the EU-China Bilateral Agreement, needed for WTO membership, was not concluded until 19 May 2000 (see above); hence for China to have offered its EU Policy paper before or soon after that date would have looked very odd by WTO membership negotiations standards which require extending equal treatment to all. There is also the already mentioned slow Chinese political decision process.

To complete the picture, one has to look into what China has been doing. In 2003, it, together with Japan, South Korea and the ten member nations of ASEAN agreed to create the ASEAN+3 'preferential trading agreement', which is yet to be finalised, but the negotiations for it go back as far as the Asian financial crisis of 1997 if not before. In other words, China has been exerting its utmost in terms of 'cooperation' in Asia; hence its relative coolness to those outside the region, including the EU; rather EU nations since although the EU's 'common commercial policy' (CCP) is conducted by the Commission on behalf of all member nations[36], trade and investment are run nationally. Not only that, but it has been aggressively building a leadership role in East Asia, marginalising Japan: witness its efforts to establish a leadership role for the ASEAN+3 when Japan was the instigator and its relegation of Japan to the sidelines in the January 2007 Asian summit, held in the Philippines; its disapproval of a permanent seat for Japan in the UNSC[37]; and the mentioned enticement of the DPRK back into the 6-nation talks, in spite of the fact that, as stressed at the beginning, in doing so it is also protecting itself against an influx of escapees from the DPRK and

---

35 It could of course be argued that China should have been concerned about its increased exports to the EU since they could have invited trade restricting reactions on the part of the EU: witness the actions taken against Chinese textiles (the bras war) and not settled until September 2005 and shoes. However, that would have hardy been the basis for entering into a 'relationship' along the lines developed here, since it would have been tantamount to asking for a 'dispute-settling mechanism', the appropriate place for which is the WTO which China joined in 2001.

36 See El-Agraa (2007a, Chapter 2) and Brülhart and Matthews (2007.).

37 'China's new clout within Asia was demonstrated last year, when Japan discovered that only tiny Singapore, was willing to come out in strong support of Japan's bid for permanent membership of the United Nations Security Council', wrote Gildeaon Rachman in his 'As America looks the other way, China's rise accelerates', the *Financial Times*, 13 February 2007.

enhancing its own security by promoting a nuclear-free Korean zone[38]. Furthermore, and again as already stated, in holding/hosting the FOCAC summit in November 2006 with all the African nations bar two and following it by the visit by Chinese President Hu Jinato to eight African nations in January/February 2007, his third in two years, it has demonstrated that it is seeking global leadership, again, even though some would counter by reiterating self-interest since much needed energy and mineral resources come to it from Africa, but that hardly negates my assertion and many would argue that the US has been doing likewise for decades and so did Britain when it ruled the waves. What is even more revealing is that although China's President Hu Jintao visited Poland in June 2004 and Germany, the UK and Spain in November 2005, he has still to visit the EU. Revealing because, as already stated the Commission has the sole responsibility for the EU's CCP, i.e. trade matters are not in the hands of individual EU nations; hence in not paying an official visit to the Commission while he is in Europe, he is suggesting that China values bilateral relations more than the China-EU Relationship. This may appear to be fine since the EU is still to have a true 'common foreign policy', but as indicated, the EU has a CCP, so when the President of China excludes the Commission from his European itinerary, his country is clearly behaving in a manner which suggests that it is more concerned with foreign policy matters than with the established EU-China Relationship. Indeed, this conduct is consistent with the mentioned insistence by China in its EU-China Policy Paper on the EU keeping off all matters not related to trade and investment: by its President visiting the Commission, China would seem to be endorsing the 'full package' of the EU-China Policy Paper[39]. And so on and so forth.

---

38   Indeed, in the early morning of 13 February 2007, the 6-nation group finally managed to reach agreement. In the 'deal, which cemented China's emergence as a significant power-broker on the world stage, North Korea agreed to close down its main nuclear reactor within two months and allow international inspectors to verify the process', the *Financial Times*, 'Washington moves towards normal relations; Pyongyang to close reactor under supervision; Japan voices doubts about deal', by Anna Fifield and Daniel Dombey. The DPRK's enticement into the deal was made possible not only because it was promised 50,000 tonnes of heavy fuel oil, food and other aid and another 950,000 tonnes of fuel oil when it provided a complete list of its nuclear programmes and disabled all existing facilities. It was also because the US agreed to commit to bilateral talks with the DPRK which would eventually lead to full diplomatic relations and would resolve within 30 days the dispute over $24 million in DPRK-linked accounts frozen 18 months earlier as part of a US-led crackdown on counterfeiting and money laundering. This important development is not quoted in the main text because the DPRK has a history of reneging on agreements, especially if what it was offered in order to secure the deal did not arrive and to its satisfaction. Nevertheless, it is historic in terms of China's success as a global mediator especially when the deal to the US more or less reversing its policy stance towards the DPRK.

39   One could of course counter by claiming that China may not be aware of the fact that the Commission has the sole responsibility for the CCP, in which case we would be going back decades, evoking a sense of déjà vu, to when Japan had to be subjected by France to the 'Poitiers incident' before it got the message that it had to deal with the Commission, not France, in the face of French intransigence of world trade rules, but one should be very surprised to learn that China is that ignorant of how the EU operates; on this, see, inter alia, Hosoya (1979), Anouil (1985) and El-Agraa (1988).

To put it in a nutshell, China sees itself not only as the major player in Asian affairs, but as the next hegemon; hence its reluctance to be perceived as being concerned with simply a bilateral relationship with the EU, especially when trade and investment are conducted on a national, not an EU, basis. This conclusion is reinforced when one realises the absence of a declared relationship with the US, the number one destination of its exports (see Figure 2) and FDI outflows and to whose currency it pegs the renminbi (or yuan). Although the latest EU data, released in 2004, show that the EU has become China's largest trader, this does not change the basic picture: in 2003 China's imports from the EU exceeded those from the US (respectively, 13.2% versus 8.2% of total Chinese trade; see Figure 3), but the opposite was true for imports (17.9% and 21.1%; see Figure 3). I have not used the 2004 EU data because it is not available in the consistent manner utilised here, but assuming that the data is correct and that the change from 2003 must, in the absence of miracles, be small, the EU must be referring to *total* trade, but the sum of these percentages clearly points to a minuscule difference. Moreover, one could argue that China's primary concern is the APEC forum; adding the US to the Asian picture depicted in this paper. After all, some would postulate that as a regional trade and investment bloc, the APEC forum is an analogous 'declared relationship' between the member nations. Such an argument would not wash, however, given the organisation's commitment to 'open regionalism', i.e. privileges are self-declared and extended to all nations irrespective of membership; otherwise why the recent drive by the US to establish preferential trading agreements with some of APECs's member nations[40]. Moreover, and vitally, to make such a contention would be in direct contradiction to China's ultimate goal of becoming the global leader. In other words, although all indications, including the existence of a large Chinese community in the US, suggest that China should be preoccupied with prioritising the development of a China-US relationship, seeking to become the next hegemon deters China from doing so, especially when the APEC forum, albeit superficially does so. This reinforces the argument in favour of appeasing the EU; one needs friends in order to assume world leadership, so what is better than a group of nations acting in unison as the EU when in reality they conduct their trade and investment individually! Finally,

---

40 At the Osaka, Japan, APEC summit meeting in November 1995, China's President Jiang Zemin announced unilateral tariff cuts of 30% in more than 4000 items, effective from April 1996, to demonstrate APEC's commitment to 'open regionalism', i.e. member nations extended their privileges also to non-members. That was a brilliant ploy because China had to make these cuts in order to stand a chance to become a WTO member! For a detailed discussion within a comprehensive coverage of China's tariff policies, see, inter alia, the Hoover Institution (2007).

one should mention China's military build-up[41] and increasing sophistication[42] which reinforce its determination to become the next hegemon.

VII. Impact of the EU recent enlargements

As argued in the previous paper (cross reference here??), the recent EU enlargements have no immediate significant impact on the EU as an international actor. They may have in the medium and long terms but in only the two areas where all or almost all of the EU nations have mandated a single person or sole institution to act on its behalf. The first is trade, where a single Commissioner is in charge of the EU's Common Commercial Policy, hence speaks on behalf of the EU in the WTO. The second is the European Central Bank which is in charge of the euro and is guaranteed absolute autonomy in carrying out its only objective of price stability in the eurozone. It therefore follows that one should not expect these enlargements to have any immediate repercussions on the EU/China relationship.

In the medium and long terms, however, these enlargements would impact on the relationship. As the acceding countries continue to register high economic growth and in the process possibly inducing the older members to behave likewise, the EU economy would acquire increasing clout in the WTO. This would enable the EU to be more assertive with its demands on China to become more WTO-consistent. At the

---

41 A recent study by the RAND Corporation (2007) estimates China's defence spending to be bet-
    ween 2.3-2.8% of its GDP, which is 40-70% higher than the official figure. It also points out that
    China doubled this expenditure between 1997 and 2003 to nearly reach that of the UK and Ja-
    pan, and it continued to grow at an annual rate of 10% during 2003-2005. Although that still
    leaves China with expenditure equal to one-fifth that of the US, growth at these rates means that
    China will become a formidable military nation within the next few decades. Indeed, China de-
    clared an increase of 17.8% in 2007, raising its defence expenditure to $45.3 billion (€34.4 bil-
    lion), thus reinforcing this trend (see 'Chinese military spending to rise by 18%', the *Financial
    Times* 5 March 2007, and 'Sharp rise in China's military spending: largest increase in 5 years
    follows criticism from US', the *International Herald Tribune* 5 March 2007). Detailed informa-
    tion can also be found at: http://en.wikipedia.org/wiki/China's_military_spedendin and http://
    www.globalsecurity.org/military/world/china/budget.htm. Moreover, Helprin argues that the
    Asian nuclear power that the US must take note of is not DPKR, but China: 'As [the US] have
    cut the stable sea-based leg of [the US's] nuclear deterrent from 37 ballistic missile submarines
    to 14, China works to build its own and a fleet that can provide protected bastions at sea as well
    as hunt down the small number of American boats on station'; see 'Nuclear threat from China',
    The Washington Post, 4 March 2007, p. B07).
    Although a study by the SIPRI (Stockholm International Peace Research Institute) (2005) pro-
    duces lower figures, indicating that China in 2005 surpassed only Japan in relative terms and
    Russia in absolute terms, it corroborates the RAND conclusion that China's military expenditu-
    re is higher than is depicted by the official budgetary figures; for the general website see http://
    www.sipri.org/contents/milap/milex/mex_database1.html and for the specific study in conside-
    ration, see http://first.sipri.org/non_first/result_milex.php.
42 On 11 January 2007, China successfully used a ground-based, medium-range ballistic missile to
    destroy its own old weather satellite from its orbit about 537 miles above Earth.

same time, this would put more pressure on China to oblige, given my argument that the driving force behind China's reciprocation to the relationship has been mainly the economic considerations. Moreover, in doing so, China would become increasingly more aware of the nature of the EU's Common Commercial Policy; hence act in accordance with it.

The same argument would apply to the increasing clout of the euro. As more members join the euro China would find it less productive to deal with the EU member nations on an individual basis. This would not only further enhance the role of the euro, but would at the same time strengthen the EU's Common Commercial Policy in the eyes of China; hence solidify the EU's position in that respect.

Finally, with regard to the items on which I reneged from my sticking to only those considerations where the enlargements would impact on the EU as an international actor (see p. ??, ie cross reference), these enlargements would reinforce those areas where the EU is gaining international clout by simply doing what is in its own internal interest. Such developments would reinforce the mentioned impacts and induce China to adopt a much closer and possibly more amicable approach to its relationship with the EU. Moreover, in doing so, China would be enhancing the prospects for its becoming the next hegemon.

VIII. Conclusion

The conclusion is simple and straightforward. China perceives its relationship with the EU within its overall future prospects which its population size, current economic surge and military build-up and enhanced sophistication suggest are enormous. Serious analysts have concluded that the Chinese do not see themselves as a rising new power, but as Asia's traditional power, now experiencing a renaissance: 'China, they believe, is regaining the status and prestige that it enjoyed until the end of the 18th century'[43]. Here, I go beyond that to argue that China sees its importance not in Asian, but in global terms, and becoming the Asian hegemon will no doubt facilitate paving the way to that higher goal. China therefore sees its relationship with the EU within how it fits into this general picture.

It is interesting to note that a day after this paper was originally finalised, Gideon Rachman[44] of the *Financial Times* wrote: 'The past decade has seen at least three major developments that demonstrate China's burgeoning global power. The first is the way that China is displacing Japan as the diplomatic and economic focus of Asia. The second is the growing power of the Chinese military. The third is the fact that

---

43 See, *inter alia*, Moisi (2007).
44 Gideon Rachman, 'As America looks the other way, China's rise accelerates' in the *Financial Times*, 13 February 2007. Also see Jim Yardley and David E Sanger, 'Nuclear accord set with North Korea: $400 million in fuel oil and other aid, but no agreement on disabling weapons', *International Herald Tribune*, 14 January 2007.

China is now developing global strategic interests'. Although Rachman offered alternative interpretations of these for global power in the future, in the light of what has been discussed in this paper, the picture should be much clearer regarding where China is heading to; hence on its position concerning its relation with the EU.

Finally, it may appear as a contradiction to conclude that the recent EU enlargements may in the medium and long terms draw China closer to its relationship with the EU. There is however no contradiction since an enhanced and amicable relationship with the EU would solidify China's international standing and improve its position relative to that of the United States; hence pave the way for China to pursue, if not all together achieve, its global aspirations.

References:

Algieri, C. (2002) 'EU economic relations with China: an institutional perspective', *China Quarterly* (London), No. 169, March.

Anouil, G. (1985) 'EU-Japan relations at a turning point', *EC Studies in Japan*, Vol. 18, No. 5, pp. 3-12.

Bhagwati, J. (2002), *Free Trade*. Princeton University Press: Princeton, NJ.

Brülhart, M. and Matthews, A. (2007) 'External trade policy', in Ali M El-Agraa (ed.), *The European Union: Economics and Policies*.

China View (2007) 'Chinese President Hu Jintao wraps up successful African trip'. http://news. xinhuanet.com/english/2007-02/11/content_5724926.htm

Commission of the European Communities (1985) 'Agreement on Trade and Economic Cooperation between the European Economic Community and the People's Republic of China – 1985'. http://ec.europa.eu/comm/external_relations/china/intro/1985_trade_agreement.htm

Commission of the European Communities (1994) 'Endorsement by the Council, held on 9/10 December 1994, of the Commission's 'Towards a New Asia strategy', COM(94) 314', *Bulletin of the European Union,* No.7/8, p. 82; No. 12, pp. 14-15.

Commission of the European Communities (1995) 'A long term policy for China-Europe relations. Communication of the Commission, COM(1995) 279 final', Brussels.

Commission of the European Communities (1998) 'Building a comprehensive partnership with China. Communication from the Commission, COM(1998) 181', Brussels.

Commission of the European Communities (2000) 'On the implementation of the Communication "building a comprehensive partnership with China". Report from the Commission to the Council and the European Parliament, COM(2000) 552', Brussels.

Commission of the European Communities (2001) 'EU strategy towards China: implementation of the 1998 Communication and future steps for a more effective EU policy. Communication from the Commission to the Council and European Parliament, COM(2001) 265 final', Brussels.

Commission of the European Communities (2006a) 'A maturing partnership – shared interests and challenges in EU-China relations. Communication from the Commission to the Council and European Parliament, COM(2003) 533 final', Brussels.

Commission of the European Communities (2006b) 'EU-China: closer partners, growing responsibilities. Communication from the Commission to the Council and European Parliament COM(2006) 831 final', Brussels.

Commission of the European Communities (2006c) 'Closer partners, growing responsibilities – a policy paper on EU-China trade and investment: competition and partnership COM(2006) 631 final', Brussels.

Commission of the European Communities (2006d) 'Commission working document, accompanying COM(2006) 631 final: Closer partners, growing responsibilities – a policy paper on EU-China trade and investment: competition and partnership', Brussels.

Commission of the European Communities (2006e) 'The EU's relations with China'. http://ec.europa.eu/comm/external_relations/china/intro/

Eglin, M. (1997) 'China's entry into the WTO with a little help from the EU', *International Affairs*, Vol. 73, Issue 3, July, pp. 489-508.

El-Agraa, Ali M. (1988), *Japan's Trade Frictions: Realities or Misconceptions?* Macmillan: London; St Martin's Press: New York.

El-Agraa, Ali M. (1990) 'The European Community's Internal Market and Japan's response', *EC Studies in Japan*, Vol. 21, No. 5, pp 128-148.

El-Agraa, Ali M. (1997) 'UK competitiveness versus Japanese industrial policy', *Economic Journal*, Vol. 107, pp.1504-1517.

El-Agraa, Ali M. (1999), *Regional Integration: Experience, Theory and Measurement*. Macmillan: London; Barnes and Noble: New York.

El-Agraa, Ali M. (2001) 'Dialogue amongst regional cooperative societies for the promotion of inter-regional cooperation towards global integration', in: Young Seek Choue (ed.), *Toward a Global Common Society through Dialogue among Civilizations*. Institute of International Peace Studies, Kyung Hee University: Seoul.

El-Agraa, Ali M. (2007a), *The European Union: Economics and Policies*. The 8th edition of *The Economics of the European Community* (1980). Cambridge University Press: Cambridge

El-Agraa, Ali M. (2007b), 'The EU/China relationship: not seeing eye to eye?', *Asia Europe Journal*, vol. 5, No. 2, pp. 193-215.

El-Agraa, Ali M. (2004) 'Is globalization causing increased poverty and income inequality?', *Journal of the BWW Society*, Vol. 1, July. Electronic journal, http://www.bwwsociety.org/journal/html/poverty.htm

El-Agraa, Ali M. and Wei, Ping Liu (2006a) 'The direction and composition of China's trade: an unexpected composition of exports for a developing nation?', *Journal of Far Eastern Business and Economy*, Vol. 3, pp.32-56.

El-Agraa, Ali M. and Wei, Ping Liu (2006b) 'Rationalising the dramatic change in the composition of China's exports', *Asia Pacific Economic Journal*, Vol. 4, pp. 1-28.

European Council (1999) 'Cologne European Council', *Bulletin of the European Union*, No. 6, pp. 7-37.

European Council (2000) 'Presidency conclusions: Lisbon European Council 23 and 24 March 2000', Bulletin of the European Union, No. 3, p. 7-17.

Fifield, A. and Dombey, D. (2007) 'Washington moves towards normal relations; Pyongyang to close reactor under supervision; Japan voices doubts about deal', The *Financial Times*, 14 February.

Financial Times, (2006) 12 January.

Financial Times, (2007) 'Chinese military spending to rise by 18%'. 5 March.

Fischer, S. (2003) 'Globalization and its challenges', *American Economic Review*, Vol. 93, pp. 1-30.

Global Security Organization (various years) China's defence budget. http://www.globalsecurity.org/military/world/china/budget.htm.

Griese, G.. (2006) 'EU-china relations – an assessment by the communications of the European union', *Asia Europe Journal*, Vol. 4, No. 4, December, pp.545-553.

178

Helprin, M. (2007) 'Nuclear threat from China', *The Washington Post*, 4 March 2007, p. B07.

Hoover Institution (2007) 'An assessment of Chinese thinking on trade liberalization'. http://www.hoover.org/publications/he/286666.html?show=essay

Hosoya, C. (1979) 'Relations between the European Communities and Japan', *Journal of Common Market Studies*, Vol. 18, No. 2, pp. 159-178.

International Herald Tribune (2007) 'Sharp rise in China's military spending: largest increase in 5 years follows criticism from US'. 5 March.

Kapur, H. (1981), *The Awakening Giant: China's Ascension in World Politics*. Sijthoff & Noordhoff: Alphen aan den Rijin.

Ministry of Foreign Affairs of the People's Republic of China (2003), *China's EU Policy Paper*. October 13. http://www.fmprc.gov.cn/eng/wjb/zzjg/xos/dqzzywt/t27708.htm

Moisi, D. (2007) 'Europe's distant mirror', *The Japan Times*, 27 January.

OECD (2006), *Science, Technology and Industry Outlook 2006*. OECD: Paris. http://www.oecd.org/sti/outlook

Pan, E. (2007) 'China, Africa and oil'. Can be accessed from the website of the Council on Foreign Relations: http://www.cfr.org/publication/9557.

Rachman, G. (2007) 'As America looks the other way, China's rise accelerates', *The Financial Times*, 13 February.

RAND corporation (2007), *China*. http://www.rand.org/hot_topics/china

SIPRI (2005), *The SIPRI military expenditure database*. http://www.sipri.org/contents/milap/milex/mx_database1.html and specifically at http://first.sipri.org/non_first/result_milex.php.

World Bank (1977), *World Development Report 1977*. Oxford University Press: Oxford.

Worldpress.org (2007) 'China to double aid to Africa'. http://www.worldpress.org/print_article.cfm?article_id=2674&dont=yes.

Yardley, J. and Sanger, D. E. (2007) 'Nuclear accord set with North Korea: $400 million in fuel oil and other aid, but no agreement on disabling weapons', *International Herald Tribune*, 14 January.

179

The Political Economy of European Studies in Europe and Asia: Programmes, Pitfalls, Prospects[1]

David Camroux

Introduction

As will become clearer in the following, this background paper i not drafted by someone who is a broad European Studies specialist - other than his undertaking a deal of research and writing on EU-Asian relations – but, rather someone who comes from the field of comparative politics with an area specialization on Southeast Asia. This particular background makes me sensitive to an important issue that also impacts upon my colleagues in Asia teaching and researching in another "area studies" specialization, namely that of the European Union. This issue is that of the tension, albeit a creative tension, between classical disciplinary allegiances (economics, law, history, even language studies etc.) and a concentration on one particular cultural or geographic area, namely Europe. During the numerous evaluation missions I have undertaken in Asia, and especially those for the ESCP programme in China, it became clear that many university administrations were reluctant to see Masters in European Studies degrees created and wanted the traditional disciplinary degrees to be maintained, with European Studies being merely an option. In Europe, specialists on Asia are confronted with a not dissimilar problem created by the fact that their career promotion depends on advancement in research (and to a lesser extent teaching) in their "home" discipline, with their area specialization being of secondary importance. Given that European Studies, by its nature, as practiced both in the EU and Asia is inter, or multidisciplinary, the tension between administrative, economic and career constraints, and the ideal way to undertake the tasks at hand, is exacerbated

In the following I wish to draw from the experience of my own institution in the European Studies programmes we offer and attempt to draw out a number of approaches that can be seen in the way European Studies curricula are developed and to what needs they respond. In the second lengthier part of this background paper this internal European experience is juxtaposed with insights drawn from the observation of European Studies programmes in Asia.

---

1 Other versions of this paper were presented at the 8th ESCP Roundtable in Beijing, 30th -31st October 2007 and also at the ESiA, European Studies in Asia Workshop, The Future of European Studies in Asia, Ateneo de Manila University, Manila 5th – 7th December 2007.

A. The Political Economy of European Studies in Europe

1. A French Example

In Europe there are strong political imperatives behind the flourishing of European Studies curricula. In particular, the development of a sub-discipline in European integration studies can be seen as a vital element in the development of the European project of an ever-closer union. They availability of both national and European funding both for the development of European Studies and the creation of a common European Research Area (i.e. the development of trans-European networks of collaborative research) in the social sciences provides additional incentives. European Studies in Europe has reached a critical mass where it has become almost a discipline in its own right. At the very least it is possible for the teacher or researcher to so "label" him or herself and still find career opportunities. This is not the case in a number of other "area studies" specialisations.

While probably all of us in the academic community would prefer to live in a world in which intellectual and scientific interest takes precedence over other considerations, nevertheless, the real world is rather different. It is, to use the words of the great American philosopher, Madonna, a "material world". In reality we have to take into account questions of demand as well as supply, or rather more simply, are our curricula and degrees marketable? With the increasing role of the private sector in higher education the imperative to ascertain whether our graduates will find intellectually and financially enriching jobs should be of concern to us. At the same time the concern to develop marketable curricula can sit uneasily with another major imperative, namely that of ensuring continuity and sustainability in our teaching and research by making sure we are grooming the next generation of scholars so as at some point in the future we of the older generation will be happily made redundant!

The situation in my institution, the Institut d'Etudes Politiques, or Sciences Po as it is more commonly and affectionately known, demonstrates this dichotomy. In point of fact we offer two Masters programmes in European Studies. The first, a Master of Research degree is housed in our doctoral school. The second, a Master of European Affairs is housed within the professionally oriented graduate school programmes of the Institute. The former programme has ostensibly as its ambition to train researchers in comparative politics and comparative sociology with a European specialization, while the latter seeks to educate practitioners in the area of European Affairs, a specialization promoted as akin to that of professional training in an MBA or a MPA. In practice, the different orientations of the two programmes do not lead to radically different results, for only about one in four or five of the Masters of Research graduate students would actually go on to write a PhD thesis and seek employment in teaching and research.

Be that as it may, it is illuminating to examine the course presentation for the Masters of European Affairs. According to the Sciences Po web site[2] the programme is designed to prepare graduates to work in four areas:

a. The European Union public service (Commission, Parliament, Council, etc)
b. National public services:
    – Permanent delegations in Brussels, embassies of non-members, representative bodies of international organisations
    – Cooperation bodies / inter-ministerial coordination bodies
    – Ministries of foreign affairs
    – National experts
c. Political professions: parliamentary assistants, members of ministerial cabinets.
d. Interest groups, lobbying: regional representative offices, corporate lobbyists, consultants and advocacy groups.

This listing would seem to suggest that European Studies programmes in Europe
and, in particular, their great diversity, are at least to some extent designed to respond to specific needs in the labour market. The question that immediately springs to mind is whether this is, or should be, the case in Asia.

2. Curricula: "Europe... where you sit, is what you see?"

To simplify it is helpful to classify European Studies curricula in Europe as taking one of four approaches. In using the term European Studies, I am using it in the sense underlying most programmes in Asia, namely that of European integration studies:

a. **Europe from an "area studies" perspective: the European Union as** *sui generis*. In this approach the unique aspects of European integration are stressed by taking generally a long-term view juxtaposing the present period of unification with previous periods of conflict and disunity.
b. **Europe from a comparative politics / comparative sociology / comparative economics perspective**. With the development of studies of what has been described as the "new regionalism" this approach would appear, in my view, to have increasingly greater currency.[3] Above all, given the sense in which regional integration worldwide is one of the ways nation states and societies are attempting to cope with globalization, the comparative regionalist school is on the ascendant.

---

2   www.sciences-po.fr/formation/master_scpo/mentions/affaires_europeenes/index.htm#2
3   On this approach, one which is largely shared by this author, see: Fredrik Söderbaum & Timothy Shaw (eds) *Theories of the New Regionalism: A Palgrave Reader*, Basingstoke, Palgrave Macmillan, 2003 and Mario Telo (ed.) *European Union and New Regionalism: Regional Actors and Global Actors in a Post-Hegemonic Era*, Aldershot, Ashgate, 2001.

c. **An international relations perspective**. As the EU has both enlarged and deepened, so has the study developed of the European Union as a global actor. The particular forms of soft power used to promote its interest expressed in the notions of civilian power Europe[4] and Europe as a normative power are coming under increasing scrutiny.[5]

d. **European Law**. Given the high level of institutionalisation in Europe, the one discipline that has now been in part captured by Europeanists is that of European law. Indeed the corpus of legislation and the professional opportunities offered for the specialised graduate is sufficiently great to ensure promising careers.

In reality, as far as I can gather, none of the above four approaches exists in a kind of pure form associated with a particular European Studies programme in Europe. This diversity is undoubtedly a source of enrichment for the whole European project.

B. The Political Economy of European Studies in Asia

1. Finding a "Niche Market"

When one turns to the Asian situation it is clear that a large number of these potential employment outlets mentioned above are not available to Asian graduates in European Studies. The various Asian foreign ministries can only absorb a limited intake of European specialists and probably they, like foreign ministries elsewhere, award a priority to language skills on the grounds that "one learns about ones geographical area of competence by being posted there". There is clearly a need to encourage the foreign ministries and other State bodies to appreciate and to value the kinds of competence obtained in a European Studies programme. Elsewhere in the public sector, the employment opportunities for graduates in European Studies are limited, or so is my initial impression. As China and India take on more assertive international roles, attempting to project their soft power, it can be hoped that employment opportunities will open up overseas in international organisations for graduates in European Studies. Once again, creating this demand will require efforts in both adapting, and communicating on the usefulness of, a European Studies curriculum. The one area of hope, is that provided by employment opportunities in the private sector. It would appear but common sense to assert that European multinationals in Asia should be the first target for employment of Chinese graduates in European Studies. Moreover as Chinese and other Asian multinationals develop and expand in relation to the world's

---

4   See Mario Telo, *Europe: a Civilian Power?: European Union, Global Governance, World Order*, new edn, Basingstoke, Palgrave Macmillan, 2007.

5   See Ian Manners "Normative Power Europe: A Contradiction in Terms", *Journal of Common Market Studies* 40 (2) 2002: 235-258 and Zaki Laïdi, *La norme sans la force : l'énigme de la puissance européenne,* Paris, Presses de Sciences Po, 2005.

largest market, namely the European Union, they should too become a niche for Asian European studies graduates. Yet have these labour market opportunity questions been really addressed in the setting up of European Studies programmes in Asia?[6]

Prior to the possibility of obtaining European Union funding various programmes in Asia had rather different outcomes. What many consider to have been then the best European Studies programme in Southeast Asia, namely that of the National University of Singapore was abolished by a fiat of the then Vice Chancellor who disbanded the sub-department in charge of the programme making it into a virtual degree.[7] At the Baptist University of Hong Kong a similar type of programme one which places an emphasis on learning one or two European languages other than English has survived. These two experiences, and experiences elsewhere in Asia have confirmed that the strong support of university administrations is vital for the continuation of European Studies programmes. With the end of EU financing for the 18 Chinese European Studies centres supported under the ESCP project, in my view, possibly at least half will disappear, not only because the critical mass of sustainable competence has not been reached, but also because the commitment of university and other authorities is lacking.[8]

The first question that confronts the organizer of a European Studies curriculum is to answer the question, why? Ever since former Commission President Romano Prodi declared that the European model of integration was an "export product" of the European Union. When one looks at the various European Commission financed European Studies Programmes in Asia - starting with the initial ill-fated three university Filipino consortium through to that of the successful European Studies programme in Thailand at Chulalongkorn University - followed by the rather atypical programme in Vietnam and finally to two heavy weight programmes, that in China, which at least in its first stage is drawing to an end and that in India which should begin shortly – they all have at their origins a willingness on the part of the European Union to make a political statement in these Asian countries. This unilateral political motivation is somewhat more subdued in the jointly financed programmes in Japan and Australia, for example.

---

6   A somewhat superficial "tracer study" on job opportunities was organized by the German con-sultancy GOPA in charge of the ESCP project. Unfortunately it was not really possible to make judgments on such a small pool of graduates given the ESCP had only been functioning for two or three years. However, this was besides the point for this particular consultancy firm the study merely provided further cash flow.

7   Indications are, however, that this will change soon and that at NUS a new programme will re-find the former autonomy and glory of its predecessor.

8   Given that China is no longer a developing country and given the massive European trade deficit with China it is going to become increasingly difficult to justify funding European Studies in China as a form of development assistance.

2. Politically Inspired Decisions and their Consequences

In Asia there are incentives to promote European Studies, incentives often, but not always, vectored through the various European Union delegations. This can only be applauded. For a political scientist, one who is often struck by the gap between discourse and action, the willingness by the European Commission to follow declarations by acts (i.e. funding and investment) is indeed refreshing. However, the ability to acquire EU funding can also have some unintended side effects, namely that certain institutions and individuals without a prior commitment to European Studies may simply re-label an existing centre or programme without providing any new content. The Asia-Europe Institute at the University of Malaya under its first director was one such blatant subterfuge. Lest the impression be given of suggesting this only occurs in Asia, there are also numerous European examples of putting the "cart" of funding, before the "horse" of a sound motivating project. For example having just undertaken for the first time evaluations within the FP 7 research programme I was struck by the disparity between applications anchored in a clear, coherent research programme and those that were merely not very subtle attempts to obtain funding, per se.

a. Partnership Mismatches in Asia

To state the obvious, in Asia, the EU has to deal with governments as they are, not how some Europeans at least would like them to be. The strongest example of political imperatives outweighing others, with the possible exception of the Vietnamese programme I shall return to shortly, is in China. The motivation behind the ESCP was essentially political, both from the European Commission and also from the Chinese Ministry of Commerce.[9] This is not to suggest in the least that political motivations are somehow inferior, or even misguided, compared to other, say, academic ones. Far from it, they are simply, different resulting in the outcomes they engender being different from those they would have resulted from a purely academic motivation. One tangible result, both in Vietnam and in China, was that the EU had to accept the organizing partner proposed by the governments of these countries: respectively the Vietnamese Academy of Social Sciences and the Chinese Academy of Social Sciences. In my view these were rather unfortunate choices, not because of the quality of institutions nor people, but simply because these two academies have different agendas from those of local universities and, even more so, of European academic partners. As

---

9   As EU-China relations are essentially economic, the interlocutor of the Commission in China, as in India, has been the Ministry of External Trade. It was it, and not the Ministry of Education, who designated CASS as the Chinese partner. In India having to work through the Ministry of Trade, who was involved in an administrative "turf war" with the Ministry of Education meant that an initial project from 2001-2 for European Studies centres in India was never implemented.

official think tanks linked to central governments their role is to advise their administrations. In the case of the Chinese ESCP this led, it could be argued, to a mismatch with the other Chinese actors in the university system. As is often the case this resulted in disagreements over orientations and access to funding. Moreover the administrative cultures were quite different leading to unnecessary tensions. At least in the Chinese case existing European Studies centres were given a new boost and some newer ones encouraged. In Vietnam the three-year programme died at the end because the Vietnamese counterpart offered no teaching and there was no effective relaying of European Studies expertise into Vietnamese universities where a receptive audience did exist. Indeed my three years of experience in the European consortium involved with the Vietnamese Academy of Social Sciences left me with the distinct impression that the latter saw the whole programme as merely a short-term rent-seeking exercise.

b. Partnership mismatches in Europe

EC supported European Studies programmes in Asia come under the auspices of DG Relex and not as is the case in Europe under DG Education or DG Research. One of the results has been that private sector consultancy groups, whose very existence depends on being well and truly attached to the "Brussels' teat", have become involved in drafting various bids. The advantage of this is that these consultancy firms possess technical competence, access to decision makers and the kind of sensitivity to the expectations of the Commission at times lacking in academic institutions. In the best cases a rather dynamic synergy can thus emerge with each party accepting his/her responsibilities and the ensuing rewards. In the worst case, these private consultancy firms can treat academic partners in a perfunctory manner, once the contract with the Commission has been won. In my over ten year's experience the most reprehensible private consultancy group I have encountered is GOPA, who as leader of a consortium with six European academic partners, won the technical assistance contract for the European Studies Centres in China programme. The contract having been won they then failed to provide a consortium agreement and, in effect, barred their partners from any major contribution to, and thus benefit from, the technical assistance contract. Furthermore, by virtually using only the human resources from one EU member state, ie their own Germany, they betrayed the pan-European nature that should be at the bottom of any cooperation with Asia. Fortunately it would seem that GOPA is an isolated case.

c. Triangular marriages

Three would appear to be the favourite number in Brussels. The Erasmus Mundus programme, for example, requires that at least three and normally five universities share in the awarding of a degree for it to be able to obtain this particular label. Marriages of two are already difficult enough, both in life and in academia, but threesomes are even more complicated. Yet the involvement of at least three partners seems to be a minimum requirement for European Studies to be able to obtain support from the European Commission, and in the case of Australia and Japan, from national governments. The difficulty is that, for many observers, generally there is a dominant partner, a subsidiary partner… and a sleeping or nominal partner. This situation is generated by two structural factors, namely possession of the required competence and, as previously intimated, variable levels of internal support provided by university administrations. In the short term these threesomes may function while the EC funding lasts but, as was the case in the first EC supported programme in the Philippines, involving De La Salle, Ateneo de Manila and the University of the Philippines, it was impossible to continue afterwards, when the previous partners returned to functioning in a competitive relationship with each other.

The most flagrant case of an engineered marriage in European Studies I have witnessed recently was the creation of the Silk Road Combined Centre in European Studies involving four universities in Northwest China, only two of which possessed some initial competence. Given that some of these partners are several hundred kilometres away from the others and, more importantly, that no financial provisions were made for joint activities, the future of this politically correct initiative[10] seems dim indeed.

d. The conundrum of supporting established centres versus new start-ups

EU delegations in Asian countries are confronted with a difficult dilemma in regard to supporting European Studies. On the one hand, their overriding brief is to strengthen relations with the host country and to promote a positive vision of the EU. On the other hand, they have to meet the expectations within Europe and amongst Asian academic institutions, on promoting academic quality. In my experience, not only in Asia but also in the United States and Australia, this comes down in practical terms to either supporting existing European Studies centres with a proven track record or helping start ups. Both positions can be intellectually and honestly defended. In recent years the tendency has been to support start-ups. The results however are mixed. To take the Japanese case, for example, while it is generally accepted that the start up consortium in the Kansai region has made great strides, the new consortium in Tokyo - which was chosen over a competing consortium with a proven track record – has been to date something of a disappointment. Once again this dilemma is something felt also in Europe, where, for example, in evaluating research proposal sent to the EC we are also at pains to make sure new candidates and new entrants should also be given a chance.

---

10   Aid to northwest China is indeed a priority in Beijing in its relations with external actors.

Final thoughts

To state once again the obvious, European Studies, like most academic endeavours, is fragile depending ultimately on individuals. We all have examples of areas of expertise in particular institutions that die with the departure of key staff. The challenge is to ensure institutional continuity that survives the absence of particular individual inputs. Once again this is both an Asian and a European challenge. To give but two examples. In Alfredo Robles, the Philippines has undoubtedly the most internationally respected scholar in European Studies in Southeast Asia.[11] Yet a lack of support for developing his expertise in his home institution and the demand for his competence elsewhere means that he has joined, like many of the Philippine's finest intellectual workers, the brain drain from this country at least temporarily. To use a sporting analogy, European Studies centres are a little like a football team requiring "strikers" as well as "defenders", goal keepers as well as the mid field that ensure final victory. Directing and managing a centre are skills that are not necessarily acquired during a career in research and teaching. A second example concerns Fudan University in Shanghai where under the long term leadership and generous commitment of Professor Dai Bingran, the European Studies Centre has been able to impose itself as one of the top two or three centres in China. The key to Professor Dai's success is the nurturing of at least two new generations of scholars who will ensure the sustainability of this centre.

Following from the previous rather personal, perhaps even quixotic, analysis let me be transparent in my own special pleading. If resources are scarce, which they are, and political will in short supply, which it may well be, both should perhaps be directed in priority to the young upcoming scholars, the docs and post-docs, who are the key to the sustainable development of European Studies in Asia. Hopefully many of the participants in this workshop would share this objective.

Conclusions

One cannot expect the demand for Asian European Studies graduates, and thus European Studies per se, to develop spontaneously. In a sense, the "suppliers of the supply", in other words, European Studies centres in Asia, will need to sell more effectively their programmes and their graduates. It is paradoxical that in Europe today graduates with good Chinese language skills, as well as knowledge of contemporary China gleaned through specialised degrees, can now seek top jobs and demand premium salaries. The objective in Asia should be to stress the importance of knowledge of the EU as an appropriate complement to skills in, hopefully, more than

---

11 His latest work, *The Asia-Europe Meeting: the Theory and Practice of Interregionalism* is due for release by Routledge early in 2008.

one European language. For this to occur, adapting European curricula in European Studies – and then developing new elements that correspond to the needs of the Asian "market" – is of utmost importance. Moreover as in Europe, significant amounts of time and effort will still be required in ensuring the support of local university administrations and national governments in Asia.

To conclude on an optimistic note. As the European Union as an entity continues to impose itself as a global actor of the first order – a rise concomitant with the beginnings of the demise of the US hegemony - so will national governments, the business community and civil society in Asian countries gradually become more cognisant of the "unidentified political object", to use Jacques Delors' felicitous phrase, that is Europe. Hopefully, as this happens, support for European Studies in Asia will strengthen at the grass roots and European Studies graduates will find the job opportunities they deserve.

The EU and Its Direct and Indirect Neighbours from the East:
The Balance of Relations between France, Germany, Poland, Russia and Ukraine as the Key to a Common Space of Stability, Prosperity and Security

Marc-Antoine Eyl-Mazzega

The fall of the Berlin wall, the break–up of the Soviet Union and the Warsaw military pact, and the reunification of Germany marked a turning point in international relations as they made possible the spread of democracy, prosperity and security to the entire European continent and ended the division of Europe into two antagonist blocks. These crucial events dramatically changed the European Union's (EU) strategic environment: the most important foreign policy and security challenge for the EU and its member states ceased to be dealing with a direct military threat and the prospect of a mutual nuclear destruction. The 'red threat' suddenly disappeared but, instead, the EU and its member states immediately had to cope with the security vacuum that was left at their Eastern boarder and the necessity to neutralize and dismantle remaining military arsenals, and enclose its Eastern neighbours into cooperative policies and regimes.

First, came the denuclearisation of Ukraine, the non–proliferation issue and the limitation of nuclear warheads between the United States (US) and Russia. This was less an achievement of the EU itself than one of some of its member states and of the US, the Group of Seven (G7) and of the North Atlantic Treaty Organization (NATO). The role of the EU, however, later became crucial in ensuring the stabilisation of the Central and Eastern European states (CEES) and their successful political and economical transition. The EU was able to prevent a return to Cold war authoritarian and conflicting schemes and these states were progressively inserted into EU–lead regimes and institutions, committed to cooperative policies, and committed to reform and Europeanize. The Council of Europe further played an important role in committing the CEES states to adopt and respect Human rights, especially the rights of minorities. At the end of the 90s, the EU and its member states also had to deal with the Balkan wars and the resulting peace building challenges, though here again, NATO played a major role.

NATO's 1999 and 2004 enlargements and EU's 2004 and 2007 enlargements were largely seen as allowing to close the Cold war chapter and were thus celebrated as Europe's eventual reunification – all the more that territorial and ethnic wars in the Balkans had been ended. For the EU, the 90s overall looked like a time of relief: the progressive elimination of conflicts and threats seemed to be paving the way for a never–ending period of peace and prosperity. EU's foreign policy agenda thus increasingly focussed on soft threats and on more global challenges: promoting human rights, fighting against global climate change and diseases in Africa, combating Islamic terrorism, solving low–intensity conflicts, managing the growing gap between the globalization's insiders and outsiders, supporting non–proliferation and the elimination of weapons of mass destruction, and dealing with the rise of China, India and Brazil as economical and political giants and 'rival partners'.

But the 90s, in many respects, precluded to very dramatic developments, which have their roots in these temporary and illusionary times. Indeed, since the 2000s, the Cold war period has caught up the EU and backfired with multiple fundamental consequences and challenges. It is now clear that neither the 2004 and 2007 EU enlargements, nor the 1999 and 2004 NATO enlargements, have solved the security and stability challenges which resulted from the break–up of the Soviet Union and which have been extended to the entire Eurasian continent. For sure, stability, democracy and prosperity have been successfully fostered in the former EU–15 neighbourhood. Nevertheless, this was just part of the job done.

Today, as EU's borders have extended, Russia and Ukraine are EU's new crucial direct and indirect neighbours. Their domestic, foreign and energy policies, let alone their insufficient degree of economical and political transformation as well as their low commitment to cooperation and alignment with EU requirements, are structurally challenging the stability, the security, the cohesion, the credibility and the prosperity of the EU. EU's future role and importance as an international actor decisively depends upon its capacity to strengthen its relations with Russia, especially by committing Russia to cooperative policies, and to ensure that Ukraine Europeanizes and progresses in its transition and nation–statehood building.

This paper argues that Russia and Ukraine now represent an equivalent challenge for the EU–27 than the Central and Eastern European states did, in the 90s, for the EU–12 and later the EU–15. The wake–up call has already rung. On the one hand, Putin's Russia is a crucial actor to the EU but has been pursuing a very assertive foreign policy agenda with objectives that oppose EU's interests and provide low commitments for cooperation in line with EU's requirements, especially in the energy domain. On the other hand, Ukraine's transition remains fragile, mostly as a consequence of its deteriorating energy security, and is challenged by the ambiguous policies of its elites, Russia's policies, and EU's reluctance to offset them. The Russia-EU-Ukraine triangle of relations has thus been increasingly a conflicting one. Issues at stake in these relations need to be identified and addressed by relevant strategies and policies.

The state of relations between France, Germany, Poland, Russia and Ukraine thus appears to be the key to the stability and security of the Eurasian continent. The intricate nature of these states' interests and their presently conflicting agendas make very clear the pressing necessity for a mutual commitment to cooperation and understanding. These states must negotiate a settlement of their conflicting relations and negotiations will especially need to focus on future enlargements of EU and of the NATO and on their relations with Ukraine and Russia, and rely on the Weimar Triangle, which could be further deepened and extended to Ukraine, could play an important role. Ultimately, the success of this bargaining will depend on EU's capacity to take distance and autonomy from the United States' policy in the region.

This paper in a fist part looks into the nature and importance of these challenges, then examines why and how the EU fails to address them and finally tries to make some constructive and realistic proposals and recommendations on how best the EU could face its responsibilities. Indeed, most contributions on EU's relations with Russia and Ukraine are descriptive, or mainstream, and miss to provide operational and global solutions to a very concerning problem.

Ukraine and Russia have emerged as the most immediate and crucial security and stability challenges for the EU

Russia threatens the balance of power on the Eurasian continent

Russia and the EU are currently preparing to negotiate a new Partnership and cooperation agreement to renew the institutional framework of their relations, although the Polish veto in retaliation to Russia's export ban on Polish meat has so far impeded the EU to agree on a common mandate for negotiations with Russia. But EU-Russia relations have been decisively shaped by Putin's accession to the Russian presidency in 2000 and by a new global environment of sustained high energy prices and scare hydrocarbon resources which have changed the importance of Russia and the way Russia behaves as an international actor. Russia is no more the same docile international actor as it was during the 90s. The EU and Russia are occupied both by bilateral and global issues which come across and Russia and the EU seem to share increasingly distant and rival interests so that cooperation has much suffered in recent times. Russia has definitely not evolved in the direction the EU would have liked or thought. For sure, the EU has profited by Russia's weakness and chaos in the 90s as it has integrated all CEES and the Baltic states in the EU and NATO, and was surprised by Russia's new assertive policies and strive for international respect and consideration. It is obvious that Russia has become an international actor that cannot be ignored any more and whose involvement and cooperation is fundamental to most regional, international and global issues. As a consequence, relations are at their lowest point and do not provide much short-term prospect for improvement. This is highlighted by:

- Global economical and political issues. Russia seems to share no interest in EU's agenda of fostering global development and human rights' protection and has increasingly turned to be an obstacle for the EU as shows its reluctance to further pressure Iran on the nuclear issue. Russia favours the status quo and a multilateral world order in which the EU and the US would not be preponderant and in which Russia would have an important, if not decisive say, at least in Eurasia, the Middle East, and Asia. This is also illustrated by its opposition to NATO enlargement and to NATO missions' extension, and its opposition to EU's position on the Kosovo issue. Russia thus aims at preventing the US and the EU from becoming too influential and at protecting its traditional allies to whom it exports strategic technologies such as weapons, energy, or civilian nuclear facilities, which are crucial for Russia's economical boom and its influence in international affairs (China, Iran, Syria, India, Pakistan). And Russia gets quite well acquainted on the short-term by political instability in the Middle East because this leads to higher energy prices.

- The energy issue. The EU is heavily dependent on Russia for its gas supplies but Russia tries to take advantage at the EU's expense of this situation: Russia uses energy as a foreign policy instrument (supply cuts to Ukraine, Belarus, Azerbaijan, Georgia, Latvia), and has been fostering its capacity to exert leverage and to maximize revenues from the energy sector. Putin has been nationalizing most parts of the domestic energy sector, centralizing power and revenues, and has been trying to extend Russia's state sector's internal monopoly position on the extraction and production to the transportation and downstream distribution sectors abroad, thus increasing its control and leverage on EU's energy supplies and its capacity to be a rent-seeker at the expense of transit states and of the final consumer. Russia is further posing a risk to EU's energy security as it limits foreign investments in its domestic production sector and refuses any third party access to its pipelines. This is a very important concern as Russia lacks investments and technologies to increase its gas output against the background of aging fields and infrastructures needing to be replaced by new ones. Furthermore, Russia's low regulated domestic tariffs bring no incentive for energy savings and Russia's domestic gas consumption is soaring, which adds to the fundamental concern that Russia could end up not supplying as much gas to the EU as the EU needs it, thus jeopardizing EU's energy security.

- The common neighbourhood issue. In its neighbourhood or 'near abroad', Russia is a destabilizing factor as it seeks to maintain the status quo and impedes any democratic or economical transformation that would weaken its relations to FSU states. Russia uses the energy instrument (blackmail through transit monopoly, gas and oil supplies, control−taking of infrastructures and local distribution networks, reduction of dependence from transit states to increase leverage and revenues and reduce the transit risk), the economical instrument (anti−dumping measures, import bans, investments and control−taking of the energy sector) and the military leverage (military basis, privileged arms supplies, military cooperation) to preserve its influence and maintain these states in its grip. FSU states are facing tremendous pressures to remain in Russia's grip and Russia feels aggressed and threatened by EU's and NATO's policies in its traditional zone of influence. Russia's attitude during the Ukrainian "Orange revolution" was precisely meant at indicating to the West that there's a red line in the EU's/ NATO's/ US's relations with the FSU states that should never be passed again. These tensions are likely to be exacerbated by the US's determination to let Georgia integrate quickly NATO in making the country part of the „Membership Action Plan".

- The democracy and human right issue. Russia recognizes that its domestic Human right and democracy records can be improved but systematically insists that democracy and human rights problems also exist in the EU /US, underpinning that problems in the EU are similar to those in Russia and paying no attention at all to EU's critics. Russia's political system is characterized by a strong presidential system and very weak checks and balances as power concentration in Putin hands' is important, there's a fragile freedom of expression and civil society and a strong intertwining between politics and economics. There has been no improvement in Russia's democratization since Putin's accession to power, and EU-Russia relations in this domain have brought no breakthrough at all. Russia's poor democracy record, that makes it look like between a managed democracy and a soft authoritarian regime, comes across with a strengthening nationalism and the idea that western forces seek to harm Russia and that Russia has to unite and stand firm. As a consequence, the emphasis is put on the Russian identity in an exclusive pattern and on the affirmation of the 'great state' and order society as a ultimate goal rather than democratic development. And the EU is incapable of having any leverage on the present situation

Thus, Russia's foreign and domestic policies have become a central foreign policy challenge to the EU. All the more that Russia's transition and stabilization is far from guaranteed as the country is about to enter a crucial electoral period (legislative election in December 2007 and presidential election in March 2008). The apparent political stabilization in Russia under Putin's rule hides very harsh power struggles as rival clans compete for the control of the political power and of billions of dollars. Vladimir Putin seems to be likely to remain in power first as Prime minister and then as President or head of Gazprom for at least an other decade but what would happen in case Putin suddenly were to disappear (accident, assassination) is completely uncertain. And Russia's economical boom is very fragile as Russia's economy is poorly diversified, is driven by high energy export revenues, is impeded by bureaucracy and a weak rule of law, and the geographical and social disparities are huge. The plan to increase state regulated domestic prices will face strong resistance from consumers and industrialists and might create inflation and decrease industry's competitiveness. Thus, Russia definitely remains unpredictable and its evolution uncertain which is further a risk to the EU.

The EU has obviously crucial interests to preserve. So far, the EU has not been able to improve relations with Russia and build the basis for a fundamental cooperative partnership, which is illustrated by the failure of the Four common spaces concept, and the upcoming negotiations over a new Partnership and cooperation agreement, which are likely to end-up in a deception. This comes despite Russia is a top foreign policy priority for the EU and despite the EU has made a lot of concessions to Russia over the last years: The EU has engaged with Russia in a strategic partnership, which it has not done with any other FSU state, and has remained passive while Russia was strengthening its grip on other FSU states as EU's relations to other FSU states have been kept at a minimal ambition in order not to provoke and risk a deterioration of relations with Russia. Putin has enjoyed a near free hand as he has strengthened the state's control over society and the power of some clans and made political and economical reforms going backwards. As an illustration, the US State Secretary C. Rice expressed her concern over a too important power concentration in Russia after Putin announced he may lead the presidential party list at the legislative election and remain Prime minister while the EU stated that "this is an internal Russian affair". And Putin was not much concerned both by EU's energy security worries, especially as he cut gas supplies to Ukraine and Belarus, and by some member states' temporary insistence on human rights issues. The current concept of relations doesn't have brought the expected changes and improvements and Russia and the EU are increasingly distant to another.

Ukraine as the other pillar of the stability and security on the Eurasian continent

Ukraine has been increasingly drawing attention since the "Orange revolution". The "Orange revolution" came as a surprise in Europe and European media and public opinion discovered the existence of Ukraine and its problems. Then, one year later, public opinion and policy makers were faced with Russia cutting off its gas supplies to Ukraine, thus leading to pressure reduction on the export pipelines to the EU. Each time, Russia was involved and played a dubious role.

Ukraine has a strategic importance for the EU and decisively influences its stability, prosperity and security. Ukraine is crucial for:

- The balance of power on the Eurasian continent, especially as regards Russia. Ukraine's central geographical location in-between the EU and Russia makes it a strategically important state, if not decisive. Ukraine borders 4 EU member states and has further more a large access to the strategically important Black Sea. Ukraine is a regional power and a central pillar of the Eurasian continent's stability. Nevertheless, Ukraine is at the core of a security vacuum that stretches from the EU's external boarder to the Pacif Ocean and that includes Central Asia, Afghanistan, Iran, and the South Caucasus. Russia, the same vacuum that suddenly resulted from the break-up of the Soviet Union at EU's then Eastern boarder, especially for Germany and Austria. Ukraine, given Russia's increased uncooperative politics, represents an asset to the EU, and cannot any longer be considered as an obstacle, especially in energy relations.
- The transformation and Europeanization of Russia. Ukraine can have an influence on Russia's transformation. Ukraine has indeed become a model of transition for all FSU states and civil societies and its democratization and Europeanization will no doubt also benefit Russia on the long run through a spill over effect.
- EU's energy security / economical stability. A large majority of Russia's gas exports to EU transit through Ukraine. Ukraine, together with Turkey, are the most important transit states for supplies to the EU. There are so far no real alternatives except through Belarus and Turkey, and even after the construction of the Nord Stream pipeline, Ukraine will remain a crucial gas transit country for Russia's exports to the EU. Ukraine is also one of the world's most important energy

consumer, which represents an important stake for EU's efforts to secure external supplies and to fight against climate change.

- The protection against "soft threats": crime, immigration, territorial disputes, proliferation of conventional and non conventional weapons, social and political violence
- The protection against environmental risks: nuclear accident, pipeline leaks, climate change as a consequence of an intensive coal consumption and of heavy pollution by industry.
- To EU's economical prosperity. Ukraine has huge economical capacities for imports, Foreign direct investments (FDI) and is a tremendous potential market for EU's exports that is steadily developing. Ukraine is a highly industrialized state, which is able to produce highly value added goods and provides a well qualified labour force. It is for example among the few states in the world that has a spatial and aeronautic industry.

Thus, EU's strategic interest is that Ukraine is committed to be cooperative and behaves and transforms according to EU's expectations that is to be willing and actively pursuing the goal of doing all what is possible to guarantee EU's stability and prosperity.

For this to happen, Ukraine must progress and complete its economical and political transition to a sovereign, stable, democratic, rule of law-based and market-orientated state.

The fundamental problem and challenge the EU is compelled to address is that Ukraine 16 years after its independence and nearly 3 years after the "Orange revolution" still poses a serious risk for the EU since the progress and completion of transition and stabilisation is by far not achieved and remains fragile. Ukraine's transition to democracy has made important progress after the winter 2004 "Orange revolution", but there's still a long way to go to catch up with European democratic institutional and normative standards (broadly, the Copenhagen criteria and the *acquis communautaire*). Despite all the political troubles and problems Ukraine has been experiencing since the "Orange revolution", there's has been no turning back to Kuchma-era times, although many structural weaknesses and deficits in Ukraine's transition have not been changed and improved yet.

Among the most major achievements, one can list:

- Ukraine's Europeaness is no more questioned: Ukraine is a European country and shares its history and values. The most striking fact is that Ukraine's national identity and nation—statehood building have been linked since independence on the belonging to Europe and the emphasis on the country's Europeaness;
- Pluralist media and press/ freedom of speech;
- civil society is strengthening, though still not powerful enough;
- improving rule of law, repeated free and fair elections;
- tradition of tolerance, inclusive civic identity, multiethnic state;

- rationalization of party system, few and stable big political parties;
- balanced state budget, economical growth;
- normalization and improvement of relations with EU/US;
- official commitment to align with the EU economical and political model/ official strategy of EU membership;

Ukraine's transformation and stabilization is still impeded by multiple intricate economical, political and societal factors which mutually reinforce each other and are of utmost importance to Ukraine's transformation, but also to EU's stability and security;

- Political instability / inefficiently functioning institutions and checks and balances / inefficient constitutional order and necessary constitutional reform to clarify responsibilities between President and Prime minister / under mature party system: fragile coalitions, strong political and personal divergences;
- Stalling reforms (World Trade Organization, Foreign direct investments, banking sector, privatizations, energy sector, etc);
- Russia's destabilizing policies and economical and political pressures, blackmail and forced concessions. Russia's systematic policy towards Ukraine threatens the country's sovereignty, security and stability and was facilitated by Yanukovych's return to power and Yushchenko's weakness. As a consequence of the Russian-Ukrainian gas agreements of July-August 2004 and January 2006 just after the gas crisis, Ukraine's vulnerability from Russia has increased and the country's energy security and capacity to implement a policy in the nation's interest have been increasingly put at risk. Russia has been successfully pursuing a strategy aimed at:
  - monopolizing Ukraine's energy supply sources and routes leading to the failure of Ukraine's diversification attempts and options and thus increasing Russia's leverage on Ukraine,
  - monopolizing and control-taking of domestic energy distribution market / economical and financial weakening of Ukraine's strategic domestic state energy sector as Naftohaz has been forced to give up its lucrative industry distribution sector to a Russian controlled near-vertical monopoly structure (Gazprom, RosUkrEnergo, UkrHazEnergo) and forced to agree to very low transit and storage prices, leading to a growing indebtedness of state monopoly Naftohaz, a loose of control of Ukraine's Gas transmission system, an incapacity to modernize and extend the network and a growing dependence on Russia and risk of debt for assets swaps,
  - making prices unpredictable and maintaining a strong increase potential, and maintaining the unreliability of supplies;
- Mismanagement of the energy sector / lack of public control and transparency/ rent-seeking behaviours/ inefficient domestic production;
- The country's East/West societal and political division / a European vs Russian model of development. Tension over Russian as a second official language / no nationwide political parties, nevertheless, with the exception of the BYUT party;

- Social tensions because of inflation, underemployment, shrinking of purchasing power;
- Disillusion within the population/ electoral disaffection / lack of confidence in the political system and in the political elites;
- Rent-seeking elites, intertwining between business / politics, betrayal of national interest because of self-serving policies : since no total support and determination of political elites for reforms, transformation resists. The slightest weakness in the determination to reform is not resisting Russia's pressure/ the pressure of backward forces;
- Increasing but insufficient foreign investments that need to be dramatically fostered;
- Bribery;
- Problematic economical restructuring despite a favourable context of sustained economical growth: the government still subsidises the mining and metallurgical industry sectors; energy prices remain reasonable / Ukraine is loosing its competitiveness as regards Russia, which is one of the main reasons that explained Russia's price increase demands which lead to the January 2006 gas crisis;
- Inflation, poorly diversified economy, economic growth largely relying on the increase of world primary resources price increases, deterioration of the current balance account deficit;
- Strong energy consumption per capita / insufficient energy efficiency progresses and renewable energy sources;

Ukraine has just elected a new Parliament on September 30, 2007. Democratic and reform friendly forces are in a majority but the country is once again striving to form a coalition as strong rivalries and political calculations undermine an 'orange' coalition building. Indeed, for now, Yushchenko tries to limit Tymoshenko's potential power and playing field if he is to nominate her as Prime minister, in playing her party against the Party of Region to be able to play the role of a referee. These elections however represent a thrid, new chance for Ukraine, and EU's interest is that a stable, democratic coalition is formed between Yushchenko's Nasha Ukraina/ People's Self Defence block and Tymoshenko's BYUT party, leaving the Party of Regions in the opposition. But it is far from certain that Tymoshenko and Yushchenko will be able to patch up their differences and that a possible coalition between their respective political forces will be stable and allow the new government to pursue the structural reforms that urgently need to be undertaken. Especially Russia will try again to destabilize Ukraine's political and economical situation and some powerful forces with economic interests in Ukraine will try to impede any major political and economical reform.

EU's relations to its Eastern neighbours: past and present developments

EU-Ukraine and EU–Russia relations today take place in a different context than EU's relations with the CEES in the 90s. This has a strong impact on EU's leverage capacity and calls for new strategies

The EU is now confronted to the necessity to engage with those FSU states which it had all through the 90s relatively neglected. And it appears that EU's leverage capacity and instruments to pursue its interests are clearly limited.

All through the 90s, the EU concentrated on the CEES states while Russia and Ukraine were not considered as the most important challenges to be met. Indeed, for one reason, the EU at the time was concentrating on the most immediate risks and threats, the CEES states, which were also the most capable of successfully transforming. It rapidly became clear that these states would be offered a membership perspective and progressively taken into the EU. Former CIS states were to remain outside, with the exception of the Baltic States. Ukraine's democratization was failing but the country was no immediate political or economical threat. And Russia's transition was stalling too, but Russia's international bargaining position was weak, Russia under Yeltsin's presidency was rather cooperative, and Russia was dealt with mostly by the G7, NATO, the Council of Europe, the Organisation for Security and Cooperation in Europe, the International Monetary Fund, the World Bank and by member states bilaterally. Thus, there was no apparent and perceived necessity to devote the same attention to FSU states as than to CEES. There was no debate over the necessity to offer Ukraine and Russia a membership perspective or on how relations with these states would be best adapted. Russia was never seriously considered as a potential member, neither was Ukraine, and the EU left to Russia the responsibility to deal with Ukraine.

Then, when facing the challenge posed by the CEES states all through the 90s, the EU possessed a very important leverage capacity as it could use the enlargement instrument and was determined to use it.

Last but not least, the EU had no rival, opponent or competitor to its policies. Russia, which could have been the most important obstacle for change, rather passively accepted these geopolitical changes. Russia was economically and politically too weak to oppose the West's policy. But Russia, if it had wished to, could have been much more a factor of impediment.

The problem is that while the EU was focussing on the integration of CEES states, it didn't realize that multiple challenges would progressively arise from Russia and Ukraine. These challenges are much linked to what the EU has been doing, or has missed to do since the 90s. The EU is now confronted with structural risks to its stability and prosperity emanating from states that all over the 90s were no immediate problem. Indeed, what builds the ground for today's problems, especially in the energy domain, hadn't surfaced and matured in the 90s.

These developments happen at a time when other challenges, temporary or structural, have arisen to the top of the foreign policy agendas and retain the attention of media, public opinion and policy makers. On the global agenda, there's Iran, Irak, Syria, Lebanon, North Korea, global climate change, relations with China, the US, and the fight against terrorism. On the EU related agenda, there's the integration of Turkey and the Balkan states, the fate of the new institutional treaty, the immigration issue, and the Lisbon agenda. All these issues are important but tend to draw the attention away on the crucial developments that now take place between Ukraine, Russia and the EU.

Today, Russia appears to be structurally reluctant to EU's policies and puts the emphasis on its bilateral, separate relations to selected EU member states in order to impede any common EU approach and policy. And Ukraine took the pragmatic decision to accept the European Neighbourhood Policy (ENP), but is by far not enthusiastic and considers the ENP as transitional. With both Russia and Ukraine, the problem is that these states' expectations and demand do not necessarily match with EU's representations and interests. And on EU's side, the problem is that there's no consensus between France, Germany and Poland over what are EU's fundamental interests, what should be the objectives of the CFSP towards Russia and Ukraine and how these objectives should be pursued. This stands in contrast to the 90s when a consensus quickly appeared on how to deal with the challenges posed by EU's Eastern neighbours. This is largely due to a different perception of interests, risks and threats, which is determined by different historical, economical and political legacies and realities, and by a long lasting special personal friendship between Putin, Schroeder and Chirac. This is also largely due to Russia's ability to successfully outplay EU member states against each other. As a consequence, there's no common foreign policy consensus towards Russia and Ukraine, and initiatives, such as in the energy domain, have failed. This is the major factor that may lead to a situation of asymmetrical vulnerability at the expense of the EU.

For sure, the EU has not done the necessary reforms in the 90s that would have strengthened its integration, efficiency and capacity to be an influential political actor, although the 90s were a rather calm and appropriate period. The 1993 Maastricht treaty was only completed by very weak institutional progresses, ultimately leading to the Nice treaty debacle. The Europeanization of EU member states was not supported enough and the deepening of integration remained too limited.

Furthermore, the EU cannot count on the preparatory transformational and stabilizing work which was done by NATO in the 90s in the CEES. NATO's role can no more be the same today, because of Russia, because NATO members are divided over the issue of further expanding, and because the potential candidates are not real proponents. And while NATO didn't face any real opposition from Russia as it strengthened its partnerships with CEES states and ultimately let them in, and ignored Russia's opposition to the Baltic states' entrance, this is no more the case today. Finally, the US' participation in NATO has become increasingly problematic when dealing with Russia.

The EU is furthermore deeply divided over the opportunity to further enlarge once the Balkan states will join, especially as regards Turkey, but also to those states that have not been offered a membership perspective yet, and first and foremost, Ukraine. This enlargement hostility stands in contrast to the fact that the EU is in its essence a project that is aimed at including new states in order to maximize peace, democracy, prosperity and stability, and that is not finite. In agreeing to a big bang enlargement in 2004 and 2007, the EU has implicitly determined which states were European and would be welcomed to join the 'club', and which would remain outside a political barrier that has been institutionally cemented and has so far proved to be irremovable. The 2004 enlargement was celebrated as Europe's reunification rather than EU's enlargement, in defining which states are part of the European political, social, economical and cultural entity and which are not. And this position with regards Ukraine is very ambiguous. Ukraine is geographically, historically and culturally a European country, which can be hardly questioned, so that it fulfils the criteria to apply for a membership perspective. The ENP has further pursued this crucial division and discrimination as the policy was named European Neighbourhood Policy and not EU Neighbourhood Policy.

EU's present strategy towards Ukraine

The EU and its member states have recognized Ukraine's strategic importance to the EU, but there are no concrete elements to support that this recognition has moved beyond rhetoric and has been translated into politics.

Since the "Orange revolution", EU-Ukraine cooperation has been fostered, relations have improved, visits have multiplied, but the EU sticks to a "honest" relationship"[1] that 'presently' rules out membership and clearly stresses that Ukraine still needs to further transform, ambiguously postponing any final decision. This comes despite Ukraine has been repeatedly calling for an EU membership perspective and despite the "Orange revolution" has increased the legitimacy of its claims. The EU supports Ukraine's transition and encourages Ukraine to further reform and stabilize. It recognizes that Ukraine has been making progress but stresses that Ukraine must further transform as the political instability that came after the "Orange revolution" has lead to some disappointment and fatigue among EU member states.

Ukraine is a 'partner state' of the ENP. The EU through the ENP offers specific incentives: cooperation in foreign policy, economical integration, eased movement of persons, etc. EU's approach is not a really tailor made policy for Ukraine, and its specificity is weak. The EU has declared Ukraine as a special case within the ENP, but still, Ukraine is part of the ENP and has no prospect to change this situation.

Ukraine has been granted the market economy status and its WTO bid has been supported by the EU. The EU and Ukraine further signed a memorandum of understanding in the energy sector, played a very constructive role on the Transnistria issue and agreed on an eased visa regime. But the ENP is an instrument that mainly targets 'soft threats' and which doesn't present enough political and economical

---

1   Steinmeier, F.W. (2006), Interview, *Frankfurter Allgemeine Zeitung*, March 6

support for Ukraine to be able to overcome its critical situation and for the EU to preserve its interests which can by far not be reduced to these 'soft threats'.

As a consequence of the 2004 EU enlargement, Ukraine's EU membership perspective is actively advocated by Poland and Lithuania. After the "Orange revolution", the European Parliament had called on the Commission to take account of the decisive turning point that had just occurred and to meet Ukraine's European aspirations. On July 12, 2007, the European Parliament adopted a report calling for an EU membership perspective for Ukraine. And a July 2007 survey showed that more and more Europeans are not opposed to Ukraine joining the EU and do not doubt this will happen. However, EU member states are divided over what to do with Ukraine, especially because there's a perception that Ukraine needs to further transform, a will not to harm the relation with Russia and because of the concern over EU's enlargement capacity. So far, France has proven to be the amongst the most reluctant state, partly because of its special relationship with Russia, but also because France focuses on the Southern Mediterranean dimension and is very reluctant to any further EU enlargement as any further enlargement is perceived as an impediment to any further political integration.

Negotiations over a new EU-Ukraine Partnership and Cooperation Agreement have started although Ukraine is presently in a weak bargaining position due to its political crisis. Nevertheless, the political issues have not been addressed so far and it seems that the Yanukovych government has not undermined the negotiations that progress well at the technical level. These negotiations provide a decisive opportunity for the EU to give a boost to its relations with Ukraine, to increase its leverage capacity on the country and to bring an incentive for reform in line with EU's security and stability interests. The negotiations are due to be finalized by the French EU presidency at the end of 2008.

The prospect for the EU to face its responsibilities and address the Ukrainian and Russian challenges
The EU must now urgently act and react, and must quickly find a new concept and strategy for its relations with Ukraine and Russia.

With regards to EU's institutional transformation, to inner relations between member states

Given the fact that the membership perspective is and will always be EU's most effective foreign policy tool, in no way should the enlargement policy be abandoned and in no way should the EU declare that after Turkey and the Balkans, the EU has reached its final external boarders. It would be a dramatic political mistake to draw definite EU boarders. The EU and its international environment are constantly changing, requiring adaptation, and the membership and the integration process offers decisive incentives for transformation and Europeanization. The 2004 enlargement to

CEES was a clear success and the EU could further apply the same receipt with those states that are in a similar situation as regards their political and economical transition. It must be very clear that the ENP cannot substitute the enlargement policy as some consider that it more or less offers the same gradual integration to the EU. The ENP may offer the same free trade zone, political rapprochement, eased movement of persons and alignment with the *acquis communautaire*, but this is just it, as it lacks the crucial membership perspective, negotiations for integration and accession funds and ultimately the consequence of being a full member of the club, that is equal consideration and treatment, the capacity to co-decide, the economical and financial support, and the security and the prosperity. The ENP will thus hardly be able to achieve its goal of suppressing barriers between the EU and Ukraine and of replacing the enlargement policy.

The EU must urgently settle the institutional issue and conclude a new institutional treaty enabling the EU institutions to work efficiently and enabling the EU to integrate further countries that are willing to join the EU. This is very important for the EU to increase its policy options and its leverage capacity. In a quickly changing international and European environment, the EU cannot afford to lay back one second and must always try to further integrate in key domains, such as foreign policy. The fact a new draft of the treaty has been adopted by the informal EU Council gathered in Lisbon on October 18, 2007 has to be much welcomed. Although the simplified treaty is likely to be ratified in most states by Parliamentary approval, its future remains uncertain as Britain may pass it through a referendum. Furthermore, its provisions need to be clarified, especially over competences of the Commission, the EU president and its near foreign minister. One can regret that the EU has lost much time and energy since the French and Dutch no which will have long lasting consequences for the EU since EU's international environment in the meantime has been changing at a very high speed. The creation of common near-EU Foreign minister is highly welcomed but this person will have to have strong charisma and must be visionary if it is to succeed.

In the domain of foreign policy, the EU member states must take the CFSP more seriously. The cost of finding an agreement involving all EU member states remains too important so that the CFSP is not attractive unless for consensual issues such as Burma, Bosnia, or the non-proliferation policy. And EU's CFSP can't just be reduced to such issues. A positive factor is that the most important provision included in the simplified treaty which is likely to be quickly adopted by EU member states is the creation of a near-EU Foreign minister, whose institutional role and prerogatives will be strengthened. This would mark a clear progress as the present High Representative for EU's CFSP has so far drawn his limited influence to a large extend on his strong charisma and personality.

But fundamentally, each EU member states, and especially France, Germany and Poland, must be convinced that it gets more rewards in seeking common solutions than individual self-minded and short-term options and policies. For this to happen, EU member states must fully take into account other EU member states' legitimate interests and concerns and consider that these concerns must be automatically taken into account. The EU enlargement has brought new visions, new interests, new concerns, especially with regards to EU's eastern boarders, and member states which perceive a different degree of dependence can't just look at their own interests, and worse, follow policies and decisions which clearly damage a member state's or the community's interests. For now, Russia doesn't perceive the EU as a coherent and relevant actor which clearly weakens the EU. EU member states should pay attention not to mix different political issues in their bargaining positions. And it would be very dangerous that resentments and anger between France, Germany and Poland further strengthen because these three countries are fundamental to the EU's credibility and capability and to the success of an EU CFSP towards FSU states. EU's capacity to speak with one voice is of an utmost importance for the EU to be credible and powerful and to be able to preserve its long-term interests. EU member state should thus be fundamentally convinced about the benefit the EU brings and can bring, and come up with reasonable and discursive positions which provide a clear commitment to the EU project, do not make particular short-term interests prevail over the community's long-term interests, and which do not instrumentalize the EU for internal electoral purposes. Thus, for Poland's interests to be better taken into account by other EU member states, it should be less Russia hostile, more EU friendly, and have a more constructive EU and foreign policies. Otherwise, its claims, though legitimate, won't be taken seriously by other members, especially Germany, which is likely to happen at the expense of Ukraine. And Germany and France should provide clear signals that they are ready to better incorporate Poland's concerns and interests.

More specifically, the Weimar Triangle forum should thus be further reinforced through an increased cooperation, institutionalization and dialogue. The most recent Weimar Triangle summit in 2006 has gone the right way but heads of states and governments should meet twice a year and not just once.

The new entrants Bulgaria and Romania have a crucial responsibility as their quick and successful transformation in the domains of fight against corruption and organized crime, strengthening of rule of law and human rights, will have a significant influence on EU's acceptance of further enlargements. Poland and Lithuania, together with the United Kingdom, should make sure that Bulgaria's and Romania's integration in the EU is successful in pressuring these states' governments to complete the transition and in being vigilant. If these two states prove to lag behind at an unacceptable distance, further enlargements, especially to Ukraine, will be largely deterred.

As regards the relation to Ukraine

Ukraine bears a strong responsibility in its development, and the Ukrainian political elite has a key responsibility in not deceiving the Ukrainian population, in not betraying the country's interests, and in not supporting the 'nothing is changing' sentiment among some EU member states. But the EU has a decisive role to play and some immediate steps should be undertaken both by the EU and individual member states in their bilateral relation with Ukraine:

- Among the two yearly Weimar Triangle summits, one should involve Ukraine. It could deal with energy issues (security of supply, nuclear, coal, energy efficiency and savings), transports, global issues, cultural and societal cooperation, education, scientific cooperation, justice and internal affairs;
- Increase technology transfers of renewable energy sources, increase the support for energy efficiency and saving measures, especially in the public sector, with the support of member states' energy agencies, EU funds and programmes, public/private partnerships and European Bank of Reconstruction and Development and World Bank loans. This would crucially foster Ukraine's competitiveness and its energy security and independence, and free-up resources to be exported to the EU. EU member states in their bilateral policies with Ukraine should particularly focus on this aspect, especially France, and take the example of initiatives lead by Germany or Austria;
- Make a common high level assessment of Ukraine's energy situation, especially regarding the issue of Naftohaz's deteriorating economical and financial situation, the Ukrainian government's political intentions, Russia's pressures, and the gas consortium project. This could be done based on the energy correspondent network that has been set up and whose achievements need to be publicly debated. Ukraine and Russia together are not part of any integrated regime of cooperation that would involve the EU, which makes no sense since Ukraine is the most important transit country for Russia's supplies to the EU. Thus, energy relations between the EU and Russia should involve Ukraine. Overall, the EU should no more consider that bilateral Ukraine-Russia relations are not of its business as they have very important indirect consequences for the EU;
- Help Ukraine preserve and develop its transit role and diversify its resources: through the building of the Nabucco gas pipeline and its junction with the Ukrainian GTS, through increased support for the Odessa-Brody pipe reversal, through support for the construction of a Trans-Caspian gas pipeline and a Trans-Black Sea gas pipeline that could supply Ukraine, through the discussion of the future modernization of Ukraine's gas transmission system and its extension. In this context, the EU could resort to its bilateral relation to Ukraine as a tool of leverage against Russia's increasingly hostile policies, especially in the energy sector for example, in offsetting Russia's strategy of strengthening its monopoly position on the upstream and downstream sectors;
- Foster Ukraine's participation in EU programmes, especially education and regional cohesion, increase EU funding, especially for the strengthening of civil society and rule of law in the Eastern part of Ukraine;
- Ease visa requirements, make them free for all persons aged under 30 years, develop consular network all over the country to facilitate visa applications and to decrease costs for applicants;
- Bilateral strengthening of technical cooperation (environmental issues, economy and industry reform and restructuring, agriculture);

- EU must integrate Ukraine into international organizations to increase is international commitments and predictability (South East European Energy Community Treaty) and the EU must take a more active role in the Black Sea Economic Forum and Baku Initiative;
- Foster citizen exchanges, such as pairings between municipalities; the mission of the OFAJE (Franco-German office for the youth) should be enlarged to Poland, Ukraine and Russia. Cultural and youth exchanges must be developed, same as university partnerships. The EU should seek to have an influence on everyone's life. From the East or West of Ukraine, every ordinary Ukrainian should personally feel the benefit of getting closer to the EU;
- Provide access for Ukraine's goods to the EU and help Ukraine not be harmed by non-tariff protection measures, such as complaining with EU's standards;
- Create specialized EU member states groups for those who perceive strong interests in Ukraine and who seek to foster foreign policy coordination and cooperation. The meetings of this group could gather the EU (Commission + Council), EU member states, experts, civil society and high level Ukrainian officials). This group would have some autonomy and the EU president, or the near-EU Foreign minister if this function is created, could then report to all member states and make concrete proposals for action;
- Lead a reflection on EU's attitude before and during the 2009 presidential election, which is likely to be as disputed and tensed as the 2004 presidential election, especially as regards possible reactions from Moscow as Ms Tymoshenko is likely to be in a good position to be elected.

When it comes to Ukraine's EU membership perspective claims, the EU should follow a new approach.

Indeed, Ukraine's EU membership objective must be considered seriously and cannot receive an over simplistic and irresponsible 'no' as an answer. The EU should no more state that the membership perspective is not on the agenda and the EU must turn its present approach into questions. An increasing engagement and support by the EU in the form of an EU membership perspective could indeed have favourable consequences on Ukraine's transformation so that the EU may well be able to repeat the success of the 2004 enlargement to CEES. Indeed, Ukraine possesses a favourable environment for a conditionality-based enlargement strategy to work.

First, Ukraine's political elite has been for long complaining about the lack of distinction made in the ENP between Ukraine and Tunisia, for example. Ukraine has also been complaining about the fact it has been denied the right to apply for an EU membership. And the prospect for economical cooperation which is included in the ENP is by far not enough to be a consistent incentive for Ukraine's political elite and population and to create a nationwide consensus and support for structural, gradual and qualitative reforms. Ukraine's transition to democracy has indeed been engaged but lacks a decisive boosting support. All major Ukrainian parties, even the Party of Regions, support Ukraine's EU integration. No political force except the Communists radically opposes EU integration. An EU membership perspective would force the democratic forces to seek to build stable coalitions and to give up their personal political calculations as population's expectations and pressures for reforms would increase. It could increase the pressure on Yushchenko to give up political calculations and to act in the fundamental interest of Ukraine. It would give a concrete political perspective and objective for Ukrainian policy makers, and help them to pass difficult reforms in blaming the EU and the price to pay in order to be in for a better future. The argument that the membership perspective is not automatically bringing change may be relevant on the short term, or on temporary periods in some particular countries, but the EU 2004 enlargement was a huge success, and EU accession of Ukraine is to take place in about 15 years ahead. For sure, the mistakes in the enlargement to Bulgaria and Romania won't have to be repeated.

It could also have a positive influence on the Party of Region which is currently a factor impeding Ukraine's transformation as this party has not democratized and normalized since the "Orange revolution" and further acts in the interests of its prominent members of the country's economical elite rather than of the nation. Ukraine won't transform if the Regions do not change and do not accept the change. EU's most important task is to transform the Regions in order to make it similar to the Polish former communists gathered in the SLD party which accessed to power in 1995. Poland's transformation was largely eased as a consequence of their commitment to reform. Thus, all emphasis should be put on changing the Regions, through socialization, through parliamentary exchange programmes, through commitments, etc. The Party of Region could change if it stands longer in the opposition, if civil society strengthens, if the population's democratic pressure for results and transparency increases, and if it is entrenched in a dense network of socialization with the EU. The EU could bring decisive incentive for transformation because it is in the interest of Donbass entrepreneurs that there's an economic integration with the EU, that there's political stability and economical development and modernization in Ukraine.

An EU integration could thus help conciliate the two Ukraine, at the condition that Western Ukrainians and the EU do not instrumentalize it as a means to turn away from Russia, and that Russia doesn't instrumentalize the issue as being an act of hostility and aggression. It could boost the support of Yulia Tymoshenko, who is the only candidate capable of having a national audience and to decrease the regional factor, which the September 30, 2007 election has provided some evidence.

Furthermore, when looking at polls, there's a great and concerning disillusion amongst Ukrainians over politics and politicians. Ordinary Ukrainians have the impression that nothing has changed, that the "Orange revolution" only replaced the names of those who profit from rent-seeking schemes and which are perceived as taking the population hostage. There's been strong inflation, the purchasing power has diminished, affairs and scandals have been ongoing, and permanent individual political struggles have fed a growing resentment. What is remarkable is that EU membership support has been nevertheless ongoing, all the more that the EU had nothing to offer and An EU membership perspective would provide a first decisive reward for the population. The EU membership perspective would further multiply foreign investments, as was the case in Romania, and foster the country's economical development.

And ultimately, the EU could make Ukraine and Turkey compete for the EU membership which could bring a further incentive for both states to foster their transformation. Moreover, the controversial issue of Turkish membership could also benefit Ukraine as it would highlight its advantages and good points. If Ukraine further transforms, it would better fulfil the formal and informal membership criteria, as it is Christian, clearly geographically located in Europe, and is peaceful as no terrorist group threatens its integrity and there's no significant point of contention such as the Armenian genocide issue. All the more that Ukraine's population is greater than Poland's, but still far less than Turkey's. On the long run, integrating Ukraine could bring a far greater consensus than integrating Turkey, all the more that Ukraine has a decisive strategic importance too. Thus, Ukraine's integration in the EU could be quicker than Turkey's, provided that the two ever take place, and possibly even favoured over Turkey's. The two countries accession would nevertheless specifically make sense as it would transform the Black Sea region and its bordering states into a zone of greater stability, prosperity and security which would benefit the EU, Black Sea member states, but first and foremost, Russia, provided that Russia is cooperative.

As regards the relation to Russia

The EU and Russia have no other choice but to strengthen their cooperation because they are in an interdependent situation and need to manage their common dependence.

Russia currently is showing no sign that it is ready to abandon its great state strategy and engage in a cooperative strategy with the EU. Therefore, relations with Russia are likely to remain conflicting and tensed in the years to come. This should convince the EU to make its strategy evolve, to be more assertive and to fear less confrontation with Russia when necessary. The EU should be a friend, a strategic partner and an ally of Russia, and bilateral relations should by all means be strengthened and developed. But the EU has already made a lot of concessions to Russia and can't anymore accept all its policies as far as they clearly oppose the EU's interests.

The EU should further stretch hands to Russia and EU member states should all clearly commit themselves to the importance of the relation with Russia, especially in opening their markets to Russian investments. But the EU should stand firm on its interests in ensuring that Russia's policies don't make the EU vulnerable, and that Russia's policies don't shape the balance of power on the Eurasian continent. The EU has presently no choice but to offset Russia's policies, especially in its neighbourhood, in developing an ambitious external energy policy. At the same time, EU member states should systematically refuse to participate in Russia's divide and rule strategy which only brings short-term benefits. The EU must also look at developing and fostering a more structural and grassroots policy towards Russia that would target civil society, with education exchanges, the free movement of persons, support to NGOs, and continue to insist on democratic reforms. It must also seek to bring Russia decisive support in the domain of energy efficiency and climate friendly technologies, and help Russia modernize its economy.

But decisively, the EU must change its strategy towards Ukraine as a much greater transformation in line with EU requirements and needs can be achieved there.

It is obvious that any more implicated EU policy towards Ukraine will have repercussions on the relation with Russia. This has so far lead the EU to keep its engagement with Ukraine at a minimum level but this can and should change as the comfortable present status quo situation is a dangerous illusion. For sure, the EU needs to strengthen its relations and cooperation with Ukraine and this will raise anger and hostility in Russia. But the EU should not undervalue the benefits a deepened partnership with Ukraine could bring, and should not overestimate the resulting costs on its relation with Russia, as interdependence with Russia is a reality and as Russia may be convinced to accept a mutually beneficial settlement of common problems of cooperation. Overall, the EU should not fear to act according to its own interests, which Russia systematically does itself, and should not be entrapped in the rhetoric of strategic partnership.

Thus, it is obvious that whatever its ultimate objective as regards Ukraine, the EU will have to either risk increasing conflicting relations with Russia, or prove Russia that EU's new strategy is not directed against it, and that conversely, it is also in Russia's own interest.

The EU must find a way of this dilemma and seek a fundamental negotiations and settlement, first within its most prominent members that are France, Poland and Germany, and then with Russia and Ukraine, in order to maximize all players' interests.

Any EU policy in Ukraine should in no way be aimed at playing Ukraine against Russia, because it would be absurd and dangerous to pursue the objective of weakening Russia or of raising a wall between Russia and the EU. On the contrary, the EU needs a strong and stable Russia, at the condition that Russia is committed to cooperate with the EU and does not jeopardize EU's strategic interests. Thus, Ukraine should in no way become the victim or object of an EU-Russia bargaining and rivalry.

Against this background, European, American and Ukrainian policy makers should think very carefully about Ukraine's NATO membership prospect, which proves to be very controversial in Ukraine and which is perceived in Russia as an act of hostility and aggression and largely fuels resentments. Ukraine, the EU and NATO should establish whether Ukraine's European prospect is not dependent upon its military neutralization. If Ukraine was to be offered an EU membership perspective, Ukraine could declare itself militarily neutral and decide not to pursue anymore the objective of integrating NATO. This would ease domestic and foreign tensions and allow Ukraine to focus all attention and efforts only on the EU membership. It would also reassure Russia and help to overcome Russia's categorical hostility. Such a move would need to be accompanied at the same time by a deepening of the NATO and EU partnerships with

Russia in order not to shape the balance of powers between the EU and Russia and avoid that Russia feels insecure and betrayed. Ukraine would thus become a bridge between the EU and Russia and this solution could be a win-win compromise for Russia, Ukraine and the EU[2]. For sure, Ukraine's renunciation to NATO could be a trump that could be used to make Russia accept that Ukraine further integrates with the EU. And given the intertwining between Russia and Ukraine, bringing closer Ukraine to the EU automatically leads to approach Russia from the EU. Ukraine should thus be encouraged to play this role of bridge, which could only work at the condition that Russia accepts to be itself brought closer to the EU. The EU could thus draw the perspective of the establishment in 15 years time of a great free trade zone going from Portugal to Russia. But for this scheme to work, the EU must distance itself from the policies of the United States, which are considered by Moscow to be hostile and aimed at weakening Russia. The EU should thus oppose to the Anti-missile radar shield system which exacerbates Russia's fears and whose utility and cost are not convincing. It should further pay attention that the US's support to Ukraine's integration to Euro Atlantic structures remains at a limited level in order not to raise opposition and suspicion in Russia. Any US involvement in the context of the EU trying to come closer to Ukraine and Russia could be counterproductive, but any US political disengagement must be counterbalanced by the EU playing a bigger role.

Conclusion

Time is running out for the EU to face and confront the decisive challenges emanating from Ukraine and Russia, and it is not wise to postpone any major political reaction until the next crisis appears. Developments in these countries could prove to be irreversible and would then have a tremendous impact on the EU. It would thus be irresponsible not to react by considering that the EU has other more important priorities to deal with. EU's relations to Russia and Ukraine build the cornerstone of the security, stability and prosperity of the Eurasian continent. In view of the developments in EU-Russia relations, and in view of Russia's policies and Ukraine's present degree of transformation, time has come for the EU to radically change its policies towards Russia and Ukraine. The possibility for a win-win settlement of conflicting issues between France, Germany, Poland, Russia and Ukraine definitely exists. Politicians from all sides now have to measure the urgency and necessity of such a settlement and take their respective responsibilities in achieving it. And EU citizens must be aware of the fact that, although the EU is a zone of stability and prosperity, the EU is not immune to geopolitical risks and threats emanating from its neighbourhood. Citizens

---

2   This would also make sense as Ukraine's militaro-industrial complex is much intertwined with the Russia, and since NATO is pursuing its rapprochement with Russia. Ukraine could also, in doing so, allow Russia to keep its Sebastopol base on the long term, provided that the agreement is renegotiated under much stricter and clearer terms.

must be aware that the EU will have to devote a lot of energy, money, efforts and persuasion to bring the required changes in line with its interests. It goes without saying that Europeans will ultimately have to accept that the EU should further enlarge in the East. It is also in their responsibility to imagine how the political project of the EU could be further improved in this context.

Of course, part of the answer to these challenges can be initiated by member-states themselves – for example, by developing their nuclear electricity production to better face the supply security issue, which is now more attractive than ever as it provides for low carbon emissions and reduces the external gas dependence. But, by no means, can these domestic initiatives replace an-EU wide policy which would target all these decisive issues.

In this respect, the 2008 French EU presidency will be crucial and will have to include a clear focus on Ukraine and Russia, even if the consequence is that the Mediterranean dimension will have to be neglected. Recent political developments may bring signs that France has started to measure the importance of changing its strategy towards Russia and Ukraine. The French president, Nicolas Sarkozy, has already announced that a key priority of his foreign policy, and of its EU presidency, will be to strengthen understanding and cooperation between the new and old EU member states. This looks promising at this is one of the most important issues this paper has drawn the attention on. Sarkozy seems to have already given a new impetus to France's foreign policy. His increased interest for CEES states marks a clear shift away from the Chirac era, which had completely neglected these states. The new tone and distance in French-Russian relations and the most recent meeting between President Yushchenko and Sarkozy in Paris on Friday October 5, 2007 – just before Sarkozy was to leave to Moscow, and that followed by Polish and Czech leaders – provide a further sign that France might be moving away from its traditional near-blind pro-Russian policy and is now ready to give Ukraine the consideration and attention it deserves. Although the exact content of talks between Yushchenko and Sarkozy were not known, and although French media have ignored this visit, comments in Ukraine have stated that Sarkozy expressed a warm support for Ukraine's European aspirations. France has also shown interest in making Gaz de France participate in the Nabucco gas pipeline project. It is clear that these apparently favourable political developments will need to be confirmed in the rethorics and in the actions, and that much will also depend on Germany's and Poland's positions.

Abbreviations:
CEES: Central and Eastern European states
CFSP: Common Foreign Security Policy
ENP: European Neighborhood Policy
EU: European Union
FSU: Former Soviet Union
NATO: North Atlantic Treaty Organization
US: United States

The EU Enlargement:
Implications on Transatlantic Relations

Zhang Ji

With the largest enlargement 2004 since the foundation of the European Union and the latest enlargement this year, 12 new countries have become the members of the EU, the most part of which are CEEC (Central and Eastern Europe countries) and former Warsaw Pact countries. The enlargement has turned EU as a largely western European organization to a cross-continent entity. Meanwhile, the enlargement has pushed the border of the Union to the regions in Eastern Europe and Middle East. Many argue that the big bang enlargement has profoundly changed the nature of the EU, and had huge implications to EU's strategic actoness and transatlantic relations,[1] in which the hot topic and key concept focus on "old Europe" / "new Europe". It is evidential that the policy divergence and political incoherence were the most obvious impacts that the big bang enlargement has brought to the EU's actorness and the transatlantic relations. However, the dichotomy of "old Europe"/"New Europe" can not explain everything that the enlargement has brought, and with the time passing its effectiveness to reason the relative long term implications that the enlargement has brought is descending.

On the base of reviewing the short term implications that the enlargement had brought to the EU's international actorness and the transatlantic relations, which had already been discussed much, this article would like to raise some questions about the previous studies, and contribute the analyses of the new developments and changes in the old/new member states dynamics, especially concerning the relations with the US and the Atlantic Alliance.

Enlarged EU: implications on EU's international actorness
Success of Civilian Power

The EU's enlargement policy has been its most successful foreign policy[2] by successfully using economic and diplomatic instruments –so called civilian power- as the strategic approach to realize the stability and maintain security in the European continent after the end of the Cold War and the collapse of the Soviet Union, not

---

1   See the discussion in: Brimmer, Esther and Fröhlich, Stefan ed. The strategic implications of European Union enlargement. Washington, DC: Center for Transatlantic Relations, Johns Hopkins University, 2005. Longhurst, Kerry and Zaborowski, Marcin ed. Old Europe, new Europe and the transatlantic security agenda. London: Routledge, 2005.
2   Smith, Karen E. "Enlargement and European Order". *International Relations and the European Union.* Ed. Christopher Hill and Michael Smith. Oxford University Press, 2005. p.271

letting Europe come "back to the future". The enlargement itself is a principal manifestation of the EU's actorness as a civilian power.

The latest big bang enlargement has a long history as a process of using many civilian leverages to expand the prosperity, solidarity and security across the continent, especially to the central and eastern Europe. At the initial stage, immediately after the collapse of the Soviet Union, the Community had set up a network of partnership and cooperation agreements (see Table 1) with NIS (new independent states of the former Soviet Union) to encourage them to initiate the democracy and market economy reforms, but not referencing to EU membership. In June 1993, the Copenhagen European Council agreed that the CEEC could join the EU and set the condition for membership, as so called "Copenhagen Criteria" (see box 1). In the following stage, the EU had used the pre-accession strategy to foster and boost the domestic reforms and promote peace and security in the region. In July 1997, the European Commission set the "Agenda 2000" to actively use membership conditionality to criticize domestic political processes and outcomes, and foreign policy choices, and express strong preference for particular change. In Agenda 2000, the Union opened accession negotiation with "Luxembourg Six" (the Czech Republic, Estonia, Hungary, Poland, Slovenia, and Cyprus) in 1997, and successively "Helsinki Six" (Latvia, Lithuania, Slovak, Malta and Bulgaria, Romania) in 1999 with different speed to push the big pressures on the candidate countries to achieve closely to the "Copenhagen Criteria". The membership conditionality has become the EU's most powerful foreign policy instrument and most influential leverage of promoting domestic changes within the NIS and shaping the post-Cold War order in the region.[3]

---

3   Reference to Smith, Karen E. "Enlargement and European Oder". *International Relations and the European Union.* Ed. Christopher Hill and Michael Smith. Oxford University Press, 2005. pp.270-291.

Table 1 The EU's agreements with neighbours

Association agreements with Mediterranean countries (Year in force)	Trade and co-operation agreements (Year signed/ year in force)	Europe (association) agreements (Year signed/ year in force)	Partnership and cooperation agreements (Year in force)	Stabilisation and association agreements (Year signed)
Turkey(1963) (customs union in force, 1996) Malta(1971) Republic of Cyprus(1972)	Hungary (1988/1988) Poland (1989/1989) Soviet Union (1989/1990) Czechoslovakia (1990/1990) Bulgaria (1990/1990) Romania (1990/1991) Albania (1992/1992) Estonia (1992/1993) Latvia (1992/1993) Lithuania (1992/1993) Slovenia (1993/1993)	Hungary (1991/1994) Poland (1991/1994) Czechoslovakia (1991)a CzechRepublic (1993/1995) Slovakia (1993/1995) Bulgaria (1993/1995) Romania (1993/1995) Estonia (1995/1998) Latvia (1995/1998) Lithuania (1995/1998) Slovenia (1996/1999)	Russia(1997) Ukraine(1998) Moldova (1998) Armenia(1999) Azerbaijan (1999) Georgia(1999) In 1997, negotiations with Belarus were suspended due to violations of democracy and human rights there.	Former Yugoslav Republic of Macedonia (2001) Croatia(2001) In 2003, negotiation began with Albania.

a. The Community signed a Europe agreement with Czechslovakia in December 1991, but the breakup of Czechslovakia on 1 January 1993 complicated matters. The Community then negotiated separate agreements with the Czech Republic and Slovakia.

Source: Hill, Christopher and Smith, Michael ed. International Relations and the European Union. Oxford University Press, 2005. p.274.

Box 1 The EU's membership conditions

The Treaty of Rome stated that 'Any European state may apply to become a member of the Community' (Article 237). The 1999 Amsterdam Treaty added that any European state that respect the principles of liberty, democracy, respect for human rights and fundamental freedoms, and the rule of law, may apply to become a member of the Union (Article 5 and 49).

The Copenhagen European Council in June 1993 declared that membership candidate countries must have achieved:

- a functioning market economy with the capacity to cope with competitive pressures and market force within the EU;
- stability of institutions guaranteeing democracy, the rule of law, human rights, and respect for and protection of minorities; and
- the ability to take on the obligations of EU membership including adherence to the aims of economic and political union (the *acquis communautaire*)

By 1999, the EU had formally added 'good-neighbourliness' to the list of conditions. The December 1999 Helsinki European Council stated that candidate countries must resolve outstanding border disputes peacefully, in necessary by referring them to the international Court of Justice (European Council 1999c, para. 4).

Source: Hill, Christopher and Smith, Michael ed. International Relations and the European Union. Oxford University Press, 2005. p.276.

We can see in this process, the EU had used the membership conditionality as the main leverage, both using carrot (inclusion) and stick (exclusion), to turn its attractive power into coercive (still through civilian) power to fulfill its strategic goals and foreign policy. The enlarged Union with the 27 member states and 450 million population pushed its border to the regions in Eastern Europe, had not just expand the prosperity, democracy and security to the former communist countries in central and eastern Europe, but also shaped the post-Cold War European order in its image. This enhances both internal and external expectation on the EU to continue using its civilian power to expand or make peace and stability in Europe and outside world. The enlarged EU has become the leading actor in the region,[4] and a model of expanding peace, stability and prosperity by civilian power.

A more solid giant or a more divided union?

The enlargement makes the EU a more influential actor in the region, but meanwhile the enlargement has also raised many problems even the crisis within the Union. The new member states accelerate the existing intra-divergence within the Union or create

---

4   Bretherton, Charlotte and Vogler, John. The European Union as a Global Actor second edition. London and New York: Routledge 2006. p.160.

new divisions in some policy domains, especially in foreign policy. The most obvious instance was the policy division toward Iraq War, and most recently, the severe bargain concerning the new reform treaty. The expanded EU's big size creates possibilities of losing some of the political cohesion that would enable Union to be a decisive strategic actor.[5] This incandesces the "widen/deepen" debate.

With very distinct national and historical features, being rather small countries (nine of them), and strong transatlantic feelings and ties, the new member states have a strong conservation about national sovereignty and a tendency to intergovernmentalism and Atlanticism. The principal consequences are[6]:

- the new member states are reluctant to more integration and deepening of the Union, but the core member states incline to deepen integrations in some areas or the Union as a whole, which would raise the problem of a "two-speed Union";
- the new member states create new coalitions within the Union to advance issues that may not be on the old member states' agendas, some countries refuse the initiative only because it came from France and Germany; and in a long-time perspective, the coalitions will vary, according to the issue in question, there will be few permanent alliances or power-blocs in the enlarged EU;
- the most part of the new member states would not want to be the "border" of the Union, but to bring its neighbors into the Union. Meanwhile the old member states are reluctant to widen the Union before resolving the institutional and policy inconsistence that the big bang enlargement has brought.

All of those opened the door of the conflicts in Union policy-making and policy coordinating, which broke out into a crisis concerning the policy towards US' invasion of Iraq. The US Defense Secretary then Rumsfeld raised the term of "old Europe" / "New Europe" to criticize the core old member states who had not supported US's conducts, and willingly encourage the new member states to challenge the big old ones in the Union. After that, many analysts and scholars use those concepts "old Europe"/ "New Europe" to describe the intra-divisions within the EU after the big bang enlargement.

5   Brimmer, Esther. "EU Enlargement and Tranatlantic Relations". *The strategic implications of European Union enlargement.* Ed. Esther Brimmer and Stefan Fröhlich. Washington, DC: Center for Transatlantic Relations, Johns Hopkins University, 2005. p.231
6   Reference to:
     Guérot, Ulrike "Consequences and Strategic Impact of Enlargement on the (old) EU". *The strategic implications of European Union enlargement.* Ed. Esther Brimmer and Stefan Fröhlich. Washington, DC: Center for Transatlantic Relations, Johns Hopkins University, 2005. pp.55-56,63,65.
     Brimmer, Esther. "EU Enlargement and Tranatlantic Relations". *The strategic implications of European Union enlargement.* Ed. Esther Brimmer and Stefan Fröhlich. Washington, DC: Center for Transatlantic Relations, Johns Hopkins University, 2005. p.231

The argument this essay wants to emphasize is that the dichotomy of "old Europe"/ "New Europe" was developed and used for political purposes[7]. It can explain the policy divergence in a short time after the big bang enlargement in some extent, but can not give the whole picture of the complex dynamics changes after the enlargement. Even thought the new member states have the national and historical difference and different policy orientation, the integration process and the Union's institution will shape the new identity and make the new policy-making environment. The new member states are still being at the adapting stage and in the transition process. As mentioned previously, the future policy variety will be more according to the special issue and it will be few permanent alliances. For the instance, the biggest "New Europe" country Poland has begun to rethought and adjust its policy towards the Union and its foreign policy[8], the domestic politics change accelerates the tendency.[9]

Which sort of the actor the EU will be?

The successfully using civilian power by enlargement policy to expand stability, security and prosperity increases the external and internal expectation for the EU to act as a civilian power in the region and in international arena. Externally, the neighboring countries (Turkey, Western Balkans, Mediterraneans, and Eastern NIS) have the high aspiration for the membership. Internally, no new member state wants to be the "external border" and wants to bring its new neighbors in. Then there exits a robust drawing dynamics for further enlargement. Meanwhile, the intra-division and the deficits of consistence and cohesion that the big bang enlargement has brought are far from taking over, which creates a strong retracting dynamics. Those two contradictory dynamics pose the question of the future development of the Union: which sort of the actor the EU will to be? And is there a "finalité" for the Union? As Ulrike Guérot argues that[10]:

The consequence is that the more the EU focuses on its 'civilisatory' project, the political project suffers; and the more countries are lining up for membership, the less

7   Sedivy, Jiri and Zaborowski, Marcin. "Old Europe, New Europe and transatlantic relations". *Old Europe, new Europe and the transatlantic security agenda.* Ed. Kerry Longhurst and Marcin Zaborowski. London: Routledge, 2005. p.18.
8   Osica, Olaf. "Poland: A New European Atlanticist at a crossroads?" *Old Europe, new Europe and the transatlantic security agenda.* Ed. Kerry Longhurst and Marcin Zaborowski. London: Routledge, 2005. pp.115-136.
9   See the reports of European Observer:
    Goldirova, Renata. "New Polish leader vows to take pro-EU course". European Observer. November 7,2007. <http://euobserver.com/9/25099>
    Goldirova, Renata. "Poland vows new era in relations with EU and Russia". European Observer. November 23,2007. < ttp://euobserver.com/9/25201>
10 Guérot, Ulrike "Consequences and Strategic Impact of Enlargement on the (old) EU". *The strategic implications of European Union enlargement.* Ed. Esther Brimmer and Stefan Fröhlich. Washington, DC: Center for Transatlantic Relations, Johns Hopkins University, 2005. p.71.

citizens in the EU member states are willing to support the project. ... (But) on the other hand, it is evident that the EU can only become a global actor, if it actively takes part in the shaping of the European neighborhood and builds up a geo-strategic dimension by giving the border countries a perspective for membership. ... This means basically, that the EU will have to face a trade-off between domestic redistribution and a global actor role.

The membership offer has been the most powerful and successful leverage for the Union to play its civilian actor role to shape the post-Cold War European order, but this leverage could not be inexhaustible, the Union could not bring all the European countries in. How to shape "A Secure Europe" according to the new strategic goals setting in ESS (European Security Strategy) in the new strategic environment, and to what extent the ENP (European Neighborhood Policy) could operate effectively without giving the eventual membership promise[11]? After the big bang enlargement, the Union should rethink its policy instruments and leverages to fulfill its strategic goals. Either to be a regional actor or a global actor, the foreign policy actorness and the military actorness should be developed and advanced in order to meet the challenges in dealing with the external relations, primarily with the immediate region and extensively in the global arena.

EU Enlargement: Implications on Transatlantic Relations

The enlarged EU has become the leading actor in the region, and a model of the civilian power in international arena. Further more, the big bang enlargement has included most part of the CEEC independent form former Warsaw Pact into the EU, which have a strong pro-American tendency and strengthened the Atlanticism camp within the EU. Those developments have significant implications on the transatlantic relations: in a short term, it had made the policy towards each other more contradictory and more complex in both side of the Atlantic, and given the new member states more weight in the transatlantic relations, which led to a crisis during the Iraq War; but for a longtime perspective, the big power relations return into the center of the transatlantic relations and the Euro-Atlantic agenda, and the integration process itself also creates both new identity and different policy-making environment.

US's responses to EU Enlargement

Contradictory perception: a closer partner or a stronger counterweighter?

Facing the enlarged EU, there are two schools of thoughts dominate perceptions of transatlantic relations in American, which are, in some extent, self-contradictory.

---

11 The question for :
Ferrero-Waldner, Benita. "The European Neighbourhood Policy: The EU's Newest Foreign Policy Instrument". *European Foreign Affairs Review,* Vol. 11 Issue 2, 2006. pp.139-142

The first school of thought argues that the EU and the US do not only share fundamental values, but can and should work together constructively on international issues.[12] They welcome the big bang enlargement to take in the CEEC and former Warsaw Pact countries and an expanded border, appreciate the cross-continental stability brought from the enlargement, and expect the enlarged EU could project the stability to its neighbors by continuing using its civilian power. Enlargement also makes the EU more legitimate on norms-based transatlantic issues, and a more legitimate and strong voice in the international arena who is American's partner, or at least not animosité.

Meanwhile, as the second school of thought, they also have a concern that seeing the enlarged EU as an alternative power in international affairs consciously balancing against the dominance of the US[13].

Europeans more or less share the American perception of the threat posed by international terrorism, conflict between Israel and its Arab neighbors, the global spread of pandemics, a major economic downturn, religion fundamentalism, and large immigrant and refugee flows. Even through the threat perception is not dissimilar across the Atlantic, there remain differences as to how to respond (or preempt) possible threats and, in particular, over the conditions for the use of military force.[14]The successful using of civilian instruments to address the problems and expand peace and stability in post-Cold War Europe create an alternative model in international affairs, which could challenge America's hegemony, especially the leadership in Euro-Atlantic arena. Such kind of concern is particularly strong referring to the development of a separate security framework and an autonomous military capability by EU. For the Americans, NATO's leadership is crucial to US dominance in the Euro-Atlantic arena, any EU's strategic capacity separate from NATO becomes a way to create a security framework based on European, but not transatlantic, foundations.[15]

---

12 Brimmer, Esther. "EU Enlargement and Tranatlantic Relations". *The strategic implications of European Union enlargement.* Ed. Esther Brimmer and Stefan Fröhlich. Washington, DC: Center for Transatlantic Relations, Johns Hopkins University, 2005. p.232.

13 Brimmer, Esther. "EU Enlargement and Tranatlantic Relations". *The strategic implications of European Union enlargement.* Ed. Esther Brimmer and Stefan Fröhlich. Washington, DC: Center for Transatlantic Relations, Johns Hopkins University, 2005. p.232.

14 Missiroli, Antonio. "Between EU and US: The Enlarged Union, Security and the Use of Force". *The strategic implications of European Union enlargement.* Ed. Esther Brimmer and Stefan Fröhlich. Washington, DC: Center for Transatlantic Relations, Johns Hopkins University, 2005. pp. 331, 332.

15 Brimmer, Esther. "EU Enlargement and Tranatlantic Relations". *The strategic implications of European Union enlargement.* Ed. Esther Brimmer and Stefan Fröhlich. Washington, DC: Center for Transatlantic Relations, Johns Hopkins University, 2005. p.232.

Dual-track policy: cooperate and divide

Such kind of contradictory perception reflects the contradictory developments result from the enlargement to the Euro-Atlantic agenda. The US addresses them with a two-track policy: cooperates with the EU in the one hand, and divided the EU in the other hand.

For the cooperate track: Firstly, the US promotes EU to project stability into regions around the EU by using enlargement or neighborhood policy, which appeals to EU's traditional preference - economic and diplomatic instruments, as so called civilian power. Secondly, the US asks for EU's cooperation in some regions or issue areas, which are not in US's crucial agenda, but the EU can play an effective role with its civilian assets or even military assets in some peacekeeping or crisis managing missions. But one of the most difficult questions is still there, that is to what extent will the EU be a military partner? Last but not least, the US appreciates the solid relationship with the Atlanticists within the EU, both the old or new member states, not just concerning to Iraq War and after war stabilization and reconstructions deals, but also concerning to anti-terrorism issue and geopolitical strategy, for instance the relationship with Russia.

For the divided track: The US's primary European strategy is to defend NATO as the primacy instrument in Euro-Atlantic strategic arena and military/defence issues, and not support, even opposite autonomous European military capabilities construction that separate from NATO. For this strategic goal, adding the short-term manoeuvre to incent Paris' and Berlin's support to Iraq War, the conservatives in the Bush administration were shaping the development of the perception of "old Europe" / "new Europe", and subsequently to willingly engage, and encourage, the intra-European divide.[16]

Enlargement's implications on relations with US

The most negative impact of the enlargement would be the severe policy division towards US, the member states divisions over the 2003 Iraq War created a crisis in the Union's common foreign policy and the transatlantic relations.

The Atlanticism/Europeanism difference has a long history within the Union, especially in foreign policy and defence construction, but had not resulted in such a crisis as 2003. Most of the new member states (still candidates in that time) are staunch Atlanticists, their integration into the EU strengthened the pro-American camp within the Union. Rhodes divides the reasons they rallied behind the US into three categories: first, band-wagoning for profit, secondly, balancing against threats to their "voice opportunities" within Europe, and, third, bridging divisions among their other partners

---

16 Lantis, Jeffrey S. "American perspectives on the transatlantic security agenda". *Old Europe, new Europe and the transatlantic security agenda.* Ed. Kerry Longhurst and Marcin Zaborowski. London: Routledge, 2005. pp.191,192

in order to preserve the viability of their membership within NATO and the broader Euroatlantic community that they have worked so hard to join over past decade.[17] Sedivy and Zaborowski add the political-strategic motives: (fourthly,) the effort to save NATO as the vehicle of US presence in Europe, be it as a guarantee against fears of potential revival of Russia's imperial behavior, and (fifthly,) balancing the "Franco-German monster".[18] The new member states' Athleticism tendency has its historical and cultural roots. They have a strong historical memory as the sacrifices of the west European appeasement and pacifism policies, and the Soviet Union's control, so they do not view the international law and multilateralism as the principles that are necessary to make the international system more peaceful just because they exist, and the foreign elites in Warsaw and Budapest were freer to endorse the interventionist policies of US in domestic.[19] So it would not likely to change tremendously the pro-American tendency in a short time, adding that some conservative leaders and parties willingly use the nationalism, troublemaking policy, or anti French-Germany manoeuvre to gain domestic support.[20]

However, the new member states' Athleticism does not always translate into automatic support for each and every American action or position on the international scene.[21] Some of the "New Europeans" are either changing their course, like Spain under the government of Zapatero, or, like the Czech Republic or Slovenia, have in fact never been decidedly uncritical of the US and staunchly Atlantist.[22] For the staunchest Atlanticist in the new member state, Poland, the instinctive Atlanticism had reached its apex and would be rethought and adjusted to take out of changes in the Euro-Atlantic security environment.[23] The policy adjustment will accelerate after the pro-business and pro-European Civic Platform replaced the conservative Law and Justice Party. After

17 Rhodes, Matthew. "Central Europe and Iraq: Balance, Bandwagon, or Bridge?". Orbis, Vol. 48 Issue 3, summer 2004. pp.423-436.
18 Sedivy, Jiri and Zaborowski, Marcin. "Old Europe, New Europe and transatlantic relations". *Old Europe, new Europe and the transatlantic security agenda.* Ed. Kerry Longhurst and Marcin Zaborowski. London: Routledge, 2005. p.20.
19 Sedivy, Jiri and Zaborowski, Marcin. "Old Europe, New Europe and transatlantic relations". *Old Europe, new Europe and the transatlantic security agenda.* Ed. Kerry Longhurst and Marcin Zaborowski. London: Routledge, 2005. p.23.
20 See: Dempsey, Judy. "Letter from Europe: A new conservatism rises in Eastern Europe". International herald Tribune. October 4, 2007. < http://www.iht.com/articles/2007/10/04/europe/letter.php?page=1>
21 Missiroli, Antonio. "Between EU and US: The Enlarged Union, Security and the Use of Force". The strategic implications of European Union enlargement. Ed. Esther Brimmer and Stefan Fröhlich. Washington, DC: Center for Transatlantic Relations, Johns Hopkins University, 2005. p.326.
22 Sedivy, Jiri and Zaborowski, Marcin. "Old Europe, New Europe and transatlantic relations". *Old Europe, new Europe and the transatlantic security agenda.* Ed. Kerry Longhurst and Marcin Zaborowski. London: Routledge, 2005. p.3.
23 Osica, Olaf. "Poland: A New European Atlanticist at a crossroads?" *Old Europe, new Europe and the transatlantic security agenda.* Ed. Kerry Longhurst and Marcin Zaborowski. London: Routledge, 2005. p.116.

outgoing Kaczynski, Tusk said he was set to place Poland back in the European mainstream, pay special attention to Polish-German relation, and consult his EU counterparts before agreeing to the US plan to place an anti-missile shield in Poland.[24]

Besides the domestic politics, the crucial important reasons should be taken account here is the integration process identity shaping and the new policy-making environment emerging after the government changes in many member states, in which the most importantly Merkel replaced Schroeder, and Sarkozy replaced Chirac. After Schroeder and Chirac, the "anti-American" camp within the EU was feeble, both Merkel and Sarkozy adopted a pro-American policy. The role of the "pro-American" camp in (and after) Iraq War, especially the biggest new member state, Poland, as the counterbalance to Franco-German leadership loses its importance. The amelioration of the German-American relations and the Franco-American relations re-puts the pig power relations to the center of the transatlantic relations. In this new context, the questions are: which role the new member states would/could play in the new context of the transatlantic relations? Whether they might to create other "problems" or "camps" to defend their "voice opportunities" in the transatlantic relations? How those will impact on the foreign policy actorness construction? All those questions should be paid attention in the further studies.

Enlargement's implications on Atlantic Alliance

The enlargement also made the ESDP construction debate more complex. Most of the new member states are reluctant to the EU military and defence construction, they strongly support US position that NATO should be the primacy instrument in Europe-US strategic arena and military/defence issues, and any European military capabilities construction should avoid duplication, decoupling and discrimination of the NATO("three Ds"). Poland insisted that the political and military development of ESDP must not challenge the US presence and role on the continent and opposes any sort of institutional duplication that may lead to a decoupling of the US from Europe. Subsequently, Poland rejected the idea of an EU-operational cell located outside Supreme Headquarters Allied Power Europe (SHAPE) and was reluctant about the establishment of a collective defence alliance within EU through "closer cooperation" as proposed by France, Germany, Belgium, and Luxembourg in April 2003 at Tervuren. Warsaw also opposed "structured cooperation" which it saw as a Franco-German attempt to sideline the pro-American new member states by setting up military criteria they could never hope to meet.[25]

---

24 Goldirova, Renata. "New Polish leader vows to take pro-EU course". European Observer. November 7,2007. <http://euobserver.com/9/25099>

25 Osica, Olaf. "Poland: A New European Atlanticist at a crossroads?" *Old Europe, new Europe and the transatlantic security agenda.* Ed. Kerry Longhurst and Marcin Zaborowski. London: Routledge, 2005. pp.126-127.

The Bush administration possessed a mix of European fears and expectations towards ESDP. On the one hand, a more substantial European defence effort would help relive the US of European and perhaps even some global defence burdens. On the other hand, serious European efforts promised to disturb what had become the normal balance of power and influence in the alliance.[26] This kind of the anxiety has persisted since the foundation of the NATO and dominated the US's attitude towards European military/defence construction (so called "yes, but" policy), which seems like to be continued in the near future.

During the Iraq crisis, the US appeared to follow the "the mission determines coalition" doctrine, "cherry-picking" allies and capabilities for an ad hoc coalition (with most of the new member states of the EU and the old Atlanticists within the EU) rather than making a serious effort to bring the entire NATO alliance on board.[27] This kind of the policy made the NATO become secondary importance, and gave the Europeanist the motivations to develop an autonomous European military capabilities separable form NATO, in order to dealing with the possible issues that the NATO could not be used to address, as the France, Germany, Belgium, and Luxembourg do in April 2003.

However, the Atlanticism camp is still relatively stronger in the military/defence issues, the enlargement has strengthened the Atlanticism camp in this policy area. The relationship with NATO will continue to be the key problem concerning the European military/defence construction. Even through Sarkozy has adopted a pro-American foreign policy, but the France still want to push for "a Europe of defence", especially "put defence high on the agenda" when it takes over the rotating presidency of the EU in the second half of 2008. Sarkozy convinced US as speaking before the US Congress, "The more successful we are in the establishment of a European defence, the more France will be resolved to resume its full role in NATO."[28] But whether the US will support his ambitions on "a Europe of defence" is still a question. The UK also called for a strengthening of the EU's military capacities, but emphasized that this "get on with using the institutions we have got to make progress" rather than set up new ones or "duplicate the work that is done either by NATO or nation states".[29] The other Atlanticists also do not want to be forced to choose between Washington and Brussels on security and defence issues. Then, how far "a Europe of defence" could go ahead? And which kind of structure would be developed to arrange the relationship between

---

26 Sloan, Stanley R. NATO, the European Union and the Atlantic Community: The Transatlantic Bargain Challenged, 2nd Edition. Oxford: Rowman & Littlefield Publisher, Inc.2005. pp.203-205.
27 Sloan, Stanley R. NATO, the European Union and the Atlantic Community: The Transatlantic Bargain Challenged, 2nd Edition. Oxford: Rowman & Littlefield Publisher, Inc.2005. p.236.
28 Beunderman, Mark. "French EU presidency to push for defence integration". European Observer. November 13, 2007. < http://euobserver.com/9/25131>
29 UK foreign secretary David Miliband's speech at the College of Europe in the Belgian city of Bruges on November 15, 2007. 24. see Vucheva, Elitsa. "EU must improve military capabilities, UK says". European Observer. November 16, 2007. < http://euobserver.com/9/25162>

NATO and Defece Europe in the future transatlantic agenda should be taken attentions.

Consequences to future transatlantic relations

As analysing previously, the big bang enlargement has made the EU a stronger but divided leading actor in the European continent. The enlargement demonstrates the Union's growing civilian actorness, and the alternative model of using economic and diplomatic leverages in dealing with external relations and international affairs, comparing with the US model. But the membership offer would not be inexhaustible, and the enlargement has also weakened the political coherency and policy consistency of the Union. The question of that "Could the EU be a de facto strategic actor without the strong foreign policy actorness and military actorness?" still be there. The EU could successfully use the enlargement policy to shape the order in the post-Cold War Europe in the past, but how about the future after the big bang enlargement?

The US has a mixed, contradictory perception about the enlarged EU and adopts a dual-track policy, both cooperate and divide. The enlargement has strengthened the pro-American camp within the EU in a short time, since the most parts of the new member states are staunch Atlanticists. But the strong anti-American camp diminished after Merkel replaced Schroeder, and Sarkozy replaced Chirac, and the instinctive Atlanticism also reached its apex in the new member states. The big change of the anti/pro-American dynamics within the EU returned the big power relations back to the center of the transatlantic relations and reduced the weight of the new member states in some extent. Meanwhile, the integration the adapting process also creates new identity and new policy tendency of the new member states. The new member states would not have to choose between Washington and Brussels ever, but would they create new "problems" or "camps" in order to defending their "voice opportunities" in the transatlantic relations?

The amelioration of the Franco-American relations does not automatically means that France would give up his Europeanism. To some extent, changing anti-American posture made the France more strong voice in the EU, and more easy to promote its EU construction plan. But whether Sarkozy could successfully persuade the US to support a "Defence Europe" is still a big question, not mentioning that the old and new Atlanticists will strongly defend the NATO as the primacy instrument in Euro-Atlantic strategic arena and military/defence issues. In the issue of the military capabilities construction, the US would continue to use the new member states as the counterweighter to the Europeanists. In this scenario, how the transatlantic relations will evolve and whether "a Union within Union" and "two-speed EU" will emerge are waiting for observing.

References:

1. Frohlich, Stefan. "The EU after the Big Bang". *The strategic implications of European Union enlargement.* Ed. Esther Brimmer and Stefan Fröhlich. Washington, DC: Center for Transatlantic Relations, Johns Hopkins University, 2005. pp.3-26.

2. Guérot, Ulrike "Consequences and Strategic Impact of Enlargement on the (old) EU". *The strategic implications of European Union enlargement.* Ed. Esther Brimmer and Stefan Fröhlich. Washington, DC: Center for Transatlantic Relations, Johns Hopkins University, 2005. pp.53-72.

3. Kiss, Laszlo J. "The Strategic Implications of EU Enlargement on Central and Estern Europe". *The strategic implications of European Union enlargement.* Ed. Esther Brimmer and Stefan Fröhlich. Washington, DC: Center for Transatlantic Relations, Johns Hopkins University, 2005. pp.73-100.

4. Brimmer, Esther. "EU Enlargement and Tranatlantic Relations". *The strategic implications of European Union enlargement.* Ed. Esther Brimmer and Stefan Fröhlich. Washington, DC: Center for Transatlantic Relations, Johns Hopkins University, 2005. pp.225-240.

5. Missiroli, Antonio. "Between EU and US: The Enlarged Union, Security and the Use of Force". *The strategic implications of European Union enlargement.* Ed. Esther Brimmer and Stefan Fröhlich. Washington, DC: Center for Transatlantic Relations, Johns Hopkins University, 2005. pp.317-338.

6. Sedivy, Jiri and Zaborowski, Marcin. "Old Europe, New Europe and transatlantic relations". *Old Europe, new Europe and the transatlantic security agenda.* Ed. Kerry Longhurst and Marcin Zaborowski. London: Routledge, 2005. pp.1-28.

7. Osica, Olaf. "Poland: A New European Atlanticist at a crossroads?" *Old Europe, new Europe and the transatlantic security agenda.* Ed. Kerry Longhurst and Marcin Zaborowski. London: Routledge, 2005. pp.115-136.

8. Hyde-Price, Adrian. "European security, strategic culture, and the use of force" . *Old Europe, new Europe and the transatlantic security agenda.* Ed. Kerry Longhurst and Marcin Zaborowski. London: Routledge, 2005. pp.137-158.

9. Becher, Klaus. "Has-been, wannabe, or leader: Europe's role in the world after the 2003 European Security Strategy". *Old Europe, new Europe and the transatlantic security agenda.* Ed. Kerry Longhurst and Marcin Zaborowski. London: Routledge, 2005. pp.159-174.

10. Lantis, Jeffrey S. "American perspectives on the transatlantic security agenda". *Old Europe, new Europe and the transatlantic security agenda.* Ed. Kerry Longhurst and Marcin Zaborowski. London: Routledge, 2005. pp.175-194.

11. Longhurst, Kerry and Zaborowski, Marcin "The future of European Security". *Old Europe, new Europe and the transatlantic security agenda.* Ed. Kerry Longhurst and Marcin Zaborowski. London: Routledge, 2005. pp.195-205.

12. Ferrero-Waldner, Benita. "The European Neighbourhood Policy: The EU's Newest Foreign Policy Instrument". *European Foreign Affairs Review,* Vol. 11 Issue 2, 2006. pp.139-142.

13. Edwards, Geoffrey. "The New Member States and the Making of EU Foreign Policy",in *European Foreign Affairs Review*, Vol. 11 Issue 2, 2006. pp.143-162.

14. Dannreuther, Roland. "Developing the Alternative to Enlargement: The European Neighbourhood Policy". *European Foreign Affairs Review,* Vol. 11 Issue 2, 2006. pp.183-201.

15. Yeşilada, Birol, Efird, Brian and Noordijk, Peter. "Competition among Giants: A Look at How Future Enlargement of the European Union Could Affect Global Power Transition". *International Studies Review,* Vol. 8 Issue 4, Dec2006. pp.607-622.

16. Rhodes, Matthew. "Central Europe and Iraq: Balance, Bandwagon, or Bridge?". Orbis, Vol. 48 Issue 3, summer 2004. pp.423-436.

17. A Secure Europe in A Better World: European Security Strategy. Brussels, 12 December 2003, < ec.europa.eu/enterprise/security/doc/gop_en.pdf>

18. Brimmer, Esther and Fröhlich, Stefan ed. *The strategic implications of European Union enlargement*. Washington, DC: Center for Transatlantic Relations, Johns Hopkins University, 2005.

19. Longhurst, Kerry and Zaborowski, Marcin ed. *Old Europe, new Europe and the transatlantic security agenda*. London: Routledge, 2005.

20. Sloan, Stanley R. *NATO, the European Union and the Atlantic Community: The Transatlantic Bargain Challenged, 2nd Edition*. Oxford: Rowman & Littlefield Publisher, Inc.2005.

21. Hill, Christopher and Smith, Michael ed. *International Relations and the European Union*. Oxford University Press, 2005.

22. Bretherton, Charlotte and Vogler, John. *The European Union as a Global Actor second edition*. London and New York: Routledge 2006.

23. Goldirova, Renata. "Poland vows new era in relations with EU and Russia". *European Observer*. November 23,2007. < http://euobserver.com/9/25201>

24. Goldirova, Renata. "New Polish leader vows to take pro-EU course". *European Observer*. November 7,2007. <http://euobserver.com/9/25099>

25. Vucheva, Elitsa. "EU must improve military capabilities, UK says". *European Observer*. November 16, 2007. < http://euobserver.com/9/25162>

26. Beunderman, Mark. "French EU presidency to push for defence integration". *European Observer*. November 13, 2007. < http://euobserver.com/9/25131>

27. Dempsey, Judy. "Letter from Europe: A new conservatism rises in Eastern Europe". *International herald Tribune*. October 4, 2007. < http://www.iht.com/articles/2007/10/04/europe/letter.php?page=1>

About the editors and contributors

 Ali M El-Agraa is Professor of International Economics, International Economic Integration and EU Studies in the Faculty of Commerce, Fukuoka University, Japan. He holds both a doctorate (PhD) and higher doctorate (DSc) from the University of Leeds, UK, and Kyushu National University, Japan. Although born in Africa, he is a naturalized British citizen, hence an EU national. He was invited to Fukuoka University in 1988 when he was with the University of Leeds, which he joined in 1971, but was associated with since 1964. There, he was Senior Lecturer, an elected member of the University's top management bodies (Senate and Council, 1978-88) and Head of the Office of University Adviser to Overseas Students (1979-82). His general academic field is International Economics, with more than twenty books (some translated into Japanese and Chinese), including Japan's Trade Frictions: Realities of Misconceptions?, and numerous articles in international professional journals. Within International Economics, most of his research is on International Economic Integration, with three books on the EU: The European Union: Economics and Policies (1980, the 8th edition of which was published by Cambridge University Press in 2007); Britain Within the European Community: the Way Forward (1983); and The euro and Britain: Implications of Moving into the EMU (published in 2002). He is entered in the first edition of Who's Who in European Integration Studies on the recommendation of the British University Association for Contemporary European Studies and was Senior International Consultant for the United Nations on regional integration during 2001 and General Consultative Advisor to the Anglo-Japanese Economic Institute (London) from 1996 to 2002. elagraa@fukuoka-u.ac.jp

---

 Andreas Vasilache, Dr., Associate Professor for European Studies at the Faculty of Sociology at the University of Bielefeld/ Germany and German Director of the Centre for German and European Studies at St. Petersburg State University/Russia.. Former Research and Teaching Assistant for International Relations and Foreign Policy Studies at the Institute of Political Science at Justus-Liebig-University Giessen/Germany. Former Fellow of the Heinrich-Böll-Foundation and of the German National Academic Foundation (Studienstiftung). In 2005 and 2006 Visiting Fellow at the Center for International Studies at the Massachusetts Institute of Technology (M.I.T.), Cambridge/ USA and at the Political Philosophy Group of the Università degli Studi di Firenze/ Italy. Junior-Coordinator and Executive Director of EU-NESCA, Giessen Junior-Representative of GARNET Network of Excellence, Director of the Europe-Asia Interdisciplinary Research Unit (EA-IRU), and Giessen Representative of the Research Network REGIMEN. Main areas of research: Theory of International Relations, European Studies, Governance Studies, Political and Social Theory, Intercultural Studies, Methodology of the Social Sciences. andreas.vasilache@uni-bielefeld.de

Cae-One Kim is the Chairman of SNU-KIEP EU Center, a visiting Professor of Graduate School of International Studies, Seoul National University (SNU), and the Chairman of International Peace Foundation.

After his graduation from Law College of Seoul National University (1961), Prof. Kim went to Brussels for further studies. He majored in European economic integration at Universit Libre de Bruxelles. His doctoral dissertation thesis (1969) was on 'La CEE dans les relations commerciales internationales' (Presses Universitaires de Bruxelles).

As Prof. at the School of Economics of Seoul National University (1971-2004) and Dean of College of Social Sciences (1995-96), he taught on international economics including European integration and trade policy. He successively served as President of numerous Korean academic associations, especially International Economic Studies (1988-89), Comparative Economic Studies(1995-97), Information-Telecommunications Policy Studies (1995-97), Korea Economic Association (2000-01), EU Studies (1994-2004) and founding President of EUSA Asia-Pacific (2001-2004). He was also founding President (1988-91) and Chairman (1993-98) of Korea Information Strategy Development Institute (KISDI), Korea Monetary Board Member (1991-94) and Commissioner of Financial Supervisory Commission (1998-99) of Korea. On his contribution to enhancing Korean-European academic relations, he was awarded of French Government Decoration, Lgion d'Honneur (1990).

In relation to publication activities, he wrote many books and articles on international economics, the EU and Korean economy including 'International Economic Order (1986, Kor.), 'Economic Reforms in the Socialist World (1989, McMillan)', 'Korean Economy at Turning Point (1996, Kor.)', Economics of the EU (2004, Kor.)', 'Is Market Integration in Northeast Asia Possible? (2005, Kor)', 'Conditions for the Successful Establishment of East Asian Economic Integration: An Institutional Approach (2006, Kor), and 'EU's Common Commercial Policy and International Commercial Relations (2007, Kor). caeonek@snu.ac.kr

---

Professor Dai Bingran is Jean Monnet Chair at the Centre for European Studies, Fudan University. He is also Vice Chairman of the Chinese Association for European Studies, Vice Chairman and Secretary General of the Chinese Society for EU Studies, Deputy Director of the Shanghai Institute for European Studies. He began European studies in the late 1970s, and has been since then chairing courses and carrying out research at Fudan and other universities and institutions both at home and abroad. His current research interests cover EU's economic development, institutional reform and external relations.

brdai@fudan.edu.cn

Dr David Camroux is a Senior lecturer seconded to the Institut d'Études Politiques (IEP) in Paris where he teaches on contemporary Southeast Asian society. He is also a Senior Research Associate within the Centre d'Études et de Recherches Internationales (CERI). His previous positions at Sciences Po were as Director of Studies at the Centre des Hautes Études sur l'Afrique et l'Asie Modernes (CHEAM), from 1994-1998, and Executive Director of the Asia-Europe Centre from 1998-2004. Prior to this, he held positions at the University of Paris XII (Val de Marne) and the University of Paris VIII (St Denis).

He studied for his first degree at the University of Sydney and his doctorate in Paris at the Sorbonne. Dr Camroux has been since September 1994 the European Corresponding Editor of The Pacific Review (London ; Routledge). He is a regular commentator on Southeast Asian and Pacific affairs for French radio and television as well as for the press. For his academic achievements he was made a "Chevalier de l'Ordre. des Palmes académiques" in July 1993 and a "Chevalier de l'Ordre des Arts et des Lettres" in May 1997.

david.camroux@sciences-po.fr

Dr. Frank Delmartino has retired in 2005 as the Director of the Institute of International and European Policy at Leuven University (Belgium). As a Jean Monnet Professor, he's still teaching Comparative Regionalism and Federalism (Leuven) and 'Changing Concepts and Perceptions of the EU' at the College of Europe in Bruges. His research focuses on institutional innovation in the EU, the process of integration and citizens' participation. In recent years he has been teaching at a variety of universities in the Far East, getting more involved in the field of Asia-EU relations.

frank.delmartino@soc.kuleuven.ac.be

Iwona Anna Hanska is currently Assistant for International Relations and Foreign Policy, Deputy executive Director in projects in Central Asia (2005-2006/2007-2009), Ph.D. candidate at the Institute of Political Science of the Justus-Liebig-University Giessen/Germany and research fellow of GARNET Network-of-Excellence. Research: International Relations, Foreign Policy, political and historic relations between Poland and Germany, transformation processes of Central Eastern Europe.

Iwona.A.Hanska@sowi.uni-giessen.de

Dr. Jian Junbo, lecturer at the Centre for European Studies at Fudan University, China.

He was born in Hunan province located in the central region of China, graduated as a bachelor majoring in politics from Nankai University (Tianjin, China) and earned a PhD degree in international relations at Fudan University (Shanghai, China). His PhD dissertation focused on the legitimacy of U.S. hegemony after the end of the Cold War, and he is now mainly concentrating on European politics, Sino-Europe relations, political theory and social theory. He is so far the author of more than ten issued academic articles as well as the participant of several international academic conferences. From 2004 to 2008, as a visiting PhD student and a scholar, he has studied at Hong Kong University, Durham University and Giessen University. He teaches European Union's politics and foreign affairs for bachelor students, meanwhile, as a student counselor, he is in charge of post-graduates studying at the International Politics Department of Fudan University.
jianjunbo@yahoo.com.cn

Marc-Antoine Eyl-Mazzega is a French-German PhD student at Sciences Po Paris/Centre for International Studies and Research (CERI). His thesis analyses Ukraine's gas policies and the role of Ukraine for Europe's gas supply security. He holds a Master's degree in international relations and has so far had several working experiences, such as at the French Embassy in Ukraine, the European Parliament in Brussels, or the BNP Paribas bank. His publications so far deal with the Ukrainian gas issue, and have been published by the CERI or the French Ministry of Industry.
marcantoine.eylmazzega@sciences-po.org

Dr. Reimund Seidelmann is currently Professor for International Relations and Foreign Policy at the Institute of Political Science, Justus-Liebig-University Giessen/Germany, Professor for Political Science at the Institute for European Studies (IEE), Free University Brussels/Belgium, Honorary Professor for International Politics, Renmin University Beijing/PRC, Honorary Professor Universitas Katolik Parahyangan Bandung/Indonesien, European Chairman of the Academic Board EU-CHINA EUROPEAN STUDIES PROGRAMME (2004-2008), and coordinator of the EU-NESCA RESEARCH DIALOGUE project. He is director of the research and cooperation project GERMANY, THE EU, AND CENTRAL ASIA (2007-2009) funded by Volkswagen-Foundation and Co-Director of the cooperation and professionalisation programme GOOD GOVERNANCE, GOOD REGIONAL COOPERATION, AND THE TRANSFORMATION OF THE SECURITY SECTOR IN INDONESIA (2006-2009) funded by the German Foreign Ministry. He works on International Relations theory, European foreign and security

policies, peace- and conflict studies, and transformation studies. In addition, he worked as consultant for political bodies and industries.
reimund.seidelmann@sowi.uni-giessen.de

Soko Tanaka, professor at the Faculty of Economics at Chuo University in Tokyo/Japan since 2003, and President of Japan Society of International Economy. He works on economic and monetary integration in Europe and East Asia. He also was professor of Tohoku Universtity 1982-2003 and professor of Hitotsubashi University 2002. tanakaso@tamacc.chuo-u.ac.jp

Toshiro Tanaka is Professor of European Political Integration, Jean Monnet Chair ad personam, Keio University and Director of Keio Jean Monnet COE Centre for EU Studies. He is a founding member of EUSA-Japan and was President (2002-2004). He was also President of EUSA Asia-Pacific (2003-2006). His recent publications in English include: "Peace and Reconciliation between France and Germany after the WW II, Journal of Political Science and Sociology, No.2, 2004. "From the Convention through the IGC to the European Constitutional Treaty", EU Studies in Japan, No. 25, 2005. With E.FUKUI and J.BAIN, "Cast in America's Shadow: Perceptions of the EU in Japan" in M. HOLLAND, P. RYAN, A. Z. NOWAK and N. CHABAN eds., The EU Through the Eyes of Asia (Singapore, Asia-Europe Foundation, 2007). tanatosi@law.keio.ac.jp

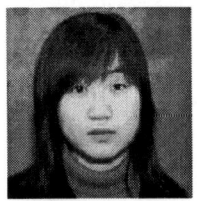

Yang Na is PhD student at the Zhou Enlai School of Government, Nankai University, Tianjin, China. She studied at Duisburg-Essen University, Germany from December 2006 to March 2007 as a program student. Her research field is European Governance and European integration. nana71_6@hotmail.com

Zhang ji is PhD candidate at the Department of International Politics, Fudan University, Shanghai, China. He was an exchange student at Sciences Po. Paris from February to June 2007. His doctoral dissertation will be about France's Policy towards ESDP. zhangji@fudan.edu.cn

Transformation, Development, and Regionalization in Greater Asia

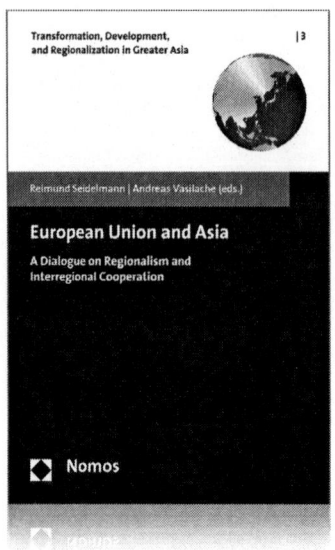

European Union and Asia
A Dialogue on Regionalism and Interregional Cooperation
Edited by Prof. Dr. Reimund Seidelmann and
Dr. Andreas Vasilache
2008, 363 pp., pb., 59.00 €,
ISBN 978-3-8329-3433-0
(Transformation, Development, and Regionalization in Greater Asia, vol. 3)

This volume gives a state-of-the-art overview of concepts and perspectives of regionalism and interregional co-operation with a particular focus on interregional relations between Asia and Europe. By combining a theoretical and conceptual approach with a strong empirical insight and regional knowledge, scholars from Asia, the Asian-Pacific region and Europe explore the political, economic, security and cultural aspects of regionalization processes and inter-regional cooperation.

The discussion of both chances and possible traps in regionalization processes and in interregional cooperation in Asia and Europe shows that interregionalism can provide a basis for good governance in a globalized world.

This publication is the fourth volume of the book series from the research and cooperation project EU-Network of European Studies Centres in Asia (NESCA): A Research Dialogue, funded within the 6th Framework Programme of the European Commission. Prof. Dr. Reimund Seidelmann is professor for International Relations and Foreign Policy Studies at Justus-Liebig-University of Giessen, Germany and at Université Libre de Bruxelles, Belgium. He is Coordinator of EU-NESCA. Dr. Andreas Vasilache is research assistant and lecturer in International Relations and Political Theory at Justus-Liebig-University of Giessen, Germany. He is Executive Director of EU-NESCA.

Nomos Verlagsgesellschaft
Tel. (+49) 7221/2104-37 | Fax -43 |
www.nomos.de | sabine.horn@nomos.de